orphic bend

orphic bend

MUSIC AND INNOVATIVE POETICS

ROBERT L. ZAMSKY

The University of Alabama Press   Tuscaloosa

The University of Alabama Press
Tuscaloosa, Alabama 35487-0380
uapress.ua.edu

Chapter 1 appeared in a previous form as "Ezra Pound and Charles Bern-
stein: Opera, Poetics, and the Fate of Humanism," in *Texas Studies in Litera-
ture and Language* 55, no. 1: 100–124, copyright 2013 by the University of
Texas Press, all rights reserved.
Inquiries about reproducing material from this work should be addressed to
the University of Alabama Press.

Typeface: Perpetua

Cover image: *Vertical Forms with Colors*, mixed media, 18 x 22 in., 2008;
from the *Ankhrasmation* series by Wadada Leo Smith; published by Kiom
Music, ASCAP, used by permission of the artist
Cover design: Michele Myatt Quinn

Cataloging-in-Publication data is available from the Library of Congress.
ISBN: 978-0-8173-6014-6
E-ISBN: 978-0-8173-9370-0

Contents

Acknowledgments

This book was made possible thanks to the many conversations over the years that echo through its pages. It is fitting that the first chapter looks at Charles Bernstein's collaboration with Brian Ferneyhough, since it was in Charles's seminar that I first learned about that opera and that the ideas at the center of this book first coalesced; fitting, too, that the book ends with Nathaniel Mackey, who graciously entertained my inchoate thoughts on his work and whose poetry and poetics have remained an abiding inspiration for what is possible in visionary lyric. I benefited, too, from exploring Charles's opera in the company of scholars, writers, and performers of the genre during the 2004 National Endowment for the Humanities Summer Seminar, "Opera: Interpretation Between Disciplines," hosted by Carolyn Abbate, then at Princeton University. An earlier version of the work on the operas of Bernstein and Pound appeared in *Texas Studies in Language and Literature*, and a substantially different version of the work on Mackey's poetry and poetics appeared in *Arizona Quarterly*. I also presented earlier work on the book at the conferences of the American Literature Association, the Modernist Studies Association, the Midwest Modern Language Association, and the Illinois Philological Association. I would like to thank the participants and interlocutors at those gatherings for their input. Many of the conversations that fed into *Orphic Bend* happened, formally and informally, at the Louisville Conference on Literature and Culture Since 1900, and Alan Golding, long-standing co-organizer and all-around impresario of the conference, deserves special recognition for helping to establish such a vibrant intellectual and creative community. Heartfelt thanks, too, to Robert Archambeau, Joe Donahue, Norman Finkelstein, Peter O'Leary, Patrick Pritchett, Eric Murphy Selinger, and Mark Scroggins.

There is the book, and then there is the life of which the book is a part. At the center of this life is my wife, Florence, whose infectious spirit of adventure and unflagging generosity have kept me afloat, and our children, Annette and Thomas, tireless joys, who have done their level best to keep things interesting. Thank you all.

Introduction

"Once and for all it is Orpheus,
Wherever there is music"
—Rainer Maria Rilke, *Sonnets to Orpheus*

—*Or*—

"Poets who will not study music are defective"
—Ezra Pound, "*Vers Libre* and Arnold Dolmetsch"

Orphic Bend explores the role of music in modern and contemporary innovative writing in the United States. The book addresses the operas of Ezra Pound and Charles Bernstein in relation to the legacy of Renaissance humanism, the notion of music and musicality as fundamentally framed by the figure of Orpheus's backward glance in the poetry and poetics of Robert Creeley, the relationship between song and place in John Taggart's postmodern pastoralism, the critical performance of voice in the sound poetry of Tracie Morris, and Nathaniel Mackey's exploration of musicality as a mode of knowledge. I argue that the profound role that music plays in contemporary writing amounts to an "Orphic bend," a rich vein of poetic practice that recalls the Orphic roots of lyric even as it posits radically new modes of musicality. In many ways, the writers considered in this study are particularly invested in articulating their relationship with modernism, a period for which music's influences on poetic practice have been well documented. As *Orphic Bend* demonstrates, though, their projects are iterations of a much older set of problematics regarding the source and efficacy of music, as well as the mechanisms and implications of its relationship to poetic language.

The definition of terms poses a real challenge to any interdisciplinary study of the arts, perhaps especially so when music is a part of the equation. What, after all, is music? If there is a score, a performance, and a recording, which is the "work"? Which is the object of study, and which bears most importantly on literary practice? Do we treat the poem on the page as analogous to a score and a reading of the poem as analogous to a performance of that score? What about the specifically textual elements of a poem, those aspects that are active primarily at the level of reading but that still would best be characterized as musical in their mode of coherence or relation? And, how does improvised music change the terms of the analogy? These questions have been the subject of theoretical debate for centuries, and I do not propose to resolve them within the pages of *Orphic Bend*; rather, the book explores how consideration of these problems, and others, shapes literary practice. That is to say, I do not presume to offer a clear, concise, and stable definition of music, nor, for that matter, even a stable continuum of definitions for music along which poetry might be placed. To be sure, there would be some appeal in doing precisely that. One could, for instance, invoke the familiar binary of music as Apollonian form and music as Dionysian expressiveness, and then plot contemporary writers according to their relative adherence to one or the other of these poles. As appealing as such a heuristic process might be, it is also immediately artificial, and it misses the often vexed nature of these terms within the practices of the poets themselves.

Orphic Bend is not a work of musical aesthetics, and it adopts the admittedly rather more awkward practice of determining the notions—which are not the same as definitions—of music that are active in the creative and critical practices of these writers. One of the products this approach yields is an understanding that music can mean radically different things to different people, even when they are thinking largely of the same musical genres or modes, as is the case with several of these poets. To frame the heterogeneity of music's meaning, my discussion is often shaped by works in musicology, musical aesthetics, and the philosophy of music. Thus, for instance, I develop the discussion of opera in the first chapter in conversation with work on opera by Carolyn Abbate, historical considerations of the role of the Orpheus myth in the foundation of the genre, and musicological analysis of Ezra Pound's opera, *Le testament de Villon*. Similarly, chapter 4's discussion of Tracie Morris builds upon Fred Moten's articulation of the performativity of Blackness, including in Black musical traditions to explore how Morris understands and embodies performed language as an efficacious act. In the final chapter, too, on the work of Nathaniel Mackey, musicological analysis of the free jazz of Don Cherry and Cecil Taylor, as well as arguments regarding music and meaning, underpin my analysis of his intensely exploratory poetics. As these discussions demonstrate, the poets included in *Orphic Bend* do not merely like music but also contribute important thinking about the meaning(s) of music.

Orphic Bend thus treats the myth of Orpheus less as a stable benchmark for artistic practice or literary history and more as a multifaceted and ever-changing set of ideals, tensions, and values, all grounded in the assertion of a fundamental identity between poetry and music.[1] The first known mention of Orpheus in classical literature consists of two words: "famous Orpheus."[2] Attributed to the sixth-century BC poet Ibycus, this fragment acts as a reverberating membrane, gathering the voices of the poet's renown and amplifying and transmitting them to later generations. In the centuries that follow, Orpheus's status as the father of lyric poetry is continuously invoked and altered as the very practices, constraints, and ideals of lyric develop.[3] What's more, beyond simply narrating the mythological ability of a poet to overcome the constraints of mortality, both his wife's (temporarily) and his own (permanently, as his severed head continues to sing), the story of Orpheus has been read as an allegory for everything from Christ's harrowing of hell to the plight of the artist and the foundation of society itself. While there are innumerable contributions to the development of Orpheus's myth, two have become the most influential: that of Ovid's *Metamorphoses* and that found in the fourth of Virgil's *Georgics*. The basic plot of the myth is generally framed in three phases: the idyllic period before Eurydice's death; Orpheus's descent to the underworld and subsequent return (following the structure of katabasis and anabasis common to much Greek drama), including the pivotal event of his glance back; and his death at the hands of the maenads, an example of *sparagmos*, or ritual sacrifice. To this skeletal plot, both Ovid and Virgil provide significant embellishments. Ovid, for instance, appends a happy ending: after a particularly horrific description of the death of Orpheus, his spirit is said to rejoin Eurydice in the underworld. Virgil makes a darker revision to the myth, and it is perhaps because of this that his version has become the most culturally powerful, particularly with respect to the use of the myth as a model for lyric poetry. While Ovid presents Eurydice as an innocent "bride . . . walking / across the lawn, attended by her naiads,"[4] when she is bitten by the serpent, Virgil frames the scene in a much more sinister way. Virgil places the myth at the root of his lesson in the keeping of bees, an allegory for the atonement of sins. The main topic of book four is how to regain bees once the hive has been decimated or lost.[5] The key, of course, is sacrifice—and twice we are told that bees emerge out of the putrifying guts of slaughtered cattle. The key figure in this narrative is Aristaeus, who has lost his bees as punishment for the role he played in the death of Eurydice. As Virgil has it, Eurydice was not merely going for a stroll with her bridesmaids when she was bitten by the serpent; she was, rather, trying to escape the unwanted sexual advances of Aristaeus. Virgil thus introduces into the story of Orpheus the threat of sexual violence and, thereby, the foundation of lyric.[6] What's more, with no recuperative reunion in the underworld, Virgil's version leaves the trauma of Orpheus's second loss of Eurydice an open wound, thus paving the way for critical endeavors that will propose lyric as based upon a primal loss, absence, lack, transgression, or fault.

Even this brief recounting of the myth suggests its capaciousness. And, in fact, Orpheus has been deployed as not merely a subject but also a paradigm in countless theoretical endeavors. As Kaja Silverman has argued, while the myth may seem anachronistic to us now, in fact, it underscores a strain of modern and contemporary critical thinking that both praises certain modes of reflection and interrogates the centrality of the individual in subject formation. I will return to her discussion in more detail, particularly with respect to Robert Creeley's verse, but, for now, it is useful to recall her enumeration of how the myth of Orpheus continues to shape our psychic lives. In contrast to the tragic, Virgilian Orpheus, Silverman looks to the reunion of Orpheus and Eurydice in Ovid's coda, which foregrounds the dream of a wholeness found only in death. For Silverman, the story of Orpheus thus resonates most strongly for how it foregrounds finitude as the most universal bond among not only humans but all living things, a sense that is precipitated by an initiatory loss, figured by Orpheus's backward glance and Eurydice's second death. As Silverman traces the influence of this structure in modern and contemporary literature, film, and critical thought, she touches on a number of writers and thinkers who either directly or indirectly reference Orpheus, including, of course, Rainer Maria Rilke, as well as Friedrich Nietzsche, Lou Andreas-Salomé, Sigmund Freud, and others for whom the Orphic occasion coincided with a reconsideration of the questions, "What is a woman? What is a man? How do they—and how *should* they—relate to each other? Is our yearning for wholeness merely a remnant of our infantile narcissism or does it refer to something real? If there is a Whole, what is it, and why do we feel so estranged from it?"[7] As Silverman notes, one of the most prominent voices of modern critical discourse shaped by Orpheus is that of Maurice Blanchot, especially in his essay "The Gaze of Orpheus," in which he proclaims, "Writing begins with Orpheus's gaze. And this gaze is the movement of desire that shatters the song's destiny, that disrupts concern for it, and in this inspired and careless decision reaches the origin, consecrates the song. But in order to descend toward this instant, Orpheus has to possess the power of art already. This is to say: one writes only if one reaches that instant which nevertheless one can only approach in the space opened by the movement of writing. To write, one has to write already. In this contradiction are situated the essence of writing, the snag in the experience, and inspiration's leap."[8] Poignantly articulating the mise en abyme that comes to dominate the tragic vision of lyric in modernity, Blanchot's discussion resonates with the role of the Orpheus myth that Silverman identifies in broader critical discourse. As Silverman argues, the reflective stance of Orpheus and the unavoidable importance of analogy as a logical gesture are central to Sigmund Freud's development of psychoanalytic practice, Martin Heidegger's sense of finitude, and Walter Benjamin's notion of history.[9] She also invokes Jacques Lacan, noting that even as he rejects the centrality of analogy, his work "helps us to see [that] the resistant force [between our sense of similarity to others and our reluctance to admit to that awareness] is the desire awakened in us by the impossible-to-satisfy demand that humanism makes upon us: the demand to be 'individual.'"[10]

In fact, although Silverman does not pursue this thread, Lacan's discourse is shaped by the Orpheus myth in even more concrete ways, particularly in the section of *The Four Fundamental Concepts of Psychoanalysis* dedicated to developing the notion "Of the Gaze as *Objet Petit a*." In "The Eye and the Gaze," Lacan echoes the critical sense of recollection as he distinguishes between the point of the subject's vision and the external ubiquity of the gaze: "It is no doubt this *seeing*, to which I am subjected in an original way, that must lead us to the aims of . . . that ontological turning back, the bases of which are no doubt to be found in a more primitive institution of form."[11] Noting the similarity between "the stain and the gaze," Lacan defines their function as "both that which governs the gaze most secretly and that which always escapes from the grasp of that form of vision that is satisfied with itself in imagining itself as consciousness."[12] For Lacan, the gaze, in "the scopic relation," is equivalent to the *objet a*, which he here defines as "a privileged object, which has emerged from some primal separation, from some self-mutilation induced by the very approach of the real."[13] As this link between the *objet a* and the gaze makes clear, for Lacan, the economy involved in the gaze is that of escape or elision. The subject is constituted by the gaze, the subject's desire is an effect of the gaze, and any object in the field of vision is only ever partially seen. That is, the scopic drive is a replay of Orpheus's failed desire to visually capture Eurydice.

Each of these strains of Orphic thought shares a key trait: they point to a crisis of the senses at the pivotal moment in his narrative. That is, the primordial poet, the very figure for the unification of poetry and music, breaks the law, commits his self-defining sin, by virtue not merely of the turn of his physical body but of his turn toward the sense of sight. This self-founding self-violation is reinforced in Blanchot and Lacan, particularly in the fact of Lacan's use of this moment as a narrative scaffolding upon which to construct the apparatus of the gaze. As such, what had been a central fault in Orpheus's character becomes a critical elision in the deployment of his story; the foundational truth of his identity is first denied by him and then, again, by the critical tradition that invokes him. Just as Eurydice suffers a second death at the hands of Orpheus, so, too, does his identification with poetry and music in this critical tradition. The poets considered in *Orphic Bend* provide us with an occasion to reclaim this identification and to ask, among other things, a question embedded, though erased, in these uses of his myth. If, for instance, the Orpheus myth provides the narrative and logical architecture for Lacan's development of the gaze, then his argument implies that all of us, inasmuch as we are subject to the workings of the gaze, are lyric poets. Or, to be more precise, to experience the processes of the gaze is to find oneself in the circumstance of the lyric poet. To be sure, this is not a point of interest to Lacan; but, it is a point that is unavoidable if the terms of the myth are to have any value beyond the generic structure of katabasis-anabasis. As such, one might ask, why is it that Lacan's development of the gaze brings us back to the text-music nexus, albeit unintentionally? What does the subject gain at this interdisciplinary juncture? As the Orphic architecture of the Lacanian gaze implies, and as many of the poets considered in this study contemplate at length, the answer is desire. That is, if the economy of the gaze is that of the *objet a*, if the machinery of the gaze is that of desire, and if Orpheus's identity as the primordial poet is shaped by this machinery, then the backward glance of Orpheus figures the retroaction of desire that is also central to the relationship between poetry and music. As I will argue, the terms and implications of this calculus function quite differently from poet to poet, but, for each of them, the link between music and poetry infuses poetic language not merely with sound or pattern but also, and most elementally, with insatiable desire: for the other, for the self, and for knowledge itself.

While *Orphic Bend* frames the work of the poets considered in its pages with the myth of Orpheus, I do not mean to suggest that all of these writers intentionally or explicitly invoke Orpheus. To be sure, some do. As I note in chapter 1, for instance, Bernstein's introduction to *Shadowtime* invokes the term "katabasis," thereby explicitly framing the subject of the opera, Walter Benjamin, as an Orphic figure. Mackey's mention of the mythical poet is even more explicit and carries throughout his work as a poet, novelist, and critic—a fact made evident not least by the fact that *Orphic Bend* derives its title from a key moment in Mackey's serial fiction, *From a Broken Bottle Traces of Perfume Still Emanate*. For the writers in the intervening chapters—Robert Creeley, John Taggart, and Tracie Morris—the relationship to Orpheus is simply not an explicit one. None of them, to my knowledge, describes his or her work in relation to the Orphic tradition. Yet, all of them work in modes that clearly recall the ideals and practices associated with the paradigmatic lyric poet, the most important of these being the conviction that poetry and music are inextricably linked.

Across the five chapters of *Orphic Bend*, the myth of Orpheus operates as a rotating prism whose different facets illuminate sometimes dramatically different aspects of the shared framework of poetry and music that is so essential to the myth. In the case of Pound and Bernstein, for instance, the relationship between poetry and music becomes the ground upon which Pound seeks to recapture the lost possibilities of the Renaissance and upon which Bernstein launches his incisive critique of Pound. For his part, Creeley very much inherits Pound's sense that poetry and music are closely linked in ways that result in a poet's particular voice, or "measure," and yet, as he internalizes the sense of the poet's measure, his work becomes shaped by the Orphic premise that the act of poetry itself is driven by the insatiable desire to articulate that which cannot be captured, including perception itself, and by the Orphic disposition toward elegy. In a further rotation of the prism, John Taggart's poetry is animated by the pastoral underpinnings of the Orphic tradition, particularly as framed in Virgil's retelling of the myth. In this vein, the unity between poetry and music links the poet to the particularities of place, ranging from a place of spiritual contemplation, such as the Rothko Chapel, to that of regional history, such as the Cumberland Valley of South Central Pennsylvania. Across his varied career, Taggart emphasizes the fundamental importance of sound in poetry, as the voice emanating from the poet's body reverberates with etymology and history, "unveiling," making new and available again, those modes of connectivity that are variously eroded, paved over, or simply forgotten. The world-building potential of Orpheus that Taggart thus mobilizes also resonates with the sound poetry of Tracie Morris, whose work explicitly claims cultural and political possibilities for the unity of poetry and music. However, whereas Taggart delves into the histories of words and places, Morris emphasizes the performative power of spoken language, foregrounding the fact that all spoken language bears cultural, communal, and personal marks of the speaker (again returning to the sense of language as a signature, or "measure"). For Mackey, the Orphic voice of the poet may well embody such individualizing marks, but it also and more powerfully reaches toward an order of knowledge in which poetry and music are nearly indecipherable from one another. In this sense, music and the musicality of poetic language are the gateways for Mackey's Gnosticism, the mechanisms of initiation into a realm not of secrets to be learned but of visionary knowing that continuously unfolds.

The nexus of poetry and music that animates the work of the writers under consideration in *Orphic Bend* recalls the interdisciplinary dynamics at the heart of literary modernism, a period for which the influences of music on poetic practice have been well documented.[14] Certainly, the most prominent figure in this trajectory is Pound, as we see most explicitly in chapter 1, but his ideas about the importance of music as a grounding or benchmark for poetry are also clearly echoed in Creeley and Taggart; just as certainly, the most important intermediary figure is Louis Zukofsky, who radically transforms and extends the possibilities of Pound's musico-poetics.[15] For some, the link to Zukofsky is substantive and concrete: Creeley was a champion of Zukofsky's work, wrote poems dedicated to him, invoked him in his critical prose throughout his career, and wrote prefaces and introductions to several editions of his work; Zukofsky plays an even more important role in the poetry and poetics of John Taggart, as I discuss in chapter 3; and Nathaniel Mackey, too, has cited Zukofsky in his critical writings.[16] While Morris has not, to my knowledge, directly invoked Zukofsky in her work, her play with the sonic register of language as meaning making clearly participates in a similar set of aesthetic principles.

Perhaps Zukofsky's most abiding contribution to our thinking about the relationship between poetry and music is from his poem "'A'—12," in which he states, "I'll tell you. / About my *poetics* . . . An integral / Lower limit speech / upper limit music."[17] This section of "A" is dated from 1950, but Zukofsky had been ruminating on this configuration of the relationship between poetry and music for nearly two decades by that time, as is found in his essay "An Objective" (1936), in which he baldly states the musical analogy: "a poem: a context associated with 'musical' shape, musical with quotation marks since it is not of notes as music, but of words more variable than variables, and used outside as well as within the context with communicative reference."[18] Zukofsky's Paterian ranking of the arts is a part of his engagement with Pound's influence, particularly as is found in his emphasis on the musical imagination as being a fundamentally formal or structural one. This emphasis on music as form is grounded in Pound's concept of *melopoeia*, the ways in which poets "charge [a visual image] by sound, or [they] use groups of words to do this," a microcosm of the importance of structures of interrelation in Pound's poetics.[19] Zukofsky expands upon this idea to enumerate three kinds of music in Pound's *Cantos*: "(a) the music of the words themselves, their sound effects, (b) the music caused by the juxtaposition of word and word, line and line, strophe and changing strophe, entire canto against entire canto, and the time-pauses between each of these, (c) the suggested music of all the *Cantos* at once: that is, as there is the entire developing and concluding music of the sonnet, not only the pairing or quadruplicating of its rhymes, there is the entire music of a single poem of length such as the *Canto* . . . an immediacy of the entire structure."[20] This range of music that Zukofsky identifies in Pound's poetry is embodied in the practice that most directly links their two projects: the invocation of the fugue as a model for poetry. As Mark Scroggins has demonstrated, one of the most important ways in which Zukofsky adapts and radically reconfigures Pound's project is in his use of the fugue as a model for juxtaposing disparate material within an ongoing, large-scale form. Whereas Pound's use of the fugue was shaped also by his investment in the notion of the ideogram, which, in his usage, as Scroggins reminds us, "is an inherently totalizing, perhaps even totalitarian form," "Zukofsky's poetics of parataxis, with all of its radical openness to the nonliterary and subliterary, is involved with a formal principle that is less form than texture. The principle of 'fugal' composition, as constantly self-generating and regenerating 'weave,' escapes the totalizing tendencies of the ideogram."[21] The sense of music as offering a "texture" or a procedure that continuously (and perhaps endlessly) unfolds rather than a form that might be apprehended lays the groundwork for the sometimes very different ways the writers in *Orphic Bend* lay claim to music's power as a model for poetry.

Each chapter in *Orphic Bend* invokes specific aspects of the Orphic legend as a frame for the practices of the poets under consideration.[22] Chapter 1, "Opera,

Poetics, and the Fate of Humanism: Ezra Pound and Charles Bernstein," explores the turns to opera by Ezra Pound and Charles Bernstein, focusing in particular on the role of Orpheus as the figure for syncretic knowledge. The chapter attends to Pound's 1933 opera, *Le testament*, and Bernstein's *Shadowtime*, which had its world premiere in 2004, and argues that Bernstein's work is a pointed and multilayered rejoinder to Pound's. Behind both of these works lies the history of opera and its grounding in Renaissance musical humanism—including, of course, the profoundly important role of Orpheus as the figure for elemental unity for writers, thinkers, and musicians of that period. Pound famously wrote his opera as a means of "criticism," an act of advocacy on behalf of its subject, the fifteenth-century troubadour, François Villon. Claiming that Villon's verses were too subtle to be translated, Pound, with the assistance of the American pianist and composer, George Antheil, set them to music by building what remains one of the most idiosyncratic of operatic architectures. Dating from the period during which Pound worked as a professional music critic for the *New Age*, and after Vorticism, *Le testament* is a virtual laboratory for Pound's intense interest in music. The goal of the opera, in Pound's typical grandiosity, was to restage and radicalize the Renaissance in order to fulfill what he saw as one of Western culture's great lost opportunities.

With *Shadowtime*, Bernstein confronts Pound on his own favored ground. While I would not suggest that the opera was produced explicitly or only as a critique of Pound, nearly every aspect of the work—from its conception, through its treatment of its subject, Walter Benjamin, and the compositional practices of both Bernstein and the work's composer, the British "maximalist" Brian Ferneyhough, and on to its performance—is in stark contrast to Pound's work. As such, the work is best understood through the lens of Bernstein's important critiques of Pound in his critical writings, essays in which he powerfully argues that Pound's anti-Semitism and fascism must not be excused away by poets or critics who admire his innovative literary practices. As Bernstein argues, the challenge of Pound for subsequent writers and critics has been how to profitably extend the radical possibilities of his work without either excusing his faults or, worse, inadvertently reiterating them. Ultimately, the chapter argues that Bernstein's work amounts to a critique of humanism itself very much in line with the work of Emmanuel Levinas.

While Bernstein's turn to opera raises a specific set of questions regarding text-setting practices, musical humanism, and the politics and ethics of aesthetic form, Robert Creeley's relationship to music, the subject of chapter 2, poses a very different challenge. To put it simply, music is of foundational and abiding importance to Creeley, but the precise nature of that importance is elusive. To frame the role of music in Creeley's poetry, chapter 2, "'Measure, Then, Is My Testament': Robert Creeley and the Poet's Music," pays particular attention to the importance of song in Creeley's early verse and its marked replacement later in his career by the phenomenon of the echo. In the early essays, Creeley's sense of musicality is synonymous with one of his favorite terms, "measure," and this, in turn, with ideas about voice and rhythm. This element of Creeley's poetics demonstrates the profound importance of Pound to his sense of poetry, deriving, as it does, so explicitly and clearly from Pound's sense of the musicality of poetic language as a signature of selfhood. This is also the aspect of Creeley's verse that is most important to Charles Olson's development of "projective verse," and, finally, it is the moment in which Creeley's own prosody is most directly influenced by musical models, here, in particular, the ubiquitous bebop of the early 1950s. As the chapter argues, the music of Creeley's voice is shaped by his articulation of competing commitments to precision, the elements of authorial control and craft that are deeply important to him as a young poet, and the prospect of receptivity, a kind of losing oneself or giving oneself over to the process of writing.

The chapter explores Creeley's frequent association of poetry and song, as indicated both in the titles of his poems and in his discussions of poetry. Creeley's sense of the music of poetry is shaped by the same tension between innovation and tradition that characterizes his broader literary practice, and his investment in the notion of the poem as song derives from what can seem to be a very old-fashioned, he would likely have said, very New England, sense of the cultural work of the poet. The final aspect of Creeley's relationship to music is found in his shift from song to variations on the term "echo" or "echoes," a project that culminates in the publication of the volume *Echoes* in 1994. As the chapter argues, the charged senses of music, measure, song, and echoes that course through Creeley's work derive from the tension between instantaneity and recursivity that figures Orpheus's loss of Eurydice. In fact, the stance and occasion of Creeley's work, the perspective from which it proceeds, extends from his intense consideration of the precise moment at which Orpheus breaks the deal and turns to look for Eurydice.

Chapter 3, "Orpheus in the Garden: John Taggart," uses the Orpheus myth as a way to frame apparently divergent compositional practices in the poetry of John Taggart, a member of the generation of poet-thinkers who came in the wake of Creeley and the New American writing. Generally identified with the objectivist tradition, especially with Louis Zukofsky and George Oppen, Taggart has explored the relationship between poetry and music since the late 1960s. Beginning with the 1981 publication of *Peace on Earth*, Taggart developed a distinctive style that combined the influences of post-bop jazz, the mid-century American minimalism of composers such as Steve Reich and Terry Riley, Gregorian chant, and the tradition of the hymnal. Although the jazz line of Taggart's discography at this point in his life would be markedly similar to that of Creeley, the influence of that music is dramatically different. If bebop leads Creeley in the direction of a short, terse, sharply syncopated line, post-bop jazz, reinforced by minimalism and chant, leads Taggart into a mode characterized by the construction of large blocks of text composed of intense repetition and slight variation of words, clauses, lines, and phrases. In early poems in this mode, such as "Drum Thing" and "Giant Steps," Taggart develops this practice in response and even homage to what he hears in the jazz of John Coltrane, with the influence of the minimalists becoming more pronounced as the form develops and expands in poems such as his meditation upon the Vietnam War, "Peace on Earth," and the monumental and masterful works "Slow Song for Mark Rothko" and "The Rothko Chapel Poem," both of which also suggest Taggart's interest in the visual arts.[23] These deeply meditative, entrancing poems contrast sharply with Taggart's next mode, which begins with the 2004 publication of *Pastorelles* and continues in *There Are Birds* (2008). Whereas his earlier work largely eschews referentiality in favor of the play of internal repetition, *Pastorelles* marks an increasing interest in description, and the nature of the musicality changes, though its importance remains. While the title poems in the collection are serial in nature, none of the poems in the book exhibit the same repetition and variation as is characteristic of the chant poems, with Taggart working, instead, mostly in shorter forms in a more identifiable lyric mode. Thematically, the collection is shaped partly by the effects of an extended drought in the Cumberland Valley of South Central Pennsylvania, where Taggart has lived since 1969, and the collection as a whole is profoundly invested in the history and geography of the surrounding landscape, a combination of concerns that also animates *There Are Birds*. In the latter collections, Taggart's Orphic project is to actuate the mutually constituting relationship between song and place.

The myth of Orpheus provides a framework for understanding an abiding but surprising consistency in Taggart's project. In spite of the obvious stylistic differences between his middle and later periods, Taggart is consistently writing within the Orphic bend. In the chant poems, Taggart deploys repetition and scale as means to develop immersive aesthetic experiences that ultimately aspire to spiritual, though not particularly religious, ends. For instance, in his poem "Peace on Earth," one of the first instances of this mode, Taggart develops the form out of a deep personal need to find an aesthetic mechanism for coming to grips with the consequences of the Vietnam War, the trauma of which is condensed into the famous image of Phan Thi Kim Phuc running naked down the road as a child, having been badly burned by a Napalm attack. The Pulitzer Prize–winning image by photographer Nick Ut became ubiquitous after it ran in the *New York Times* in June 1972 and, in the poem, becomes a talisman of the war as a personal trauma, even a sin for which we must all, as Americans, seek absolution. The prayerful mode of the chant poems as seeking forgiveness continues as they reach their apex in a pair of long poems for the American painter Mark Rothko, who, himself, saw his abstract art as a kind of religious iconography. In the poems of *Pastorelles* and *There Are Birds*, the focus of this prayerful mode shifts to the landscape and the history inscribed upon it. Across these striking shifts in form, though, Taggart's work draws its energy from the Orphic task of bringing poetry and music together as a means of reestablishing a lost unity between selves and the landscapes that carry our histories.

Chapter 4, "Eurydice Takes the Mic: Improvisation and Ensemble in the Work of Tracie Morris," argues that the sound art of Tracie Morris profoundly shapes the curve of the Orphic bend in contemporary literary practice by confronting the troubling status of gender in the Orpheus myth. If the myth of Orpheus traditionally figures the intimate relation between poetry and music, it also relegates the woman to the status of either the unwitting, silent, and sacrificed beloved or the undifferentiated horde of vengeful maenads. Morris rejects this silencing of the feminine even as she powerfully lays claim to the manifold Orphic potential of poetry as sound. The chapter pays particular attention to two publications from 2018: *Who Do with Words*, based upon Morris's engagement with J. L. Austin's theory of the performative that was the subject of her doctoral dissertation at New York University, and *Handholding: 5 Kinds: Sonic, Textual Engagements*, which consists of her written and sonic responses to the work of other artists. As companion pieces, these two books represent an important advance in our thinking about the role of music in innovative writing, as Morris claims that the fundamental expressive act of the utterance is in itself performative. In doing so, her work resonates powerfully with current discussions about the relationship between performativity and Blackness, particularly as developed by Fred Moten in his trilogy, *consent not to be a single being*. Morris's text and sound-based art are both grounded in the notions of ensemble and improvisation that Moten elucidates, deploying the utterance as a performative that is at once deeply political and fantastically visionary.

The final chapter, "'Orphic Bend': Music and Meaning in the Work of Nathaniel Mackey," is the culmination of the book's argument. The book takes its title from a seminal event in Mackey's serial fiction, *From a Broken Bottle Traces of Perfume Still Emanate*: the fictional band's release of its first album. The band, a world music–oriented group of experimental musicians located in Los Angeles during the late 1970s and early 1980s, provides Mackey with an opportunity for extensive and elaborate contemplations on the expressive, even discursive, potential of music and the musical properties of discourse. The fiction is in epistolary form, presenting the reader with letters written by a character who goes by the initial "N." (not coincidentally, the same as Mackey's own first initial, Nathaniel) and addressed to a character referred to as "Angel of Dust." After searching for a new drummer, developing a new name for the band, and experiencing a mystifying series of events during which speech-bearing, comic strip–like balloons emerge from their instruments during a number of performances, the band finally releases its much-awaited first album, *Orphic Bend*.

I adopt the title of this album from Mackey's fiction and make his work the final subject of the current study to indicate the significance of his place in this discussion. I will state it baldly: no other living writer bears such a deep-seated and thoroughgoing relationship to music as does Mackey. There are certainly contenders, especially among writers influenced by jazz (including, most significantly, Amiri Baraka); but, the distinction of Mackey's work is the degree to which he has internalized the relationship between poetry and music. As Mackey treats music as a subject in his critical writing and as a theme in both his creative prose and his poetry, and as he develops distinctive modes of musicality in both his creative prose and his poetry, he both reclaims and recasts the epistemological condition that has defined Orphic poetics for centuries.

Mackey approaches the material of his art form, language, in a manner much like a musician would approach those of musical expression. The distinction is important. Mackey does not, with exceedingly rare exceptions, seek to approximate the sounds of the music that are so important to him. He does not incorporate blues forms, as did Langston Hughes and Sterling Brown, for instance; nor does he write in a way that seeks to replicate or approximate the innovations of free jazz, as William J. Harris has so astutely observed in Amiri Baraka.[24] The distinction I am drawing is that the musicality of Mackey's poetry is not that of imitation; he does not locate a musical mode outside of poetry and then write in such a way as to bring the poetry closer to its sister medium. Rather, he writes, in both poetry and prose, as if language and music are always already so closely related as to be nearly versions of one another. As I discuss in detail in the chapter, this is evident in his prose depictions of the fictional musical performances, in which music is matter-of-factly granted the status of discourse and in which his own compositional habits can best be described as musical. In many ways, this creative prose is something of a primer for Mackey's poetry, in which his investigations of serial forms, patterning of sound and idea, and teasing at the limits of what is knowable propose music and musicality as unique modes of knowledge.

The writers considered in *Orphic Bend* demonstrate the ongoing vitality of the relationship between poetry and music in innovative writing. As intensely innovative as their work is, it also thus participates in some of the very oldest debates regarding the nature of poetic language and the cultural work it performs. This does not, however, diminish their inventiveness; rather, it demonstrates how and why this inventiveness matters. Focusing their attentions on the musicality of poetic language, redefining the parameters of what we mean by musicality, these writers continuously expand the possible domain of meaning.

1

Opera, Poetics, and the Fate of Humanism
Ezra Pound and Charles Bernstein

Orpheus is the figure of elemental unity. As the performer whose work moves the animals and even the rocks and the trees, he bridges the gap between the chaos of the natural world and the order of civilization; as a demigod, he touches both the human and the divine realms; as a mystic, a priest, and a pedagogue, he acquires knowledge and imparts it to his disciples; as the bereaved lover who follows his beloved Eurydice down to Hades, he crosses the boundary between the worlds of the living and of the dead; and, as the archetypal poet, he possesses the singular ability to unite words and music. Interestingly, throughout the vicissitudes of his ordeal, this final aspect of his character is constant. So much so, in fact, that it persists even after he is torn limb from limb by the maenads. The dismemberment of Orpheus' body is both the fittingly dramatic conclusion to his myth and the premise for a final, enduring mystery: his severed head continues to sing as it floats down the river Hebros toward Lesbos, where it will engender the very birth of lyric poetry. Even when all else is rent asunder, Orpheus retains the unity of text and music.

This persistent link between poetry and music within the myth of Orpheus belies the difficulty of the relationship between the two sister arts. In fact, the unity is precisely a mythical one, and the arts of time, proximate though they may be, share a history not of identity but of metaphor, and they are often in competition with one another. Music and poetry each invoke the other, sometimes as an ideal toward which to aspire, and sometimes as a temptation necessary to resist. During cultural moments when concepts of reconciliation and unity predominate, their relationship often takes on allegorical significance, and it often does so under the aegis of Orpheus. Such was certainly the case for the Renaissance as its fervor for Neoplatonic unity gave rise to opera, and such is also the case for writers of the modernist and postmodernist eras, when the dreams of underlying unity seem lost. This shift in worldviews, bracketed by the centuries dominated by humanism, is imprinted in the genre of opera in perhaps unexpectedly poignant ways because of the profound degree to which the genre is linked to the humanist ideal. While artistic practices are always enmeshed in the cultural, philosophical, and political tensions of their moment, opera is unique as a veritable petri dish of Renaissance musical humanism. There is perhaps no other instance in which theory so clearly precedes artistic practice, with opera emerging out of the debates over musical composition and text setting that preoccupied the early humanists.[1] Notions of unity are central to opera from its very earliest stages—unity of words and music, unity of the past and the present, unity of different modes of knowledge, unity of the expressive subject—ideals that reach their apex in the nineteenth century with Richard Wagner's conception of the *Gesamtkunstwerk*. Early opera is also shaped by the epochal shift underway during its founding: a shift from feudal order to a nascent bourgeoisie, the birth of modern science, and the establishment of modern subjectivity.[2] In many ways, opera bridges this gap, recalling the institutions and modes of the past and projecting the possibilities of the future in a combination of aesthetic spectacle and Orphic mystery. As opera participates in the humanistic project of reclaiming the best of the past in order to establish a better future, the practical ideal of unifying words and music becomes an allegory for unity writ large. And, just as political idealism belies the inequities and outright prejudices of practice, so too does the proposed unity of words and music prove elusive.

Opera is often understood as the product of a great compromise between musical and textual demands, a way of thinking about the genre that lays bare the value judgments of aesthetic purists.[3] As Slavoj Žižek wryly summarizes, from this perspective, opera is "a stillborn child of musical art," one that "always has to rely in a parasitic way on other arts (on pure music, on theater)."[4] While Žižek typically embraces this always-already compromised nature of the genre, others have been much less generous. Even Brian Ferneyhough, the composer whose work, *Shadowtime*, is the subject of this chapter, has previously pronounced opera "a mostly closed book."[5] Coming to opera from the literary angle instead of the musical one hardly elevates the genre; such a perspective only accentuates the other, no-less-happy side of this art-as-compromise, namely, the treatment of the text in operatic text setting. As I will discuss in more detail below, it is utterly conventional in operatic practice to transform the source text of the libretto so much as to render its semantic content unavailable in performance. While it may be true, as the music purists have it, that opera lets itself be shaped by the demands of narrative (plot and character development, for instance), the resulting artwork is hardly a model of elocutionary clarity. And, if we need to follow the details of a story's plot, the place to look is in the program, not the stage. Nor is this loss of narrative clarity the limit of text setting's effects on the libretto; the very poetics, from the concept of the work as a whole to the microcosmic level of sound play, is governed by concerns that are much more properly understood as either musical or dramatic. That is to say, writ large or writ small, the *poeisis* of opera does not simply set a libretto but, much more significantly, makes something new out of it.

This troubled status of the text in opera is the central point of contention between Ezra Pound's *Le testament* and Charles Bernstein's *Shadowtime*, two iconoclastic contributions to the genre which take head-on the foundational issue of text setting that makes the genre seem such a risky choice for a poet and such a besmirched one for a composer. In *ABC of Reading*, Pound described his motivation for setting the work of the fifteenth-century French poet, François Villon, admitting, "technically speaking, translation of Villon is extremely difficult because he rhymes on the exact word," such that "I personally have been reduced to setting [Villon and Catullus] to music as I cannot translate them."[6] Bernstein's treatment of his subject, the life and work of Walter Benjamin, could hardly be more different. The synopsis of *Shadowtime* presents its ambitious scope and critical angle: "*Shadowtime* is a thought opera. . . . In its seven scenes, *Shadowtime* explores some of the major themes of Benjamin's work, including the intertwined natures of history, time, transience, timelessness, language, and melancholy; the possibilities for a transformational leftist politics; the interconnectivity of language, things, and cosmos; and the role of dialectical materiality, aura, interpretation, and translation in art. . . . *Shadowtime* inhabits a period in human history in which the light flickered and then failed."[7] As we will see, whereas Pound's opera develops out of and exhibits an intense level of attention to Villon's language, Bernstein's investment in Benjamin's ideas results in a radically different work. In the profound differences of approach to the form of opera, *Shadowtime* contrasts and contends with Pound's operatic turn, not merely as an element of Bernstein's ongoing critical engagement with Pound's legacy but also as representative of the larger challenge of accounting for humanism in contemporary innovative writing.[8]

While there are certainly stylistic and contextual differences between *Le testament* and *Shadowtime*, there is also a great deal that invites their pairing. To be sure, Pound's opera is ultimately the highly idiosyncratic work of a self-taught amateur, while *Shadowtime* is the result of Bernstein's collaboration with one of the most widely recognized and influential of contemporary experimental composers, the "Maximalist" Brian Ferneyhough. Nevertheless, these works are more than incidental forays into the genre, and they bear more than an incidental relation to one another. Pound turned to opera after working as a music critic for

The New Age for four years, and he spent more than a decade developing *Le testament*, often with the assistance of other composers and musicians, most notably George Antheil. Distinct versions of the opera appeared in 1921, 1923 (the Pound/Antheil score, considered the opera's "urtext"), 1926, and 1933, in addition to a 1931 adaption for BBC Radio.[9] In fact, *Le testament* is a key instance of Pound's working out of his ideas about the relationship between poetry and music.[10] *Shadowtime*, I would suggest, is a similarly crucial part of Bernstein's oeuvre as he grapples with his modernist predecessors, not least of all Pound, and the larger, longer intellectual traditions that underwrote their projects. It also represents a sorely underappreciated aspect of his substantial oeuvre, his work in musical theater.

The relationship between the turns to opera by Pound and by Bernstein can be found first in their choices of subject, François Villon and Walter Benjamin, respectively. Both Pound and Bernstein construe the lives of their subjects as allegories for larger historical moments, and the operas most profoundly demonstrate the results of their searches to represent the significance of Villon and of Benjamin in their formal innovations. Just as Bernstein reads the circumstances of Benjamin's suicide as symptomatic of the failure of modernity, Pound's Villon "represents also the end of a tradition, the end of the medieval dream, the end of a whole body of knowledge."[11] As Pound and Bernstein contemplate the work of their predecessors, each of whom embodies a cultural nadir, the decision to work in opera is a loaded choice of genre, since opera itself is so thoroughly infused with humanist ideology. To put it rather schematically, Pound's Villon is the embodiment of that period that immediately precedes the very Renaissance that will give rise to opera, while Benjamin's life coincides with the historical moment often invoked as that of opera's death, and his work breaks from the humanist tradition both in its Frankfurt School materialism and in its mysticism. That is to say, broadly speaking, *Le testament* and *Shadowtime* are both attempts at epochal intervention by way of aesthetic form; more specifically, the conflict between the operas is staged by way of their respective treatments of two features central to the operatic tradition: the allegorical use of Orpheus and the practical challenge of text setting.

The figure of Orpheus as the model of unity has underwritten the invocation of his story for millennia, and it is of particular importance during the humanist epoch extending from the Renaissance to the present day. For the poets, musicians, artists, and thinkers of the Renaissance, Orpheus served as a patron saint for the project that would come to be known as "humanism"; more than merely a symbol of what they might hope to achieve, he was the very embodiment of the Neoplatonic ideal. Particularly for the early humanists, the myth of Orpheus amounted to a figuration of their project in at least two important ways: the ancient source of his myth satisfied their classicist penchant, and the narrative itself

resonated with the key challenges confronting the humanists, including the uni-
fication of disparate fields of knowledge, the linkage of the past and the present,
humanity's role in the natural world, and the relationship between aesthetics and
truth. That is to say, for the humanist thinkers of the Renaissance, the narrative
of Orpheus represented the possibilities and the challenges of syncretic knowl-
edge and fundamental unity, and the figure of his character embodied the possi-
bility of the achievement of this ideal. As such, for the Renaissance humanists,
Orpheus becomes, as Patricia Vacari has argued, "the prototype of the human-
ist's artistic genius."[12] As is typical of such a perpetually protean character as Or-
pheus, the humanist Orpheus also embodied a fundamental paradox between the
Apollonian and the Dionysian capacities of music.[13] On the one hand, Orpheus
is the clear champion of Reason, as he plays Apollo's music to tame the chaos of
Nature and establish the order of civilization; and yet, he is not merely scientistic
or calculating. He is also seen as a mystic, even a shaman, who possesses unique
knowledge of both Nature and the supernatural, whose ways might reveal to hu-
manity the syncretic truths it seeks. Ultimately, this paradox within the Renais-
sance understandings of Orpheus encompasses both the notion of the human as a
political animal and the artist as a seeker after hidden, divine truth.

   The invocation of Orphic unity as the model of artistic genius persists after
the Renaissance, although it goes through important transformations during the
Romantic period. While the role of Orpheus in Romantic and post-Romantic
thinking is a vast and vexed topic, one of the more compelling points is the shift
in the power relations perceived in the myth of Orpheus and the effect of this
shift on the ideal of truth in music and, by extension, the musicality of poetry.
For the Romantics, Orpheus is no longer the voice of Reason, which is variously
seen as diminished, polluted by day-to-day pragmaticism, or quite simply and
profoundly flawed. As the Romantics displace Reason in favor of Imagination,
their relationship to the Orphic vision of the poet also changes.[14] While theories
of correspondences and reconciliation clearly retain and even accentuate the syn-
cretic ideals of the Renaissance, for the Romantics, the truths that underscore
these correspondences are no longer those of a syncretism forged by Reason but,
rather, those of revelation. For the Orphic Romantic genius, the ideal of a gen-
eralizeable, universal truth is displaced by the sublime, enabled by an increasing
emphasis on the individuality, even the necessary idiosyncrasy, of the imagina-
tion. Such is clearly the case with another poet who, like Pound and Bernstein,
saw in opera an aesthetically important opportunity, Charles Baudelaire. In his
1861 essay, "Richard Wagner and *Tannhäuser* in Paris," Baudelaire begins by fram-
ing the subjectivism of the essay that follows: "May I, in the course of the fol-
lowing appreciation, be allowed to speak often in my own name," and goes on to
both assure the reader that this rhetorical stance will insure his own "sincerity"
and to hope that, "in recording his own impressions, [he] will also be recording

those of some unknown supporters."[15] Providing a passionate and detailed reading of Wagner's oeuvre, Baudelaire closes his discussion by describing the unique qualities of a genius—"An artist, a man really worthy of that great name, must surely have in him something essentially *sui generis*, by the grace of which he is himself and not someone else"—and famously proclaims Wagner to be "the most genuine representative of modern man."[16] Baudelaire identifies the unique quality of Wagner's genius as "passion" and interestingly concludes the essay by commenting on the possible legacy of Wagner's challenge to operatic conventions. While he is as yet unsure as to whether Wagner will succeed in his project to "reform" the genre, his final comments suggest that the success of the opera is already assured, as long as we understand success appropriately. Whether the opera will elicit imitators or usher in a new style, which he considers likely, even if it proves a failure, it will have succeeded in opening up a radically new vein of artistic possibility, one that ultimately derives from the unique sensibilities, the unique genius, of Wagner.[17]

The relationship of Baudelaire's response to *Tannhäuser* to the development of the Orphic disposition in poetry can be usefully understood in the broader context of Romantic notions of individualism. In Baudelaire's response, even as he articulates the "total unity of effect" achieved by the power of the opera, he is clear that the truths he perceives are not so much general and universal as they are radically personal. In this, his appraisal of the opera resonates powerfully with Wordsworth's 1800 "Preface to the *Lyrical Ballads*," in which he justifies the idiosyncrasy of his project on the grounds that attending closely to common language allows buried, encrusted truths to bear forth. Perhaps more to the point for Pound and Bernstein, the writings of Ralph Waldo Emerson similarly demonstrate a profound emphasis on both the revelatory nature of the Orphic poet's relationship to truth and the intense uniqueness of that truth.[18] In essays such as "Nature," "The American Scholar," and, most poignantly, "Citation and Originality," Emerson powerfully argues for the poet's need for radical individuality of thought, a need clearly founded on Emerson's belief that the role of the poet is one of Orphic revelation. In fact, in "The Transcendentalist," as the poet's access to truth is extrapolated into the broader prospects of transcendental moments of clarity, Emerson's sense of the relation between truth, the individual, and the world at large becomes darkly pessimistic, both because of the fleeting nature of moments of transcendental insight and because of our inability to successfully act upon them or communicate them to others. This Romantic turn inward also affects the Romantics' notions of the relationship between poetry and music, as the relationship between the arts is abstracted into the realm of Keats's "unheard music." The unity of the arts becomes individualized and abstracted, and the image of Orpheus takes on the colors of the self-regarding, even narcissistic, poet.

At stake in this evolution of the idea of Orphic unity is much more than simply the representation of a mythological character; rather, at stake is the very status of humanism. Given the profound role played by Orpheus in Renaissance thought, it is perhaps inevitable that any subsequent representations of Orpheus amount to either direct or indirect commentaries upon the humanism for which he stands. On the one hand, the humanistic ideals articulated during the early Renaissance and revisited and refined by later generations continue to under-write beliefs such as universal human rights, secular justice, and essential human dignity. However, and at the same time, our recent history of modern fascism and genocidal war are also demonstrably horrible culminations of the dark un-derside of humanism. This uncomfortable paradox has made the problemati-zation, if not the repudiation, of humanism a central preoccupation of recent intellectual history, as is found in the line of thought that extends from the emer-gence of psychoanalysis to the advent of structuralism and the several iterations of poststructuralism and that provides the intellectual foundation for Bernstein's project and that of other language poets. As language writing has sought to re-spond to its cultural and political climate, its most obvious point of departure and attack has often been the troubling political legacy of modernism. But, in fact, the arguments put forth by this "loose affiliation of unlike individuals," in Bernstein's words, recalls perhaps nothing so much as the theories and defenses of poetry that preoccupied the writers of the Renaissance.[19] The line of poetics that extends from Pound, through the Black Mountain poets and poets of the San Francisco Renaissance, and on through Lyn Hejinian's open form poetics, Ron Silliman's Marxist-inflected critiques of syntax and grammar, and Susan Howe's interrogations of history recalls arguments made over poetic form, the role of lyric, the relationship between literary predecessors, and so on that pre-occupied Renaissance writers in works such as Philip Sidney's *Defense of Poetry,* Thomas Campion's *Observations in the Art of English Poesie*, George Puttenham's *The Arte of English Poesie*, and so many others. As profound as the effect of post-structuralist thought undoubtedly was for the Language poets, and as deeply as it has often allowed them to critique underlying notions of subjectivity and agency, their very emphasis on poetry, even reconstrued, as the venue in which these arguments were to be made recalls the power ascribed to poetry by the think-ers of the Renaissance and suggests that what language poetry did was to not so much extinguish the concept of the human as to radically reconfigure its param-eters and possibilities. This, at least, is certainly the case with Bernstein, one of the most powerful voices in the group. A key component of this work for Bern-stein has been his coming to grips not only with modernism but also specifically with Pound.[20] As such, Bernstein's critical response to Pound and the profoundly problematic aspects of his legacy is a local skirmish in the larger debate over the possibilities and liabilities of humanism as such.

While Bernstein's critical response to Pound and his legacy has taken place most explicitly in his prose work, with the publication, setting, and performance of his libretto, *Shadowtime*, their relationship is placed squarely and perhaps unexpectedly onto the operatic stage. With this turn to opera, Bernstein takes on the art form that is not only most closely associated with Renaissance musical humanism but also profoundly important to Pound. What's more, in their respective turns to opera, both Pound and Bernstein directly take up the features of the Orphic ideal and, in the case of Bernstein, the character of Orpheus himself. Whereas Pound turns to opera in an attempt to revive, radicalize, and modernize the prospects of humanism, Bernstein's turn to the genre is an important moment in his ongoing critique not only of Pound but of the humanist project more broadly. As I will discuss below, Bernstein's commitment to the capaciousness of poetic practice as a means of critical intervention in the habits of the humanist tradition echoes Emmanuel Levinas's call for a radical attentiveness that mitigates against the exertion of the self onto the Other. For Bernstein, the possibility of this openness lies within the purview of a poetics that is more concerned with careful listening to and for the otherness of the Other than it is with trying to speak to and for one another. In the place of a drive toward a singular, unifying voice, Bernstein proposes a poetics of multiplicity and contingency as the basis for reconceived literary and artistic practice. In *Shadowtime*, the prospects of this poetics are brought to bear on the task of text-setting that lies at the heart of opera, and which is also infused with opera's roots in Renaissance musical humanism.

Opera was developed as a systematic, nearly scientific attempt to revive the unity of words, music, and drama that the members of the sixteenth-century Florentine *camerata* believed could be found in classical Greece. The fact that Greek music was unknown and unknowable only fueled the fantasy construction of a lost and ideal art capable of feats far beyond anything associated with contemporary musical practice. The intellectual environment out of which opera arose was infused with the Neoplatonic thought of Marsilio Ficino, Giovanni Pico della Mirandola, and other humanists, whose work provided the conceptual basis upon which opera was built. As Peter Kivy summarizes:

> Five major conclusions were reached by the "philosophes" of opera. . . . They are, first, that music exerts power over the souls and characters of men; that it can change them, morally, for the better or worse, and raise their emotions. Second, that this emotive arousal and moral manipulation is accomplished through "imitation" or "representation" of human character and emotions. Third, that (as Plato apparently believed) by music's "representing" or "imitating" human character or emotions one can only mean its "representing" or

"imitating" human speech and other expressive behavior. Fourth, that Greek drama was a "musical performance" of some kind—that in some sense or other it, or part of it, was sung. Fifth—but only by inference, as the texts bear no witness here—that Greek music was neither contrapuntal nor chordally accompanied: in other words, completely monophonic.[22]

Of the conclusions noted by Kivy, what most interests us here is the link between classical *mimesis* (that possibility for music to "'represent' or 'imitate' human character or emotions") and the persuasive power of music and the resulting practice of text setting. As Kivy's catalogue suggests, the particular mimetic power of music and the rhetorical ends to which it can be put lent it unique weight in the formation of a person's character. Given the clearly pedagogical intent of Pound's aesthetics, it is worth reminding ourselves how Plato conceived of the role of music in pedagogy. The standard place to look is book 3 of *The Republic*, in which Plato argues:

> Education in music is most sovereign, because more than anything else rhythm and *harmonia* find their way to the inmost soul and take strongest hold upon it, bringing with them and imparting grace if one is rightly trained, and otherwise the contrary. . . . And further, because omissions and the failure of beauty in things badly made or grown would be most quickly perceived by one who was properly educated in music, and so, feeling distaste rightly, he would praise beautiful things and take delight in them and receive them into his soul to foster its growth and become himself beautiful and good. The ugly he would rightly disapprove of and hate while still young and yet unable to apprehend the reason, but when reason came the man thus nurtured would be the first to give her welcome, for by this affinity he would know her.[23]

In Plato's discussion, appropriate musical training is both a prophylactic against the possible infection of the ugly and untrue and, at the same time, a method for habituating the soul to what is true and beautiful. Interestingly, Plato sees this capacity for aesthetic discernment as something that can be fostered and nurtured before a person's intellectual maturity—aesthetic judgment, in this framework, is made available to the young and as yet incompletely educated, while reason is acquired only in maturity. It is this profoundly, even elementally, pedagogical conception of music that raises the stakes of text setting. Putting words to music brings language into the higher, musical order of beauty in one of two ways: it locates and heightens a musical beauty already present within the words, or, much more likely, it transmutes the words into the realm of the musical. Ideally, the musicality of the text setting serves as a warrant for the profundity of the text and integrates it into the Platonic unity. In practice, the very impossibility of the unity between words and music, the fact that language's semantic register will always draw it away from pure form, compels the genre toward endless formal innovation.

The practice of text setting that lies at the heart of opera thus embodies the humanist belief in a fundamental, if hard-won, syncretism that runs through even apparently disparate discourses. As F. W. Sternfeld has noted, this Neoplatonic idealism results in a certain irony at the heart of operatic text setting, as is found in the compositional practice of Claudio Monteverdi: "As an opera composer, Monteverdi starts from the words of the libretto, where the characters express themselves in words. . . . But only some words (some stories, some emotions) are capable of being transformed into music ('cantare,' 'armonie'). When this is the case, communication through music (notably, but not exclusively vocal music) as the vehicle of expression is possible. In this case, the words give rise to the music, but are ultimately left behind, because inspired song ('canto') supersedes them, we are 'translated' (to use a biblical term) into another realm."[24] Ultimately, the work of operatic text setting is not to heighten or punctuate anything like the beauty of the language on the page, nor even necessarily to dramatize the text as it is written, but, rather, to find an abstracted, emotive, musical corollary to the text. Since opera was to be a musical form, the text simply had to give— ironically, having chosen a poetic text because of its beauty, profundity, and emotional impact, the composer does away with it precisely as a means of faithfully attending to it. This conceptualization of text-setting practice immediately raises the question of just what is being taught in and through opera. Certainly, much of the meaning of opera resides in the content of its stories: it is no accident, for instance, that the story of Orpheus figures so prominently in early opera. Nor, for that matter, is it incidental that Pound's opera features a text by François Villon, nor that Bernstein's focuses on the life and work of Walter Benjamin. It is just as certain, though, that the edification offered by language set to music is something quite apart from even the most poignant narrative content: it is located in the form itself. Put quite simply, the transmutation of a source-text into the libretto of an opera amounts to a Neoplatonic search for the form hidden yet immanent within the text. As the humanists sought to recover the truths of syncretism and unity in the laboratory of opera, the genre became a microcosm of their overarching faith in the pedagogical role of art.

The Neoplatonism that underwrites the advent of opera resonates with Pound's ventures in operatic composition. His work in this area began in earnest after his Vorticist years, a period during which, as Charles Altieri has argued, Pound's literary work was largely grounded in his desire to recast Renaissance humanism in modernist terms. Altieri develops the notion of "expressivist humanism" as the outcome of Pound's project to restage and radicalize the Renaissance and focuses on the iconoclastic possibilities of humanistic thinking. As he frames humanism with respect to Pound, Altieri argues that "humanism is above all a set of practices and themes devoted to the process of idealizing the potential of human agents to produce and respond to certain values not typical of any social marketplace and not derived from some transcendental doctrine but carried in a privileged set of exemplary actions."[25]

In this framework, literary canons are established as a means of perpetuating "projected 'best selves' and thus shaping our behavior as ethical agents."[26] The major distinction that Altieri finds in Pound's rethinking of humanism is that Pound "makes the expressive individual a set of active qualities rather than a set of determinate contents, and he teaches us to read for the force these qualities might exist [sic]. The art work becomes a display and a test: it is possible to give form to an infinite range of qualities by synthesizing a system of equations, and the capacity of those equations once created to serve as instruments intensifying the perceptions and resistances of others becomes the public measure of the value in private acts. Art expresses not worlds or selves but ways of seeing and arranging the world."[27] What Altieri identifies in Pound is the degree to which the challenge of reclaiming humanism in the face of modernism is met by individualistic formal means. The pedagogy of aesthetic form involves the characters of both the artist and the audience. On the one hand, artwork for Pound exhibits the will of the artist, a demonstration of the strength of the artist's character to be most convincingly located in the force of the artwork's internal self-organization—success with artistic form is a kind of guarantor of the *virtù* of the artist; at the same time, this formal success presents a challenge to the reader, whose responsibility it is to ascertain and learn from the unique qualities of poetic form.

In Pound's work in music theory and composition after World War I, his "expressivist humanism" is increasingly configured as arising from an artist's rhythmic precision. Pound's notion of rhythm during this period is both complex and all encompassing. In *Antheil and the Treatise on Harmony*, for instance, a work partly devoted to his early collaborator on *Le testament*, the composer and pianist George Antheil, Pound proposes that "music is a composition of frequencies," a claim meant to underline his thesis that ultimately even harmony is a kind of rhythm because pitch is measured by the frequency of sound waves over time; rhythm is thus the most elemental aspect of artistic expression.[28] The Antheil essay explicitly addresses this topic in the context of Vorticism, noting, "The Vorticist Manifestos of 1913–14 left a blank space for music; there was in contemporary music at that date, nothing corresponding to the work of Wyndham Lewis, Pablo Picasso or Gaudier-Brzeska."[29] After the war, Pound found the corresponding figure in Antheil, whose musical inclinations satisfied Pound's conception of a possible Vorticist music: "The article on Vorticism in the Fortnightly Review, Aug. 1914 stated that new vorticist music would come from a new computation of the mathematics of harmony not from mimetic representation of dead cats in a fog horn (alias noise tuners). This was part of the general vorticist stand against the accelerated impressionism of our active and meritorious friend Marinetti."[30] Pound sees Antheil's compositional practices as demonstrating a sense of precision that corresponds to the particular circumstances of modernity. Far from the Art of Noise (the "dead cats in a foghorn") of the Italian Futurists, "Antheil has not only given his attention to rhythmic precision, and noted his rhythms with an exactitude, which we may as well call genius, but he has invented new mechanisms, mechanisms of this particular age."[31] For Pound, the precision of Antheil's music is that of an intricate, solid, and moving object: "a construction or better a 'mechanism' working in time-space, in which all the joints are close knit, the tones fit each other at set distances, it can't simply slide about."[32] This "mechanism" operates at the level of the rhythm within the piece, in the relationships between instruments and voices, and even within the acoustic qualities of and performance practices associated with individual instruments. Thus, for instance, in Antheil's piano playing Pound hears someone who transmutes his detested instrument by playing it like a modern: "There is the use of the piano, no longer melodic, or cantabile, but solid, unified as one drum. I mean *single* sounds produced by multiple impact."[33] Treating the piano as the percussion instrument it is, Antheil's precision demonstrates an energy that Pound sees as authentic to its historical moment.

If Antheil ultimately proved to be only a temporary brother-in-arms, Pound had a much more long-standing exemplar in the figure of Villon. And while the essay on Antheil can read as a veiled or opportunistic promotion of Pound's own aesthetic agenda, his advocacy for Villon seems to be born of humility and admiration—if not a sense of defeat at his inability to translate the intricacies of Villon's language. In his 1934 essay, "Dateline," Pound recalls his work on the Villon opera as an example of one of his favored modes of advocacy: "Criticism via music, meaning definitely the setting of a poet's words; e.g. in *Le testament*, Villon's words . . . this is the most intense form of criticism . . . [with the exception of] Criticism in new composition."[34] Pound wears his Neoplatonic belief in the efficacy of music on his sleeve, here, as he proposes text setting and musical composition based upon a poet's work as the highest orders of critical engagement with that work.

With the Villon opera, Pound's belief in the efficacy of Villon's prosody was put into practice when he prepared a broadcast version of it for BBC radio in 1931. In this adaptation of the opera, Pound maintained his intense commitment to the acoustics of Villon's voice—the musicality of his language—even as he sought to bring Villon to an unprecedentedly broad audience. In fact, the medium of radio provided Pound with a powerful tool for the construction of his "expressivist humanism," because it turns the abstract concept of voice into the physical reality of a radio voice existing only as sound waves in the air. As Margaret

Fisher has argued, the radio production of opera was also an ideal opportunity for Pound in his quest to reinvigorate the relationship between poetry and music that he thought had reached its apex in troubadour practice, since, "voice on radio offered the promise of pure sonic contour in a time-based medium, the opportunity 'to cut a shape in time.'"[35] For Pound, as the radio audience listened to Villon's words, duly elevated via musical setting, they came into direct contact with the form of his aesthetic, that lasting manifestation of his *virtù*. As Pound works to bring the prosody of Villon's language to the BBC public, his attention to the aurality of Villon's text "mitigates the distance of time, translation, and perception through a music that retains the sonic surface, texture, and movement of the original voice."[36] It is in this sense that the ideal of mechanical precision is linked to that of the poet's own indelible voice. Far more important than the content of Villon's poetry to Pound is its aural movement that Pound believed could be precisely replicated in performance and broadcast through the radio. As Fisher summarizes the link between Pound's experiments with the new technology and his more archaic interests: "Electricity in the air became Pound's vorticist key to unlock medieval 'forms,' by-products of mental powers so highly charged that they ventured beyond, or existed outside . . . the everyday mentality to become the cultural engines that powered a society: love, and *virtù*."[37] The radio production of the opera was ultimately much more than simply an opportunity to reach a broad audience; the real value of broadcasting Villon's text is that in the medium of radio, Villon's words become pure sound, and thus provide the listener with unimpeded access to the expressivity of his form.

As Fisher's discussion suggests, Pound's work on the opera is something of a laboratory experiment based on his ongoing theoretical and historical concerns with the relationship between poetry and music. Pound's prose writings, of course, are replete with comments on the topic. In *ABC of Reading*, for instance, he describes melopoeia as the process of charging words or groups of words with sound[38] and famously asserts that "poetry atrophies when it gets too far from music."[39] In his 1918 discussion of Imagism, "A Retrospect," he clarifies the rhythmic relation between poetry and music when he advises, "as regarding rhythm: to compose in the sequence of the musical phrase, not in the sequence of the metronome."[40] He returns to the concept of rhythm in the "Treatise on Metre" appended to *ABC of Reading*, flatly stating, "Rhythm is a form cut into time."[41] The historiographic element of Pound's interest in the matter is evident in his 1913 essay, "The Tradition": "It is not intelligent to ignore the fact that both in Greece and in Provence the poetry attained its highest rhythmic and metrical brilliance at times when the arts of verse and music were most closely knit together, when each thing done by the poet had some definite musical urge or necessity bound up within it."[42] These examples, drawn from Pound's writings before and after the war, before and after the Vorticist years, before and after having written his own music and operas, not only point to Pound's dedication to the idea that poetry would be reinvigorated by a greater attention to its historical affinity with music but also show that what animated this dedication was a Neoplatonic belief in music and the musicality of poetry as providing access to some otherwise unknown and unknowable truth.

Pound dwells on the nature of this musical truth as he develops his companion theories of Absolute Rhythm and Great Bass. R. Murray Schaefer has argued, "Pound first conceived of *absolute rhythm* as something existing above the abrasions of workaday art. It was the breath-pattern of the master artificer, above analysis."[43] Pound first deploys the idea of Absolute Rhythm in the introduction to his 1910 Cavalcanti translations:

> Rhythm is perhaps the most primal of all things known to us. It is basic in poetry and music mutually, their melodies depending on a variation of tone quality and of pitch respectively, as is commonly said, but if we look more closely we will see that music is, by further analysis, pure rhythm; rhythm and nothing else, for the variation of pitch is the variation in rhythms of individual notes, and harmony the blending of these varied rhythms. When we know more of overtones we will see that the tempo of every masterpiece is absolute, and is exactly set by some further law of rhythmic accord. When it should be possible to show that any given rhythm implies about it a complete musical form—fugue, sonata, I cannot say what form, but a form, perfect, complete. Ergo, the rhythm set in a line of poetry connotes its symphony, which, had we a little more skill, we could score for orchestra.[44]

Pound revisits the concept of Absolute Rhythm in the "Credo" section of "A Retrospect": "I believe in an 'absolute rhythm,' a rhythm, that is, in poetry which corresponds exactly to the emotion or shade of emotion to be expressed. A man's rhythm must be interpretative, it will be, therefore, in the end, his own, uncounterfeiting, uncounterfeitable."[45] Pound's discussions of Absolute Rhythm are marked by his commitment to an intense individualism, an almost primal authenticity, and an aesthetic of precision, qualities that are held together through the force of Great Bass, which Schaefer likens to "the keel of a ship, exerting a centripetal pull over everything above it."[46] Through the ever-evolving notions of Absolute Rhythm and Great Bass, Pound grapples with the concept of truthfulness of temporal form—that is to say, a radically conceived musicality—as the measure of a poet's voice.

Pound's understanding of rhythm results in a treatment of Villon's text that differs markedly from the conventions of operatic text setting. He does not transmute Villon's text into a higher musical order; rather, he identifies the brilliance of Villon's text within the musicality of its language. The truth of Villon's *virtù* is embedded within his prosody, and Pound's task as composer/text setter is to highlight that truth and bring it forth to the audience. To put it plainly and in stark contrast to the conventions of operatic text setting described by Sternfeld, Pound derives the opera's rhythm from a microcosmic level of attention to Villon's prosody, with a resulting score that was effectively unplayable in its original form. In spite of various phases of simplification and clarification by Pound and Antheil, the score remains incredibly fragmented and jarring, a fact addressed by many of Pound's best commentators. For example, Fisher draws our attention to the eight lines of Heaulmière's aria, which "bear some of the more difficult mixed meter . . . (bars 194–198: 15/32 to 5/8 to 7/16 to 6/16 to 2/8, and bars 203–213: 11/16 to 3/8 to 19/32 to 2/4 to 3/8 to 11/16 to 7/16 to 2/8 to 3/16 to 2/8)."[47] In *Musical Aesthetics and Literary Modernism*, Bradley Bucknell similarly considers Villon's first aria, "*Et Meure Paris*," noting the lines "are set over seven bars, each of which possesses a different time signature: 11/16, 3/4, 5/8, 7/8, 2/4, 5/8, 11/16."[48] Daniel Albright, in *Untwisting the Serpent*, attends to the superimposition of time signatures at this same moment in the opera, observing, "*Le testament* does not use time signatures in the ordinary sense; the time signatures (evidently devised by Antheil) appear in parentheses beneath the bars when necessary—which is often after every bar. Thus in the first five bars of the first number, we have 11/16, 3/4, 5/8, 7/8, and 2/4 . . . [and in the piece "*Dame du ciel*" there is a sequence of three bars in 33/16, 21/8, and 36/22; . . . [in] the soprano line, . . . [while] the orchestra plays beneath this in 8/4, 8/4, and 5/4."[49] In passages such as these, Pound's interpreters draw our attention to the intense and intensely idiosyncratic rhythmical contours of the opera, and they rightly frame these as the moments when the work is most deeply involved in its own project. What interests me about these formal characteristics of the opera is that they derive from Pound's rejection of harmony as an illusion (perhaps a delusion), and thus directly engage the role of music in humanist thinking. In this respect, Pound's text-setting practices can be read as a corrective to those of the Renaissance humanists. Whereas harmony was a central part of their quest for unity, Pound's opera attempts to capture Villon's "uncounterfeiting and uncounterfeitable voice" by attending to the poet's own rhythmic signature.

Pound's attention to Villon's voice in *Le testament* is thus an expression of the Vorticist-rooted aesthetic ideal by which he distinguishes modern artistic practices. In *Antheil and the Treatise on Harmony*, he compellingly frames the distinctive feature of modernist practice in contrast to Richard Wagner, whose *Gesamtkunstwerk* can be read as the culmination of the existing operatic tradition's ideal of unity between music and text (and drama). As Pound describes:

> There are two aesthetic ideals, one the Wagnerian . . . [in which] you confuse
> the spectator by smacking as many of his senses as possible at every possible

moment, this prevents his noting anything with unusual lucidity, but you may fluster or excite him to the point of making him receptive; i.e. you may slip over an emotion, or you may sell him a rubber doll or a new cake of glass-mender during the hurly-burly.

The other aesthetic has been approved by Brancusi, [Wyndham] Lewis, the vorticist manifestos; it aims at focusing the mind on a given definition of form, or rhythm, so intensely that it becomes not only more aware of that given form, but more sensitive to all other forms, rhythms, defined planes, or masses.

It is a scaling of eyeballs, a castigating or purging of aural cortices; a sharpening of verbal apperceptions. It is by no means an emollient.[50]

It is Neoplatonic pedagogy of aesthetics with an acerbic wit. Pound's amusing allusion to Wagner signals his departure from the aesthetic ideal of the Gesamtkunstwerk, and yet, the work of his own opera does not eschew unity; rather, it reframes the basis upon which unity is achieved. Instead of abstracting a musical form from the text, Pound's efforts in *Le testament* are aimed at the kind of precision he noted in the summation to a 1918 review from *New Age*: "In affairs of tempo the *beat* is a knife-edge and *not* the surface of a rolling pin."[51] Or, perhaps more poignantly, in his 1913 essay "The Serious Artist": "By good art I mean art that bears true witness, I mean the art that is most precise."[52] Sounding a note that will reverberate throughout twentieth-century poetics, he goes on to consider what qualifies as great poetry: "In poetry I mean something like 'maximum efficiency of expression.'"[53] Throughout these comments, Pound demonstrates his consistent commitment to a modernist aesthetic of precision and radical authenticity. For Pound, text setting poses both a great challenge and a tremendous opportunity for the musically true voice of a poet to be heard.

Pound's rich conceptualization of voice is dependent upon an Orphic notion of a unified and authentic subject with expressive, form-making potential, an assumption that lies at the core of Bernstein's contention with Pound. Bernstein has written on several occasions about the challenge of Pound's legacy to contemporary innovative writing, consistently arguing that "contemporary poetry's response to Pound is to enact a poetry that does not fragment for the sake of a greater whole but that allows the pieces to sing their own story—a chordal simultaneity at pains to put off any coherence save that found within its own provisional measure."[54] Cautioning against the comfort of disinterested formalist readings, Bernstein notes, "while one may prefer to dwell on the formal innovations of *The Cantos*, the meaning of these innovations can be adequately appreciated only after we consider the context of their fascist roots. If we are to take Pound, or ourselves, seriously, then we must grapple not with the 'structures themselves' but with the political and historical contexts in which these structures emerge."[55] In such discussions, Bernstein presents a sharply critical take on the slippage between Pound's ideals and his practice. While Altieri recuperates the humanistic ideals that motivated Pound's literary innovations of the Vorticist period, thus seeking to more carefully align Pound's work with his intentions, Bernstein locates in Pound a fundamental misreading of his own work. As Bernstein argues:

> Pound vilified fragmentation and abstraction as debasing the "gold standard" of language, yet his major and considerable contribution to the poetry of our language is exactly his rococo overlayings, indirection, elusiveness. His fast-moving contrasts of attitudes and atmospheres collapse the theatre of Ideational Representation into a textually historicist, unfinishable process of composition by field—a field of many voices without the fulcrum point of any final arbitration, *listening not judging*: a *dis*integration into the incommensurability of parts that marks its entrance into the space of contemporary composition. Insofar as contemporary poetry does not wish simply to admire or dismiss Pound's work but to come to terms with it, these competing dynamics must be reckoned with.[56]

What Altieri identifies as Pound's conscious "undoing of categorical judgment without anxiety about origins,"[57] Bernstein suggests is a way in which Pound's texts slip out of his authorial control, much to Pound's chagrin. In fact, throughout the *Cantos*, whether Pound is drawing from the tradition of Japanese Noh drama, economic theory, contemporary or historical political events, or Greek mythology, the very organizing force behind the poems is none other than Pound's own authority as an expressive subject. That is to say, the very prospect of art as "a display and a test," as Altieri puts it, not only proceeds from but seeks to reify the expressive self of the poet. In this gesture, humanism is recast by establishing authority not by relation to a tradition but via the authority of the individual self. The promise of the *Cantos* and in Pound's poetics more broadly, as Bernstein sees it, is not found by more closely aligning Pound's practice with his ideals but, rather, by building on the failures of that practice. For Pound's poetics to be comprised ultimately of a "*dis*integration" of the source material is a productive failure within his schema that provides his work with its lasting importance. For his poetics to have achieved the coherence that he sought and that Altieri attributes to the figure of the author would mean the perfection of a totalitarian ideal.

Bernstein elsewhere expresses his discomfort with the idea of the poet's autobiography as the guarantor of aesthetic validity in art. While consistently at pains to emphasize the individual and site-specific aspects of poetic practice, Bernstein is equally careful to distinguish such considerations from facile notions of voice, which ultimately devolve into measures of artistic sincerity, and insists, instead, on poetry as linguistic artifice. In this vein, Bernstein advocates for a poetics of the limit, one that actively resists conventional notions of Orphic unity and constantly both seeks and creates difference. In his essay, "Time Out of Motion," Bernstein acknowledges that "the poetic force of expressing what has been repressed or simply unexpressed—whether individual or collective—has been considerable," yet he maintains:

> There is also the necessity of going beyond the Romantic idea of self and the Romantic idea of the spirit of a nation or group (volksgeist) or of a period (zeitgeist), a necessity for a poetry that does not organize itself around a dominant subject, whether that be understood as a self or a collectivity or a theme— writing, that is, that pushes the limits of what can be identified, that not only reproduces difference but invents it, spawning nomadic syntaxes of desire and excess that defy genre (birth, race, class) in order to relocate it.
>
> All these multifoliate creations of language chime—some would say clang—at once; so that there *is* an acoustic locus to English-language poetry: the negative totalization of many separate chords, the better heard the more distinct each strain. Difference is not isolating, but the material ground of exchange; though perhaps it is a dream to hope, in these times, that the pleasurable labor of producing and discerning difference can go beyond the double bind of group identification/individual expression and find idle respite in blooming contrariety—the sonic shift from *KA* to *BOOP* in which the infinite finitude of sound and sensation swells.[58]

In this insistence on the "acentric locus of English-language poetry," it should not go without saying that Bernstein, by way of a parenthetical phrase, aligns literary genre with "birth, race, class." The point being, of course, that for Bernstein, identity does not precede literary activity but is constituted within and through it. As such, the responsibility of the poet for constantly creating new genres by pushing the limits of conventional literary discourse is prerequisite to opening new possibilities of identity, a much more radically provisional and exploratory process than that envisioned by Pound. We should also not miss Bernstein's use of musical metaphors precisely as he puts the assumption of an expressive subject under pressure; describing the multiplicity of English-language poetry as "chiming" or "clanging," and advocating for "the sonic shift from *KA* to *BOOP* in which the infinite finitude of sound and sensation swells," Bernstein's figurative use of music, here, invokes music as an order of knowledge preferable for its capacity to sustain difference within itself.[59] Bernstein presents the landscape of contemporary poetry as a dissonant soundscape, one that becomes only increasingly dissonant the better we listen to it. In this attention to difference, a desire for the ever-increasing possibilities of poetry as an activity in the world, we can locate the base of Bernstein's critical response to Pound. For if Pound's ideal of poetic force is ultimately centripetal, constituting forms that draw together disparate materials, Bernstein's poetics is persistently centrifugal as it seeks to generate new possibilities for poetry. That is, for Bernstein, inasmuch as "difference is not isolating but the material grounds of exchange," and poetry's greatest responsibility is to ceaselessly create new fields of possibility within language, poetry is the very mechanism of human interaction.

In passages such as these, Bernstein's turn to musical metaphors suggests an idealization of music that is familiar among modern and contemporary writers. For this metaphorical language to work, we must accept first poetic language and then the postwar literary scene as tenors for which the common vehicle is music. As such, part of what is curious in these passages is that a poet as intensely textual as Bernstein turns to musical metaphors as a way to figure his arguments about the politics of poetic form and contemporary writing. Such a gesture raises the question of what conceptual space music occupies in Bernstein's imagination and whether its function from that space is similar to the idealization of form in Pound. The answer is that Bernstein neither seeks nor finds in music a formalizing ideal but, rather, one that provides both a conceptualization of the difference he so values and a mechanism for producing and pursuing such difference. This is one of the central themes of his treatments of poetry in performance, most prominently in the introduction to his anthology *Close Listening* (1998), in which he argues, "while performance emphasizes the presence of the poem, and of the performer, it at the same time denies the unitary presence of the poem, which is to say its metaphysical unity."[60] Bernstein goes on to argue that the variety of presence that poetic language achieves in performance "creates something of the conditions of hearing (not just listening to) a foreign language—we hear it as language, not music or noise; yet we cannot immediately process its meaning."[61] That is to say, in the poetry performance, we encounter the physical presence of language, its distinct sound, in a way that may be quite different from the way the text works on the page, and in a way that demands a different range of critical attentions to account for the poem as *heard*. As such, even as Bernstein advocates for incorporating poetry in performance as an integral part of our critical understanding, such a shift in understanding serves not to clarify a particular poem but to proliferate its possibilities; similarly, attending to the idea of poetry in performance as a category of critical analysis will not serve to clarify issues of voice, speaker, prosody, and so on, but will instead usefully (and perhaps perpetually) complicate them. That is to say, while music, musicality, and sound are for Pound unique signatures whose centripetal force implies a metaphysical order, for Bernstein, music draws our attention to sound, and sound draws our attention to the materiality of language, to the embodiment of language in the act of performance—music as *sound* leads us forever outward, is centrifugal.

In their notions of unity and difference, Pound and Bernstein thus present two very different relationships to the humanist tradition: one that seeks a "modern renaissance of the Renaissance," in Altieri's phrase, and one that would more radically recast humanism by basing our relations with the past, with one another, and with ourselves not upon essential sameness but upon perhaps insurmountable and even irreconcilable difference. In this sense, we might expand upon a comment made by Fabrice Fitch in the liner notes to *Shadowtime*: "The adventures of Benjamin's 'shade' have distinct echoes of Greek myth, particularly the Orpheus legend. . . . This allow[s] [Ferneyhough] to speculate on the paths that the genre *might* have taken during the early stages of its development, when its definition and conventions (for example, the boundary between oratorio and opera) were yet to become fixed or standardized. . . . Seen in this broader historical context, *Shadowtime* begins to make more sense: neither 'anti-opera' (Ferneyhough: 'I have no intention of blowing up opera houses') nor 'anti-anti-opera,' but '*ante*-opera.'"[62] A similar framework might be brought to bear on the opera's relation to the history of the genre: that *Shadowtime* is neither anti-humanist (it does not seek to blow-up humanistic institutions of learning, for instance), nor anti-anti-humanist (it does not try to reinforce traditional humanism in the face of a critical onslaught), but *ante*-humanist. If *Le testament* is testimony, above all, to Pound's expressivist humanism, then *Shadowtime* both mourns the failures of that ideal and contemplates an alternate course of events from those set in motion half a millennium ago. If opera as we know it embodies a complex set of choices about the relationship between text and music, then *Shadowtime*'s radical reconsideration of this fundamental feature of opera amounts to a reconsideration of humanism itself. However, as is evident from the synopsis that prefaces the opera, even as Bernstein's libretto and Ferneyhough's setting of it place traditional notions of humanism under a great deal of duress, *Shadowtime* vigorously maintains the pedagogical aims so central to the humanist project: to articulate a meaningful relationship with exemplary predecessors (Benjamin), to formulate modes of relation between disparate discourses (music, poetry, and Benjamin's philosophy), and to develop, through art, more authentic and more ethical relations with others.

Although it feels a bit risky to consider Ferneyhough's compositional practices alongside Pound's, not least because of Pound's amateurism and Ferneyhough's complex sophistication, there are at least three points of contact between this aspect of *Le testament* and *Shadowtime*: the status of musical history, the treatment of source texts, and the relationship to the Orphic tradition. Given the desire of each opera to return to the roots of the genre, it is perhaps no great surprise that they both run through miniature histories of music. As Daniel Albright has argued, while *Le testament* does not develop in a conventional sense, it does work through a series of styles, ranging from troubadour song to modernist avant-gardism. Albright takes the opera's last number, "Frères humains," as a case in point and contrasts Pound's use of the same Villon text with that found in Kurt Weill and Bertolt Brecht's *Threepenny Opera*. He suggests, "Instead of Weill's anger and insistence, Pound hears in it resignation, almost empty wind. An opera that began in a relentlessly monodic fashion has at last achieved if not harmony, at least a fully coordinated counterpoint—an ending that gives a sense of completeness."[63] By contrast, Albright concludes that *Le testament* "is a grave comedy, in which styles themselves are dramatis personae."[64] This observation provides a compelling point of comparison with *Shadowtime* inasmuch as it similarly performs a kind of primer on music history, and does so by way of a compartmentalization of the musical material that, if anything, is even more radical than that of *Le testament*.

Shadowtime is divided into seven scenes, two of which (scene 2 and scene 6) are described as "Barriers," each demarcating shifts in the opera. The first barrier, scene 2, is an eighteen-minute interlude for solo guitar, "marking the beginning of the journey of Benjamin's avatar (shadow or dream figure) from the represented historical times of Scene I to the nonhistorical time of the unfolding opera";[65] the second barrier, scene 6, titled "Seven Tableaux Vivants," imagines Benjamin's Angel of History as Albrecht Durer's Melencolia. The sense of fragmentation continues within scenes. For instance, scene 2 "is made up of 128 small fragments, some of them lasting 2 or 3 seconds, some of them lasting maybe 15 seconds, which are played continuously."[66] As with Pound's opera, in which shifting musical styles function as a structural allegory of Villon's life, and perhaps the universal state of man (achieving "if not harmony at least fully coordinated counterpoint" on the gallows with our fellow thieves), the fleeting forms of classical music in *Shadowtime* speak to the exhaustion of a tradition.

Shadowtime's break with the tradition that underwrites *Le testament* is further evident both in Bernstein's libretto and in Ferneyhough's treatment of it. Whereas Pound's sense of Villon's musicality determines everything about his resulting composition, *Shadowtime* is a study in contradiction. Ferneyhough has described text and music as being "two world systems, those of verbal/conceptual *as opposed to* musical discourse" (my emphasis), with the difference between them an "impossible fracture" ("Words and Music"). The resulting intense fragmentation, stylization, and layering of Bernstein's text in the setting of *Shadowtime* sometimes virtually and often fully obliterate intelligibility. Such is the case, for instance, in scene 3, whose title, "The Doctrine of Similarity," is an adaptation of the title of Benjamin's essay, "The Doctrine of the Similar," in which he characteristically interweaves his materialism and his mysticism, and suggests that the significance of occult knowledge lies largely in the notion of "the 'similar'" and that "such insight . . . is to be gained less by demonstrating found similarities than by reproducing processes which produce such similarities."[67] We can locate such a process of reproducing similarities in the three pieces titled "Amphibolies I (Walk Slowly)," "Amphibolies II (noon) [instrumental]," and "Amphibolies III (Pricks)," which punctuate scene 3.[68] The title "amphibolies" is an alteration of "amphibole," from the Greek meaning to throw or hit on both sides, and is used to designate "an ancient casting net."[69] As we will see, this meaning of the word underwrites the procedure of Bernstein's libretto as it casts text about, but there are other meanings of the word that are equally operative. In the synopsis, Bernstein describes the title as "suggesting mineral ambiguities,"[70] a phrase that rather offhandedly combines two additional fields in which the term resonates: mineralogy and logic. For, mineralogically speaking, an "amphibole" (pronounced "amphi-bowl") designates a grouping of dark-colored, flaky rocks, while, logically speaking, an "amphiboly" (note the different pronunciation) is a variety of ambiguity in which the construction of a sentence or clause allows for it to contain multiple distinct meanings. In the very choice of word for the title, then, these pieces revel in the richness and multiplicity of language.

However, even as the naming of these pieces suggests a poetics of drawing out unsuspected similarities in a word, the movement through the three "amphibolies" demonstrates how Bernstein's commitment to poetry as the production of difference extends Benjamin's interest in processes that produce similarity. This can sound paradoxical—with one talking about differences and the other similarities—but their connection lies in their investment in the similarities of process as opposed to those of product. Bernstein conceives of poetry as a difference-producing machine; drawing out the disparate applications of the same Greek roots in "amphibole" is a poetic act not because it brings to light unnoticed similarities between rocks and reason (obduracy would be far too easy a target), but because it encourages us to think about the stunningly different implications that accrue to common roots over time. For his part, Benjamin is committed to finding similarities that already exist not in the world but in a notion of language as "the highest application of the mimetic faculty," an archive of "non-sensuous similarities or non-sensuous correspondences" that functions most like clairvoyance.[71] For Benjamin, one of the clearest examples of these "non-sensuous similarities" is to be found in the comparison of words for the same thing in different languages. The similarity is not at all between the two words themselves but in their relationship to their common signified, a relationship that Benjamin argues was once fundamentally and directly onomatopoeic and now accessible only through a kind of linguistic reverse engineering. This preoccupation with similarity and difference in the libretto suggests an ethical dimension to the opera's pedagogical intent that would be familiar to early humanists. As Joel Bettridge has argued, *Shadowtime* is clearly a work with a moral at its center, however, "the libretto is not interested in moral teachings or lists of ethical behaviors. It aims to locate ethics in the attempt to read carefully, to interpret our texts and each other well."[72] As the play of difference in Bernstein's adaptations of "amphiboly" demonstrates, to read well means not to arrive at the right conclusion but to participate in an endless act of inquiry and interpretation. In the postmodern Orphism of *Shadowtime*, uncertainty is elemental, and contingency is foundational.

The resulting drama of difference production and interrelation is played out over the three "amphibolies" pieces both in Ferneyhough's use of musical form and in the text of Bernstein's libretto. Ferneyhough's use of canon, in which multiple voices imitate one another, functions as a formal corollary to the notions of similarity, difference, and repetition that are central to the opera. In the libretto, this concern, which the synopsis describes as being ultimately one of "life in extremity," is evident in Bernstein's shifting the order of repeated words. The first part of "Amphibolies I (Walk Slowly)" reads:

Walk slowly

and jump quickly

over

the paths into

the

briar. The

pricks are points on a

map

that take

you back behind the stares

where shadows are

thickest at

noon.[73]

The text is then followed by two phonically based variants, but only the words from this first part return in "amphibolies" 2 and 3. These two later pieces each go through a clear pattern of throwing the text back and forth. In "Amphibolies II (Noon) [instrumental]," the text of the first "amphibole" is reversed line by line and word by word, to read: "noon / at thickest / are shadows / where / stares the behind back you,"[74] and so on. The third and final "amphibole" maintains the line order of the second and reverses word order within the lines, putting the words within lines back in their original order: "Noon / thickest at / where shadows are / you back behind the stares,"[75] and so on. There is one exception to these permutations of words: the three-word line, "the paths into" does not change from poem to poem. Thematically, this makes sense because, as the synopsis tells us, scene 2 is the first scene after the transition "of Benjamin's avatar . . . from the represented historical times of Scene I to the nonhistorical time of the unfolding opera."[76] But the line also seems key to our understanding of this moment in the opera, offering us multiple paths into this aesthetic field in which Benjamin's life and ideas serve as the shared signified treated by two distinct languages, that of Bernstein's poetry and that of Ferneyhough's music. That is to say, as Ferneyhough aptly summarizes it, "like the writings of Benjamin himself, 'Doctrine' concerns itself in the first instance not with presentation but with 're-presentation,'"[77] with the similarity between the text and the music found not in their affinities to one another, but, rather, in the nature of their relationships to both Benjamin's ideas and his life as paradigmatic of modernity.

In this treatment of Benjamin, we find the opera's engagement with one of the most important touchstones of operatic tradition, the myth of Orpheus. Just as the form of opera is an expression of humanist classicism, so too do its thematic preoccupations tend toward the ancient world. Particularly in early opera, the myth of Orpheus seemed irresistible—most famously in Monteverdi's *L'Orfeo* and Peri's *Euridice*, but also in countless other examples. Orpheus also prominently returns in the first reform opera of Christoph Willibald Gluck, *Orpheus and Euridice*. The myth of Orpheus has obvious appeal for opera inasmuch as it articulates the very ideal of uniting poetry and music, but the importance of the myth goes beyond the story line. As Sternfeld argues: "When one examines the voluminous literature dealing with Orpheus . . . one cannot help feeling that the figure of Orpheus stands for more than the well-known plot suggests superficially. The multitude might be touched and diverted by the traditional tale, but those who know, who have been initiated, perceive a deeper meaning. For them Orpheus becomes a sage, a courageous seeker after divine wisdom, a conqueror of death, a religious prophet (if not the founder of a religious cult, Orphism), an *allegory* for Apollo, Dionysus, Osiris, or Christ."[78] This allegorical use of Orpheus is clearly at play in Bernstein's opera, even explicitly so. The synopsis describes scene 4 as Benjamin's "Orphic descent into a shadow world," and the second piece from the scene is titled "katabasis," the hero's descent into the underworld. As such, the opera seems to fall in line with the habits of the genre, as Sternfeld continues: "In [medieval] moralizations [of the myth of Orpheus], Orpheus' descent equals Christ's harrowing of Hell. To a humanist the analogy of such a descent, such a katabasis, with that of Ulysses in Homer's *Odyssey*, with Aeneas in Virgil's *Aeneid*, and, last but not least, with Dante under the guidance of Virgil in the *Divine Comedy*, would be obvious. It is the symbolism of the *figura* of Orpheus that distinguishes him from other musical figures of antiquity (such as Arion or Amphion)."[79] Insofar as *Shadowtime* proposes Benjamin as yet another figure to map onto the myth of Orpheus, the opera seeks not only to honor Benjamin, not only even to demonstrate his life as paradigmatic of modernity, but also to put his ideas into aesthetic practice. It is useful to recall Pound's use of Villon in this light. While Villon does not go through katabasis, he is nonetheless an Orphic figure who serves a symbolic purpose similar to what Sternfeld identifies in the humanist response to the broad applicability of the myth of Orpheus. For Pound, Villon is far more than merely an important predecessor; as a troubadour, he practiced the ideal of poetry closely aligned with music; as a rogue and an outlaw, he embodied Pound's vision of the poet as an embattled and misunderstood outsider; as a major figure of the ubi sunt tradition, Villon participated in the crisis between past and present that forever occupied Pound. As such, Pound's strict fidelity to the sound patterns of Villon's language, his desire to broadcast them to the public, and his determination for the total unity of effect all function to give voice to Villon as a figure of Orpheus, come back from the dead and singing.

The stark difference in the Orphic treatment of Benjamin lies in the simple fact that he is not resuscitated. While "*Shadowtime* projects an alternative course for what happened on that fateful night," as the synopsis tells us, the opera does not work to reunify Benjamin as operatic tradition does the dismembered poet-singer, either literally by altering the events of the story (as was particularly common for operatic performances intended for the court) or figuratively by uniting words and music. In fact, the opera is so permeated by images and varieties of fragmentation—from its splitting of Benjamin into his historical self and his avatar and the interrogations of Benjamin conducted variously by "Three Giant Mouths," "the two-headed figure of Karl Marx and Groucho Marx joined to the body of Kerberus,"[80] to the range of historical figures and Ferneyhough's text-setting practices—that the very idea of reunification is deemed implausible. As such, if Orpheus is a figure for Benjamin in the opera, he is a figure not for magical reunification (of poetry and music, of the dismembered body, of modernism recuperated) but for the power of dispersed and irreconcilable parts. In this sense, the opera recovers the dark or even macabre elements of the Orphic legend as described by Carolyn Abbate: "[Orpheus's] dismemberment . . . entails a split between singing voice and human body in terms that suggest the work of those accustomed to butchery. A terrible physical reality is precondition for the miracle—coexisting within the miracle, side by side. To be complacent about the head, to say it is just a metaphor, thus may reflect willed blindness to the awful aspects of Orpheus' fate, and to a symbolic force that is allied with horror, and not with poetry alone."[81] The sense of grotesque horror that Abbate describes as an essential element of the Orpheus myth's economy also underwrites *Shadow-time*. As the synopsis tells us, "*Shadowtime* inhabits a period in human history in which the light flickered and then failed."[82] This is not an opera of redemption in which similarity and sympathy rule the day, and in which the awful aspects of Benjamin's fate are turned into heroic metaphor. This is an opera that considers the underside of disembodiment as taken literally. In its very rejection of conventional representation or dramatization, the opera emphasizes the historical specificity, the actualness and factualness of Benjamin's death as he tried to escape the all-too-real violence of occupied France. At the same time, Benjamin does live on in the opera inasmuch as it takes his ideas as compositional principles—the opera itself becomes an example of what might best be described as Benjaminian praxis.

The complex symbolic role that Benjamin thus plays in the opera again resonates with Abbate's discussion of the Orpheus myth as being about the double-edged power of music. As Abbate suggests, "In one view, power is in a work per se, in another, in its execution. Power may reside in the transcendent aspect of music that rests above its own precipitation into live performance. Or it may reside in the performer, who produces the immanent matter of the moment. As a master symbol for the performance network, Orpheus' postmortem singing reflects the former, suggesting an Orpheus-puppet moved by Apollo, who speaks through heads and lyres as well as through women and men. As a minor symbol of musical power, however, it can also imply an Orpheus who is the source of all sound, a body part that sings through residual energy."[83] Benjamin's symbolic function in *Shadowtime* can be understood following Abbate's scheme. To a great extent, *Shadowtime* operates in precisely the Apollonian realm of music as disembodied idea, as pure form—this is, after all, a self-described "thought opera." And yet, at the same time, in the very great degree to which the opera resists ideas of unification, it emphasizes the importance of if not the physicality of performance, then the ineffability and ephemerality of it. In its profoundly irreconcilable fragmentation, the opera emphasizes the violent premises of the Orpheus myth that Abbate draws to our attention, and it does so in a way that both revisits those very first operatic invocations of Orpheus and demonstrates a very different set of choices that might have been made about setting text to music. In its grimmest logic, the opera suggests that Benjamin's suicide is not only a significant moment in human history but also the logical conclusion of the humanism of that history, a terrible culmination of events set into motion centuries before his birth. What the opera presents us with, though, is not anti- or post-humanist opera but an opera that wants to reclaim a humanism that revels in artifice and difference as ways of perpetually resisting the risks of orthodoxy, a humanism that embraces the polyphonous, poly-vocal, polycultural, and polymorphous.

In its desire to thus radically recast the bases and implications of humanism, *Shadowtime* powerfully resonates with the critique developed by Emmanuel Levinas. In *The Humanism of the Other*, Levinas argues that "the crisis of humanism in our times undoubtedly originates in an experience of human inefficacy accentuated by the very abundance of our means of action and the scope of our ambitions."[84] In Levinas's analysis, the failure of humanism is ultimately that of the ego, and he proposes to reconfigure a humanism based on a radical receptivity to the Other, what he describes as "a new concept of passivity."[85] In doing so, as Tony Davies has argued, Levinas "retains an ethical register denied to those for whom the human is simply an effect of structure or discourse. Humanity is neither an essence nor an end, but a continuous and precarious process of becoming human, a process that entails the inescapable recognition that our humanity is on loan from others."[86] Tellingly, Bernstein alludes to Levinas in precisely these terms in his essay "State of the Art," arguing that "what poetry belabors is more important than what poetry says, for 'saying is not a game' and the names that we speak are no more our names than the words that enter our ears and flow through our veins, on loan from the past." He concludes, "when we get over this idea that we can all speak to each other, I think it will begin to be possible, as it always has been, to listen to one another, one at a time and in the various clusters that present themselves, or that we find the need to make."[87] Listening instead of speaking, multiplicity instead of exactitude, receptivity instead of expressivity: these are the terms in which the formal innovations of *Shadowtime* reenvision humanism.

If *Shadowtime* can thus be read as a rejoinder to Pound, it should also be understood in the context of Bernstein's other work in musical theater, collected under the title *Blind Witness* and published in 2008. The work in *Blind Witness* professes its affinity with Gertrude Stein and Virgil Thomson, Bertolt Brecht and Kurt Weill—particularly the opera *Blind Witness News*, the repetition in the libretto for which brings to mind *Four Saints in Three Acts*. The libretti in *Blind Witness* are strikingly different from those in *Shadowtime* in their use of character, dialogue, plot, and other conventions of musical theater. The music, too, could not be more different from the intense intellectualization of *Shadowtime*. The composer for the settings of the three operas in *Blind Witness*, Ben Yarmolinsky, consistently works in conventions of popular music and show tunes, and as he describes his text-setting practices in the introduction to the collection, "there is a consistent attempt . . . to follow the rhythms and cadences of our language as it is spoken. . . . The music was evoked by the words."[88] If this line brings to mind Pound's practice in *Le testament*, the suggestion is confirmed when listening to the operas, in which Yarmolinsky's syllabically based text-setting practices are unmistakable. Formally, the three operas in *Blind Witness* thus exist in profound tension with *Shadowtime* and contribute significantly to the breadth of Bernstein's engagement with music. Their difference from the mode of *Shadowtime* can partly be understood by the fact that they are not as powerfully inflected by a specific engagement with the traditions and conventions of opera; and yet, they are also of a piece with *Shadowtime*, bearing the resemblance of their projects in their titles. The titles of *Shadowtime* and *Blind Witness* attest to a circumstance in which vision is both necessary and circumscribed. Bernstein's work articulates this paradox with its disparity of styles (characteristic, also, of his broader oeuvre), ultimately as a rejection of that line of idealizing the signature of the individual that underwrites Renaissance notions of *virtù*, Romantic individualism, and Pound's belief in the "uncounterfeiting and uncounterfeitable" rhythm of an artist's language. For Bernstein, as we hear in *Shadowtime*, the subject, like the Orphic poet, is not a set of positive qualities, nor even a conglomeration of material features, but a locus of receptivity and responsiveness.

2

"Measure, Then, Is My Testament"

Robert Creeley and the Poet's Music

Orpheus' error seems then to lie in the desire which moves him to
see and to possess Eurydice, he whose destiny is only to sing of her.
—Maurice Blanchot

If I can just hear your pretty voice,
I don't think I need to see at all
—Jack White

Charles Bernstein's intervention in the history of modern and post-
modern opera that was the subject of the preceding chapter brackets a period of
innovative American literary practice that was very much indebted to many of
Ezra Pound's key tenets, including his sense of the importance of music to poetry
and the singularity of the poet's voice. For the poets of the New American Po-
etry tradition, those who were either published in Donald Allen's seminal 1960
New American Poetry anthology or closely affiliated with those who were, Pound,
in conjunction with William Carlos Williams and Louis Zukofsky, were the el-
ders whose work framed a trajectory for exploratory, innovative writing outside
of the stifling confines of mainstream and academic poetry; many of these poets
were also powerfully influenced by music, including the emerging bebop of the
period, which played a foundational role for writers such as Amiri Baraka, Allen
Ginsberg, and Jack Kerouac.[1] In his poetry, Baraka develops perhaps the closest
stylistic relationship to bebop among his peers, a relationship that is underscored
by major writings on jazz at the time.[2] For his part, Ginsberg famously described

his 1955 poem *Howl* as "a jazz mass,"[3] while Kerouac builds upon the model of bebop to establish his conception of "spontaneous prose."[4] The prevalence of music as a touchstone for these and other writers of this period speaks to the vitality of the Orphic model of lyric even as the changing practices of both music and poetry fuel one another.

Among the most prominent poets identified with the New American Poetry whose work is shaped by his engagement with music is Robert Creeley, and the role of music in his poetics is both profound and vexing; profound because music is a common point of reference for Creeley, yet vexing because he does not discuss it at length, rather invoking it as a conceptual marker or aesthetic analog to the project of poetry. Early in his career, Creeley's sense of music and its influence on the practice of poetry are deeply shaped by two major forces: the bebop of the 1950s and the emphasis on the meaningfulness of poetic form in the work of predecessors such as Pound, Williams, and Zukofsky. Taken together, these lines of influence underscore Creeley's fierce commitment to the ideal of the individuality of the poet's voice. During and after his time at Black Mountain College, the catalog of his musical influences expands, particularly through the work of John Cage, whose exploration of aleatoric composition reinforces Creeley's interest in the field composition practices of his contemporaries Robert Duncan, Charles Olson, and Jack Spicer, a major development in his career that is first powerfully registered in his collection *Pieces* (1969). Creeley's serious interest in music continues throughout his life and work, with him often peppering his essays and interviews with references to music and musicians, and the broader role of the aural imagination in his poetry is evident in his later work as he repeatedly turns to the phenomenon of the echo. It is the conceptual space occupied by music in Creeley's poetry and poetics that is my interest in this discussion. While the most obvious element of Creeley's music, as with any poet's, is heard in his relationship to the acoustic materials of language, its most resonant aspects in Creeley's work are found in the figural role of Orpheus's backward glance. That is to say, the particular music of Creeley's verse derives from the intensity and self-awareness with which he variously explores, resists, and performs this paradigmatic gesture.

At the heart of the tragic vision of the myth, Orpheus's gesture is both bodily and ocular, the backward glance that seals Eurydice's fate in the underworld. Perhaps the most well-known modern treatment of this moment is that of Maurice Blanchot in his seminal essay "The Gaze of Orpheus," in which he contemplates the gesture and its consequences as providing the very conditions of possibility for lyric, framing a fundamental and necessary flaw, trauma, or lack at the core of the art. As Blanchot argues, Orpheus's look back betrays a crisis of confidence on his part, a radical self-doubt that focuses on the relative reliability of the auditory and the visual senses and that hinges upon the notion of the gaze as a mechanism of entrapment. Had Orpheus trusted the sense with which he is rightly identified—sound—he would have known Eurydice's presence; his confidence flags, though, and Orpheus desperately looks back, violating the terms of his agreement as he seeks the comforting confirmation of vision. Blanchot's twist on this chain of events is to argue that the absence of Eurydice was, in fact, that which Orpheus sought in the first place; the lack whose space is demarcated by where she once stood becomes paradigmatic for lyric as the articulation of absence.[5] Gerald Bruns picks up on Blanchot's reading of the causes and consequences of Orpheus's gesture, similarly considering the role of desire in the poet's turn and attending to the conflict of the senses articulated in the myth. As Bruns argues, there is a slippage or derailment on the part of Orpheus in Hades; while "the task of Orpheus is to bring light out of darkness," the truth is that "Orpheus, however, cannot bear *not* to see Eurydice in her concealment. It is not her beauty that he desires but Eurydice herself, Eurydice in darkness, *as* darkness, the essence of the night (the other night): Eurydice the foreign and inaccessible (*autrui*). It is as though Orpheus were responding to a deeper claim, an exigency more powerful than his essentially philosophical task of restoring Eurydice to the light of being."[6] For both Blanchot and Bruns, the tragedy of the Orpheus myth encapsulates the economy of lyric, which sees it as the desire to represent that which is unrepresentable.

The occasion of Orpheus's backward glance provides a dynamic point of conflict between spatial and temporal metaphors. For his part, Blanchot touches on the temporal aspect of Orpheus's look back when he describes song as an experience through which Orpheus seems to meld with form itself. As Blanchot argues, "only in the song does Orpheus have power over Eurydice. But in the song too, Eurydice is already lost, and Orpheus himself is the dispersed Orpheus; the song immediately makes him 'infinitely dead.' He loses Eurydice because he desires her beyond the measured limits of the song, and he loses himself, but this desire, and Eurydice lost, and Orpheus dispersed are necessary to the song, just as the ordeal of eternal inertia is necessary to the work."[7] For Blanchot, song is not recuperative or ameliorative of Eurydice's loss; rather, song is the manifestation of both her loss into the underworld and Orpheus's own loss of self, first to his grief and then to the excessive expressivity of song as its sound departs the very body from which it issues. As Blanchot's discussion shifts attention to the temporal art of song, it also suggests that the configuring role this gesture plays lies in how the gesture itself structures a temporal experience, a process that is then restaged within the experience of lyric as a temporal form. This sense that the gesture at the heart of lyric is the experience of making the backward glance emphasizes lyric's identity as a temporal (as opposed to spatial) art, and, thereby, sounds its affinity, fraught though it may be, with music. Bruns is even closer to the mark with his description of the scene: "Passage into the day is the movement of the true, the movement of negation that brings life (of a certain sort) out of death. The task of Orpheus is to clarify this movement, to give it form, to bring out its beauty, its harmony and fullness, its intelligibility; it is to make truth radiant. This is the meaning of Eurydice or the work of art: the radiance of truth."[8] The task of the poet is to give form to motion, it is, to crib from Susan Howe, to "articulate sound forms in time." Even Bruns's concluding image, "the radiance of truth," denotes the radiation of the light of truth. As Bruns contemplates the influence of Eurydice's vanishing on the gaze of Orpheus in Blanchot's narrative, *"Celui qui ne m'accompagnait pas,"* he turns Blanchot's famous dictum that "writing begins with the gaze of Orpheus" on its head, and, in the process, turns back toward the realm of the acoustic: "If writing begins with the gaze of Orpheus it is because this gaze no longer unveils what it sees. . . . In such a space seeing is reduced to listening."[9] For Bruns, Orpheus's confrontation with the absence of Eurydice, triggered by the initiating gesture of the backward glance, does not so much reinstantiate or recuperate the aural as it maintains it as the elemental, fundamental, minimal state to which the senses devolve. Even when Orpheus sees the nothing that is Eurydice, he still can't help but listen.

The contemplations of Orpheus's backward glance by Blanchot and Bruns suggest the allegorical richness of the moment. There are several threads running through these readings of Orpheus's turn: the initiating crisis of confidence in the sense of sound, its displacement by sight, and (for Bruns) the return of the superiority of the acoustic; the resulting loss of Eurydice (and, for Blanchot, Orpheus himself) as a necessary trauma, a sacrifice performed so that lyric might come forth; and the gestural basis of lyric that suggests that lyric is not a depiction of a temporal experience but its inscription into language. These elements of the Orpheus myth, the initiating trauma of his glance back and all that is configured within that gesture, frame the role played by music in Creeley's poetry and poetics, a role coursing through the development of one of the most important terms in his lexicon, "measure." In his early years, Creeley's thinking about the measure of poetry very much extends from Pound's equation of poetic form with the *virtù* of the poet, along with the cobbled precision of Zukofsky and Williams. Throughout his commentaries from the 1960s, Creeley routinely echoes and explicitly invokes Pound's dictum that "rhythm is a form cut into time," including in his essays "A Note on Ezra Pound" and "Why Pound!?!" As the punctuation of the latter essay suggests, Creeley is well aware of the deeply troubling nature of Pound's political legacy, and yet, he also recalls that as a young poet in the 1940s he longed for an elder who took the craft of the art seriously, finding Auden effete and Stevens overly philosophical. Creeley interweaves Williams's "Asphodel, That Greeny Flower" with Olson's defense of Pound and Pound's own principles of *logopoeia, phanopoeia,* and *melopoeia.* The essay moves, then, from Williams—"The measure itself / has been lost / and we suffer for it. / We come to our deaths / in silence"[10]—through Olson's account of Pound's heroic forging of a poetics of the "space-field," to Creeley's own wondering at whether Pound's having "moved upon the active principle of intelligence, the concept of *virtù*," is not the penultimate value of his work, perhaps outdone only by "the effect of reading Pound, of that experience of an energy, of ear and mind, which makes a language man's primary act."[11] For Creeley, beyond the significant value of Pound's principle is the experience of the work itself, the experience of all that is encompassed in his sense of the poet's measure. For Creeley, the measure of the poet is an Orphic register that links the voice of the poet, the prosody of his practice, with the act of his intelligence and the truth of his self.

This notion is further developed in Creeley's later essay "A Sense of Measure," which again interweaves Pound, Williams, and other members of "the company." Here, Creeley cites from book 5 of *Paterson*:

> Learning with age to sleep my life away: / saying   .
>
> The measure intervenes, to measure is all we know.[12]

I have retained the spacing between "saying" and the period of the first line to show the empty space, which provides the occasion for what Williams describes as "the measure." This measure, we should note, is not the thoughts in the speaker's head as he contemplates the fatigue of his aging body; it is not a continuation of the preceding thought. The measure is an intervention, a distraction from the speaker's thoughts, a measure that then switches from noun to verb as it designates the challenge of the poet to become cognizant of just such extraintentional mental and emotional events. Creeley further develops the relationship between attentiveness and form that shapes what he means by "measure":

> I am deeply interested in the act of such *measure*, and I feel it to involve much more than an academic sense of metric. There can no longer be a significant discussion of the meter of a poem in relation to iambs and like terms because linguistics has offered a much more detailed and sensitive register of this part of a poem's activity. Nor do I feel measure to involve the humanistic attempt to relate all phenomena to the scale of human appreciation thereof. And systems of language—the world of discourse which so contained Sartre et al.— are also for me a false situation if it is assumed they offer a modality for being, apart from description. I am not at all interested in describing anything.
>
> I want to give witness not to the thought of myself—that specious concept of identity—but, rather, to what I am as simple agency, a thing evidently alive by virtue of such activity. I want, as Charles Olson says, to come into the world. Measure, then, is my testament. What uses me is what I use and in that

complex measure is the issue. I cannot cut down trees with my bare hand, which is measure of both tree and hand.[13]

Rejecting the distancing effects of classical prosody and the hubris of humanism, Creeley seeks in the idea of "measure" a register of his self as action in the world, the recursive relationship between his self and language, "what uses me and what I use."

In his essay "A Poem Is a Complex" (1965), Creeley extends his thoughts on "measure" by both naming the analogy between poetry and music and framing the resulting paradox. He notes, "I think for myself the primary term is that words can move in the measure of song, although I do not wish to confuse poetry with music. But in a poem I tend to hear whatever can be called its melody long before I have reached an understanding of all that it might mean."[14] For Creeley, poetic composition happens first in the ear. While this might be read to simply mean that the poet first hears the sound patterns of the emerging poem, the qualifications in his language suggest that something more complicated is at play. He twice denotes the distance between poetry and music—first explicitly, noting that they should not be confused, and then by the qualification, "whatever can be called its melody"—and so carefully frames an analogical relationship between the two arts, the poignancy of which resides in what he means by the "measure of song." To what extent and in what ways, then, are the song's measure, the measure that is his testament, the measure that is the articulation of the relationship between his self and language, and the "measure of both tree and hand" the same "measures"? Collating these uses of the term, we find that Creeley's "measure" works in several registers: it marks a temporal unit, suggesting that a poem is akin to a musical phrase that arises from the poet's recursive relationship with language, a kind of musical signature in words; it is a unit that delineates the defining limitations as characteristic of physical objects, including trees and hands; and it is an activity in which the particular truths of things are apprehended. Encompassing these notions, then, Creeley's verse is an act of measurement, of sounding the limits of the self within language, within time, and within experience. In this measure, the asymptotic proximity of poetry and music are underscored by the notion of musicality, in which the poet undertakes the impossible Orphic task of inscribing within language that which has always already gone.

The emphasis on attentive immediacy that emerges in this discussion of Creeley's sense of measure underscores the importance of bebop to his early poetics. Like many poets, writers, artists, and other creative workers coming of age in the period immediately following World War II, Creeley registers the rhythmic innovations, the energy, and even the cultural ethos of bebop in his early poetry.

As he reflects in "Notes Apropos 'Free Verse,'" perhaps the overriding lesson from bebop was to be found in how it manipulated time:

> For my own part I feel a rhythmic possibility, an inherent periodicity in the weights and durations of words, to occur in the first few words, or first line, or lines, of what it is I am writing. Because I am the man I am, and think in the patterns I do, I tend to posit intuitively a balance of *four*, a foursquare circumstance, be it walls of a room or legs of a table, that reassures me in the movement otherwise to be dealt with. I have, at times, made reference to my own interest when younger (and continuingly) in the music of Charlie Parker—an intensive variation on "foursquare" patterns such as "I've Got Rhythm." Listening to him play, I found he lengthened the experience of time, or shortened it, gained a very subtle experience of "weight," all by some decision made within the context of what was called "improvisation"—but what I should rather call the experience of possibility within the limits of his materials (sounds and durations) and their environment (all that they had as what Pound calls "increment of association" but equally all they had as literal condition, their phenomenological fact). There is an interview with Dizzy Gillespie (in the *Paris Review*, No. 35) in which he speaks of rhythm particularly in a way I very much respect. If *time* is measure of *change*, our sense of it becomes what we can apprehend as significant condition of *change*—in poetry as well as in music.[15]

I have quoted this passage at length to demonstrate the terms of Creeley's appreciation for bebop. In a gesture central to his thinking about music and musicality, he begins by foregrounding rhythm as deriving from the particular patterns of his mind thinking. That is, for Creeley, the sonic contours of the poem derive from the habits of attention and thought specific to the poet at work. Thus, for him, as he finds himself innately invested in figures of four, he identifies with Parker's rhythmic improvisations as a means to ground his own prosody. What's more, insofar as Creeley sees the projects of poetry and music as fundamentally aligned on this point of using time as the condition of change, the task of the Orphic poet becomes to explore and exploit the malleability of time through language.

The role of temporality in Creeley's Orphic poetics is at the center of his essay "Form" (1987), which focuses on his poetry of the 1950s. Creeley prefaces the essay with the title poem from his collection, "The Whip" (1957). As he so often does when recalling his writing and lifestyle in the years immediately after the war, Creeley here notes the emotional difficulty of the situation—from the general postwar cultural trauma to his own personal challenges, both romantic and existential. Struggling to find his voice as a young poet, Creeley found not just inspiration but a model in jazz. As he recollects, he carefully qualifies his invocation of jazz, "Not that it's jazzy, or about jazz—rather, it's trying to use a rhythmic base much as jazz of this time would. . . . It isn't writing like jazz, trying to be some curious social edge of that imagined permission. It's a time one's keeping."[16] As Creeley rejects both the formal imitation of jazz and its thematic treatment, he frames the relationship between his poetry and jazz as that of the parallel procedures by which time is made material and retained within each medium.

Creeley's reflections on how jazz influenced his early formation as a writer are remarkably consistent throughout his career. As his comments suggest, the influence of jazz can be heard primarily in the nature of his relationship to the materials of his medium, rather than in theme. While this can certainly devolve for some writers into weak imitations of jazz rhythms (a risk he is aware of in his insistence that his poems are "not jazzy"), for Creeley, the stylistic register is significant because this is the realm wherein the poet achieves his voice. That is to say, as he remarks with respect to "The Whip," the time one is keeping through the rhythmical signature of the poem is an instantiation of the poet's particular mind thinking. The stakes for form are thus very high indeed for Creeley, as his exploration of poetry as a register of the rhythm of an individual's thinking mind and speaking voice is powerfully shaped by Pound's arguments, which propose the rhythm of the poem as both an opportunity and an ethical responsibility faced by the poet. Later in his career, Creeley sheds somewhat the weight of Pound's influence in his thinking about the relationship between poetry and music, but he still situates their association on the grounds of temporality and identity. For instance, in a radio interview conducted by Julia Brown in 1983 for the "Territory of Art" radio show produced by the Museum of Contemporary Art in Los Angeles, Creeley seamlessly associates the development of 1960s innovative jazz with that of the Second Viennese School. In the interview, titled "Attitudes Toward the Flame" and available on PennSound, Creeley directly addresses the role of music in his writing, drawing attention to the temporality of music as related to his writing processes. Creeley seems to situate avant-garde jazz and the practices of twelve-tone composition on a continuum, extending from temporal maximalism to minimalism. Creeley recollects, "Time in that situation was so altered from the usual habituations I'd known . . . Ornette Coleman, John Coltrane . . . anyone who was trying to see 'how long can we expand the situation.'" He then immediately counters this commentary on the elasticity of time in post-bop to its reduction by Anton Webern, whose work, Creeley says, posed the question of "how long did it have to be to be there."[17] Creeley reads Webern's work, here, as an experiment testing the limits of finitude faced by the Orphic poet.[18] If the challenge of this poet is to capture that which is, like Eurydice, always already disappearing, then what is the smallest quantity of that subject—Eurydice or time—necessary for its presence to be registered in the work?

As this discussion makes clear, for Creeley, it is not merely that music and poetry bear an analogous relationship but that the idea of the "measure," as both noun and verb, underwrites both music and poetry, linking them in the artist's Orphic project. That is to say, for Creeley, music is a capacious, if nebulous term that goes to the core of what poetry does as both an individual and a social practice. In this light, one of the more striking aspects of Creeley's early and mid-career work—that contained within the first volume of his *Collected Poems*—is the prevalence of the word "song" and similar terms in the titles of poems. The word appears in more than twenty poems, presenting an ever-inchoate theory of music and its role in poetic practice for Creeley. As "songs," these poems are concrete instances of Creeley's Orphic poetics, and they bring a number of features to the fore: song as an instance of the sense of measure as fundamentally related to the poet's subjectivity; poetry as an act that participates in a social and communal tradition, often signaled in Creeley's work through his adoption of conspicuously archaic or anachronistic diction, modes of address, and forms; the song of poetry as infused with a specifically literary tradition, heard in Creeley's echoing of the verse of previous poets; and, finally, the sense of song and the music of poetic language as instantiations of the gesture of the turn that is so central to the story of Orpheus and the broader lyric tradition.

Many of Creeley's song poems demonstrate the importance of the literary past to his Orphic measure, as they show him working in a conspicuously antiquated mode. For instance, in the poem "Old Song," collected in 1968 in *The Charm*, Creeley deploys a form that seems to be a stripped-down ballad, with stanzas of two lines instead of four and patterned end-rhymes, as well as diction that can only be described as anachronistic. In the first line, the speaker's term of endearment for his beloved is "love," a term whose subtle anachronistic quality is reinforced in the second stanza's description of the impending sunrise "over yon sea."[19] In "Chanson," from *For Love* (1962), Creeley similarly adopts a mode that is strongly rooted in the past, as is evident in both the title of the poem and its subsequent lines. The poem begins by reinforcing the suggestion of Old World tradition in its first line, with Creeley writing in French: "Oh, le petit rondelay!"[20] Creeley's key terms, here—chanson and rondelay—shape most of what comes in the poem. As it continues, the poem sings of the speaker's aging and links its own identity as song with that of birds in the first line of the second stanza: "as when for a lark / gaily, one hoists up a window / shut many years."[21] The lark for which the window is opened, here, is of course both a bird, whose song is the "rondelay," an invocation of the pastoral tradition with which the roundelay as a form is identified, and a whim upon which the speaker acts as he throws open the window. As such, the speaker in these lines opens the window to let in not only the bird but also the entirety of the pastoral tradition, reflecting upon a bygone mode as he himself ages. The echoes of a previous literary and linguistic epoch continue in the next stanza, as the speaker refers to his beloved as both "the lady" and "madame." Then, in a rather curious gesture, the final stanza begins with, "etc." and concludes with a repetition of the first stanza, thus coming full circle as the song that it is. That insertion, though—"etc."— bears consideration. While this brief poem has somewhat playfully, somewhat touchingly considered aging and human relationships, this abbreviation reminds us that the thematic content is utterly familiar, and perhaps even risks being banal or cliché, but this familiarity of the song is precisely its necessity. As he will say in one of his many poems titled "Song" in *For Love*, "It still makes sense / to know the song after all."[22] For Creeley, it makes sense to know the song because knowing the words to the song situates one within a living cultural tradition (and ensures the ongoing vitality of that tradition); what's more, doing so integrates the reader/listener/song-lover within an entire structure of relationship that is embedded within and (re)activated through the song, much as Orpheus's singing establishes social order through its articulation of form.

The Orphic underpinning of the reasons that it might still make sense to know the song become clear in several of the more prominent poems from *For Love*. For instance, the poem "A Song"[23] begins by recalling Creeley's Poundian terminology in "Music Is My Measure," where the song is described as a "testament." As he does in the essay, Creeley, as did Pound, links song with an elemental quality of identity or person, although here it is a quality sought after rather than one simply possessed or expressed. This "song" is divided into three sections, the first of which contemplates the speaker's desire. The first lines of the poem both link song and testament and suggest that they are not exactly the same thing: "I had wanted a quiet testament / and I had wanted, among other things, / a song."[24] The enumeration of testament and song, here, both denotes them as two objects of the speaker's past desire and delineates them as different. In the lines that follow, song comes to the fore, with the speaker describing what it would have been, the phrasing of desire in the past conditional completely sealing it off from the possibility of ever coming to pass. In this melancholy tone, the poem first describes the song as "a like monotony," which resonates both with the sense of ongoing, predictable boredom and the perpetuity of a singular sound, or tone. Then, song becomes "(a grace / Simply. Very very quiet // A murmur of some lost / thrush, though I have never seen one."[25] As the lines continue to qualify the sense of the song the speaker desires, transforming it from a "monotony" to "a grace," the poem also reduces the song to a minimal state, a mere "murmur." The section concludes, then, with the odd assertion that the speaker has never seen a "thrush," perhaps the most common of the passerine birds in North America and Europe. How can it be that the speaker has never seen a robin or a blackbird? Of course, the claim is clearly figurative, and that figuration hinges on the conflict between the aural and the visual senses. To this point, the poem has articulated the vocal and aural desires of song, and it is this, the "murmur of some lost / thrush," that the speaker has never seen, not the thrush itself. Having, by definition, not seen the murmur, the variety of his desire is acoustic in nature. This peculiar invocation of the "thrush," in the context of the tension between the aural or acoustic world and the visual one, brings to mind Thomas Hardy's "The Darkling Thrush," which is marked by the eruption of the song of the thrush onto the bleak winter landscape. That is, Creeley seems, here, to be writing Hardy in reverse, thus enacting a naturalistic optimism from which the speaker feels removed. For his part, while Creeley's thrush is "lost," his speaker's senses are on the side of the birds, attuned, as they are, to song.

As the poem continues, it shifts its focus from the interiority of the speaker's desire for song to an addressee. In typically enigmatic Creeley fashion, the section begins with a relative pronoun whose point of reference is uncertain: "Which was you then. Sitting."[26] It is not at all clear what the speaker links "you" to. The grammar and punctuation of the opening sentence present a number of possibilities. Although the sentence seems to make a direct assertion, the slipperiness of "which" troubles the line, which reads as much like a question as it does a statement. The referent could be to the thrush, perhaps suggesting that the speaker does not see the "you" he seeks any more than he sees the thrush; or, perhaps the line refers back through the many qualifiers of song from the preceding section. That is, "you" could be equated with an unknown addressee, the murmur, the grace, or even the eponymous "song" of the poem as a whole. As the lines continue, the poem again emphasizes a sense of minimalist stillness, as the addressee sits, "at peace, so very much now this same quiet. / A song."[27] Again, the lines bring music into proximity with silence, the two, here, seeming to be versions of one another.

In this instance, Creeley's sense of music resonates powerfully with that of the French philosopher, Vladimir Jankélévitch, in *Music and the Ineffable*. A French moral philosopher and theorist of musical aesthetics of the generation that worked through the years of World War II, Jankélévitch is relatively little known in American critical discourse for reasons that are themselves quite interesting, although he and his work dramatically influenced Roland Barthes, Catherine Clément, and Emmanuel Levinas, among others. In *Music and the Ineffable*, Jankélévitch links music and love (and duty) in a way that is familiar to Creeley's poem, arguing that "music has this in common with poetry, and love, and even with duty: music is not made to be spoken of, but for one to *do*, it is not made to be said, but to be 'played.' No. Music was not invented to be talked about."[28] He continues, "With this [musical act], there is nothing to 'think' about, or—*and this amounts to the same thing*—there is food for thought, in some form, for all infinity; this charm engenders speculation inexhaustibly, is inexhaustible as the fertile ground for perplexity, and the same charm is born of love. Infinite speculation, as soon as it becomes exhilaration pure and simple, is analogous to the poetic state."[29] Jankélévitch's invocation of the charm reminds us that Orpheus's poetry is, quite literally, enchanting, just as Creeley's poem attends to the insatiability of the song's charm. For Creeley, the charm of the poem thus carries within it both the possibility of its own continuation, its "gross perpetuity," and the weight of responsibility for he who would sing it. As the poem concludes, "A song. / Which one sings, if he sings it / with care."[30] For Creeley, as for Jankélévitch, this near-silent-song, this "murmur," this "grace . . . very very quiet" of a song in the singer's aural imagination would be that activity in and through which the Orphic poet would articulate his relation with the beloved.

In "A Song," then, Creeley presents song in an asymptotic relationship to silence as a means of emphasizing the intensity of both the Orphic poet's desperation and the responsibility assumed by someone who would sing the song. In so doing, he also moves song toward a minimal sense of sound, much as he noted in the music of Webern, and thus problematizes our common sense of how we might think about music—if nothing else, it must remain the art of sound. The questioning of the relationship between music and sound, of what else might constitute the musicality of poetic language, is perhaps most profoundly explored in "Air: 'Cat Bird Singing,'" also from *For Love* and a poem that, like so many of Creeley's "songs," involves a conspicuous link to the past. Here, that link is found in Creeley's use of the term "Air" in the title as a way of indicating the poem's proximity to song. Titling the poem an "Air" situates it in conversation with the Renaissance tradition of the air, a lyric to be performed with lute accompaniment, and, more specifically, the work of Thomas Campion, whose *Book of Airs* from 1601 contains more than one hundred songs with lyrics by Campion and music by himself and Philip Rosseter. Campion, of course, is himself a notable figure in discussions about the relationship between poetry, music, and the musicality of poetic language, as found both in his *Art of English Poesie*, from 1602, and in his experiments with adapting Greek quantitative verse into English. The link to Campion is not incidental to the poem's title, and Creeley makes it explicit partway through the poem, describing the melody of his beloved's speech as "what Campion spoke of // with his / follow thy fair sunne unhappie shadow."[31] I will come back to the Campion poem, but first I want to consider how Creeley's poem gets there. The remainder of the title, "Cat Bird Singing," would at first glance seem to anticipate a boisterous or at least confident tone in the poem, since the term's idiomatic usage designates someone who is sitting in a privileged position. This tone is utterly absent from the poem, though; and, in fact, in its opening the mood is rather brooding or even foreboding. The poem begins, "Cat bird singing / makes music like sounds coming // at night."[32] The first line presents three terms whose articulation sets up the tension of the poem, "cat," "bird," and "singing." Creeley breaks the term for the bird, "catbird," in two, thus introducing several vectors of tension into the poem. On the one hand, there is the name of the bird, a "catbird," whose name rings ironic in the context of Creeley's emphasis on the truthfulness of voice inasmuch as the bird's name derives from the fact that its call sounds like the meow of a cat. The separation of the terms, then, emphasizes the irony in this voicing, as "cat bird singing," instead of "catbird singing," introduces the contest between predator and prey. And it is this contest, indeed, that the poem sings. The predatory sensibility of the poem is taken up again in the next two stanzas, as "the trees, goddam them / are huge eyes. They // watch, certainly, what // else could they do?"[33] As he so often does, Creeley again introduces multiple units of meaning by inserting line breaks into what is an otherwise straightforward sentence. Here, the most powerful example is the first line of the third stanza, "watch, certainly, what." The lineation creates three sound units—"certainly," bracketed by the nearly alliterative "watch" and "what." As much as these sound units are foregrounded in the lines, though, they also inflect the meaning of the lines. Here, the emphasis falls on the activity of perception, and the line moves quickly from a sense of precision to wonderment or questioning. This is, of course, immediately reversed in the next line, as the sense of the words again falls into a fatalistic mode.

The next stanza continues the figural linkages between the "cat bird singing," the speaker, and the beloved. From the beginning of the poem, the relationship is triangulated, as Creeley's division of the name of the bird into its two constituent parts gives us "[a] cat" and "[a] bird singing," a gesture that exteriorizes what would be the catbird's song and assigns it to a bird in a tree (thus also providing the tree with the eyes that watch the speaker). This shift goes on to link birdsong with the voice of the beloved: "My love // is a person of rare refinement, / and when she speaks, // there is another air, // melody—what Campion spoke of // with his / follow thy fair sunne unhappie shadow."[34] As Creeley's speaker further attends to his beloved, he adopts an anachronistic voice and explicitly invokes Campion. The speaker's description of his beloved as a person of "rare refinement" once again shows Creeley slipping into a mode whose diction and manner of address seem to belong to a bygone era. So, too, does the argument of the lines, as the beloved's voice is described not as speech but as song, "melody," as essential and life-giving for the speaker as is the air he breathes. The link, then, to the Campion is one of the poem's most interesting gestures. The ellipsis at the end of the line seems to draw the reader out of Creeley's poem, demarcating a temporal span to be filled with a trip to the bookshelf for a look at the Campion. At first, it seems to extend from a certain insufficiency in the speaker's own descriptive language; unable to capture the beauty of the beloved's voice, he turns, instead, to the ready reference of a well-known poem.

However, this reading misses the emotional economy of Creeley's Orphic relationship to both the beloved and the past. His speaker does not invoke

Campion because he does not have his own descriptive language; rather, he qualifies the "melody" of his beloved's voice by identifying it with "what Campion spoke of." That is, there is not something so clichéd and simplistic as a timeless beauty in his beloved's voice but, rather, a whole mechanism or articulation of emotional relation that is replayed time and time again between different individuals; quoting the Campion in the poem is an example of why it still makes sense to know the song. That is to say, there is a form to the relation between the speaker and his beloved that is heard in the measure of her voice. The elements of that form are carried not within Creeley's own poem, though, but within Campion's poem as it dramatizes light's pursuit by shadow. One reading of Campion's poem would link its argument with that of the Creeley poem; this reading would emphasize the sly melancholy of Campion's contemplation of ill-fated love with the speaker's adulation of his beloved in Creeley's verse. This reading, of course, is not wrong, but it misses the trigger of Creeley's turn to Campion, which has much more to do not only with a poet's ear, his sense for the music of language, but with the way the poet's musicality is a measure of himself. In these lines, for instance, Creeley turns to Campion by way of rather peculiar, almost clumsy phrasing—"what Campion spoke of // with his." The phrasing and lineation seem to be determined partly by prosodic concern. The evolving vowel pattern of the first line, from a's to o's, contrasted by the vowel rhyme of the second line; the first line's prepositional weight and the emphasized possessive mode of the second; the alliterative link between each line's first word: all draw out the allusion to Campion, bringing attention to the act of allusion itself and emphasizing the relationship between Campion and his verse. That is, the emphasis of these lines falls on "with *his*," claiming the Campion poem as an acoustic signature, his own verbal testament. In Campion's poem, then, his signature is characterized both by his use of rhythm, meter, and rhyme—all typical of his "airs"—as well as in the economy of the relationship between sun and shadow, whose tension animates the poem. In this sense, Creeley's nod to Campion is much more than simply a literary allusion; it is an Orphic invocation of a literary predecessor whose work resounds through his beloved's voice, which carries within it the melody of a poem, its unique manner of unfolding in time, from nearly four centuries earlier. Campion's "tune" is carried, embedded like an acoustic artifact, in the measure of the beloved's voice.

The allusion to Campion marks an abrupt turn in Creeley's poem, as it quickly draws to a close. Having aligned the voice of the beloved with Campion's "airs," the speaker immediately collapses the terms of the bird's name that have until now been separated throughout the poem, "cat bird" becoming, "catbird, catbird," and again ringing the anachronistic tone of "O lady" as the speaker desperately pleads, "O lady hear me. I have no // other /voice left."[35] The closing lines make starkest a contrast that has operated throughout the relationship between Creeley's and Campion's poems. Much as was the case with the echoes of Hardy in the earlier poem, here, even as the Campion sounds through and seemingly gives shape to the voice of Creeley's beloved, the two poems are dominated by attention to different senses—the visual drama of Campion's poem is transformed in Creeley into one of sound. While Creeley's speaker alludes to the Campion poem as a way to describe the "melody" of his beloved's voice, the poem itself is defined by its attention to the visual contrasts between the sun and the moon. One of the most powerful effects of this change is found in the conclusion of Creeley's poem. Whereas Campion's poem is a study in the permanence of cyclicality, Creeley's poem concludes with the speaker acknowledging the roughness or insufficiency of his own voice as he begs merely to be heard. That is, the trajectory of Creeley's poem is outward, not cyclical, with the speaker, on his last breath, his last air, dispersed in and through his appeal to the beloved's aural recognition. And it is here that we can locate the final Orphic tragedy of this poem. The speaker has appealed for his testament to be heard by a beloved whose emotional world is defined by the endless, cyclical machinations of lovers' pursuits; the speaker only hopes, perhaps in vain, to pierce the bubble of her "other air."

The adoption of apparently anachronistic modes and lyric dispositions, such as Creeley's invocations of Hardy and Campion, is, in fact, a claim on Creeley's part about the ongoing vitality of the Orphic project. Creeley quite literally turns to the past, invoking and activating past poetic practices so as to lay claim to their continued efficacy. The retroactive structure of this aspect of Creeley's work, his reaching into the past to make it new, is also played out in the recurring figure of the turn in his poems. That is to say, Creeley's turn to poetic modes sometimes centuries removed from his contemporary moment is a performance of the act of the poet on his part, the significance of which is underlined by the repeated images of turning, return, recurrence, repetition, reflection, and other varieties of *fort-da* experience that pepper his work. As found in the two volumes of his *Collected Poems*, for instance, it is noteworthy that his first poem is titled "Return" and one of the last poems from the posthumously published *On Earth*, titled "Here," reads, "up a hill and down again. / Around and in — // Out was what was all about / but now it's done. // At the end was the beginning, / just like it said or someone did. // Keep looking, keep looking, / keep looking."[36] Until the repetition of the two-word phrase over the last two lines, the poem seems to be an exercise in tracking the physical and, ultimately, temporal movements of perspective; the final line, then, partly offers a way out, through the admonishment to keep looking. And yet, its repetition also re-instantiates the sense of cyclicality articulated earlier in the poem. As such, looking does not, in fact, offer a way out but, rather, the available means by which to perpetuate the poem's quest, which seems to have resolved into an awareness of life's cyclicality.

Between the bookends of these formulations of repetition, recurrence, and return, Creeley, throughout his career, frequently develops and deploys similar gestures, with lines such as "look forward to go back";[37] "now to go back, I cannot";[38] "in the company of love / it all returns."[39] As even these brief snippets demonstrate, Creeley does not merely endorse the process of turning as a mode of critical reflection or privileged apprehension; neither the poet nor the speaker he constructs can so easily attain such an Archimedean point. Rather, the project of much of Creeley's poetry arises from the fact that perception itself is embedded in the unfolding of events. As a result, Creeley's poetry does not merely represent or describe the process of turning but, instead, almost compulsively articulates and instantiates it as the very procedure of poetry itself.

The preponderance of the Orphic turn as not merely an image but a gesture and a form in Creeley's poetry is one of the most powerful manifestations of his Orphic disposition. To put it baldly, I would suggest that the turn in Creeley is, in fact, a key element of his measure, of his music, even more so than the prosodic signature through which the musicality of his verse is perhaps more obviously identified. That is to say, Creeley's performance of the turn, and his often self-conscious thematization of it, show him to engage with what Kaja Silverman has identified as the paradigmatic function of Orpheus's glance back. As Silverman argues, this moment figures the role of reflection more generally in Western critical thought, examples of which she finds in writers and thinkers ranging from Sigmund Freud to Martin Heidegger and Walter Benjamin. As she says with respect to Freud, "his therapeutic practice is based on the act of turning around to look at the past and the belief that this can make the past happen again, in a new way."[40] Noting the role of the turn in Heidegger and Benjamin, she argues that they "also attribute redemptive power to the act of turning around. . . . The Heideggerian 'turn' is a turn toward infinitude . . . [and] the Benjaminian 'turn' is also a turn toward analogy. The present is connected to the past through unauthored correspondences. . . . These correspondences are revealed to us at moments of danger through objects that are 'blasted' out of the 'continuum of historical succession' and journey toward us."[41] For Creeley, the prospect of the "redemptive power" of the turn is much more problematic, and so his work is most often situated precisely within the act of turning itself. It is in this sense that he, as Benjamin Friedlander has argued, attempts to capture experience such that he might successfully transmit not a representation of that experience but the experience itself to the reader. Drawing upon Benjamin's critical lexicon for experience, Friedlander usefully categorizes this aspect of Creeley's work into three modes, the "immediate," the "self-conscious," and the "retrospective."[42] As Friedlander argues with respect to Creeley's use of echoes in his poems, a topic I will treat in more detail later in this discussion, echoes appeal to Creeley at least partly because "repetition, even a mechanical one, provides reassurance that the scene of writing and the scene of reading—two distinct moments of experience—can, and indeed must, coincide."[43] Even though this reassurance is certainly a fleeting one, as Friedlander notes, it is also important because it allows Creeley to "shape and so predict a future moment, providing thereby the possibility of a shared experience."[44]

One of Creeley's most poignant articulations of the figure of the turn is found in a poem that bears the term in its title, "The Turn." The poem begins by again visiting the intra-gender tension that shapes so much of *For Love*, here in a scene underscored by Orpheus's paradigmatic glance back: "Each way the turn / twists, to be apprehended: / now she is there, now she."[45] In typical fashion, Creeley breaks this stanza before the commonplace, "now she's there, now she's not," is completed—that comes in the next stanza—leaving the reader, instead, in the presence of "she," a presence redoubled by the line, "now she is there, now she." It is the preceding line that interests me most, though, for how it configures the action of the turn with which the poem commences, this turn that "twists, to be apprehended:" The punctuation of this line and Creeley's subtle shifts in grammar trouble what might otherwise be a very straightforward depiction of turning around to see. In these lines, though, it is the turn itself that is presented as twisting, not the speaker, in a gesture that brings to mind nothing so much as Ouroboros with a Möbius strip. That is to say, in these opening lines, the conventional notion of turning to acquire an Archimedean point is replaced with that of a turn that turns upon itself, apprehending itself, not something exterior to it. This complication of the gesture of turning around, then, sets up the introduction, "now she is there," which seems to be not so much the presentation of a person or character in the material world as it does an object in the negative space made possible by the turn's action.

Turning upon itself, the poem articulates, like a whirlpool, a void to which Creeley attributes the feminine pronoun: "she" could just as easily read "Eurydice." The next stanza continues to consider the role of the absence of "she," noting that, "having gone," she "went before / the eye saw."[46] Again, though, Creeley complicates the apparent sense of his phrases and clauses, beginning the next stanza with the "nothing." So, it is now *both* the case that she went before the eye saw, it saw nothing, *and* that she "went before / the eye saw / nothing," implying, at least, the eye perhaps did see something, that shadowy, empty space where Eurydice had been. As the stanza continues, it engages with Orpheus's legendary ability to move the animals, rocks, and trees, here, demonstrating that power to be a mute fantasy, as "the tree / cannot walk, all its / going must be violence."[47] In the place of Orpheus's magic, this poem has the clamor of machinery: "they listen // to the saw cut, the / roots scream. And in eating / even a stalk of celery / there will be pathetic screaming."[48] Having flatly denied even the efficacy of Orpheus's prescribed vegetarianism, the poem returns to its initiating concerns with desire and recollection. In this penultimate stanza, in fact, Creeley yokes these two elements together, first announcing the truism, "But what we want / is not what we get," and then posing the facetious and ridiculing question, "What we saw, we think / we will see again?"[49] In the next stanza, the poem concludes with a series of pronouncements, "We will not. Moving, / we will / move, and then / stop."[50] Again, Creeley's lines capitalize upon the multivalence of words, here particularly with respect to "will," with his lines invoking the sense of "will" as a species of desire and conviction as much as an innocent helping verb. What's more, this emphasis on the act of will is interwoven and contrasted with the sense of forward motion. First, we move whether or not we will to do so; then, we move following our will, although the sense of volition is far from certain and we do so only to immediately, then, "stop." The trajectory, here, is temporal more than it is spatial, as we move through time, and toward death, toward that abiding sense of finitude that Silverman identifies in the Orphic disposition. In the context of this poem, which began with the images of turning upon oneself, the conclusion seems bleak, indeed, as it proposes death as the only and unavoidable end to our constant desire to recapture, to reapprehend that which has gone before.

The complex role of reflection that animates "The Turn" becomes a prominent feature in Creeley's later poetry and is often characterized as an acoustic or aural phenomenon. This development in Creeley's sense of measure is perhaps most evident in the predominance of the term "echo" in his verse, both as a title and as a figure, which effectively displaces the notion of "song" from earlier in his career. Just as an overview of the first volume of his collected poems reveals how often he invokes song in the titles of his poems, a similar perusal of the second volume, from 1975 to 2005, is telling for the term's almost total displacement by the term "echo." In fact, there is an odd and certainly unintentional symmetry between these two halves of Creeley's career: whereas the first volume contains more than twenty poems with the word "song" or some closely related term in the title and five poems bearing a variation of the word "echo" in the title, in the second volume there are only a handful of poems explicitly linked to song by their titles, while there are nearly thirty poems titled "echo" or "echoes." If the song poems find Creeley theorizing about the music of poetry as an act of sounding the literary past, measuring the linguistic present, and attending to the contest between the senses, then the role of aurality that underscores these concerns comes powerfully to the fore in the echo poems. As the Orphic concerns and preoccupations of the song poems are transmuted into the echo poems, one of the more interesting effects of this change is on Creeley's sense of music and musicality, those hallmarks of measure that provide the durable signature of the poet's particular mind thinking.

Not surprisingly, many of the echo poems also seem to be revisitations of the

moment of Orpheus's glance back. In the poem "Translation," for instance, the
reverberation of sound seems to offer an alternate, even contrary, continuation
of the story of Eurydice's second loss. The poem again contrasts the senses of
sight and sound, proposing a by now familiar faith in the continuity of the aural:

> You have all the time been
> here if not seen, not thought
> of as present, for when I looked I saw nothing, when
> I looked again, you had
> returned. This echo, sweet
> spring, makes a human sound
> you have no need of, facts
> so precede, but you hear, you
> hear it, must feel the intent
> wetness, mushy. I melt again
> into your ample presence.[51]

The second line's pun between "here" and "hear" proposes a presence of "you"
that is unknowable to either vision or thought. It is, indeed, as if the addressee
of the poem exists as some kind of ongoing sonic entity. As the poem continues,
Creeley presents two looks, two glances on the part of the speaker. The first,
it seems, is looking proper, the ocular desire, which yields nothing; the second
look, though, is of a different order, as "you had / returned," as an aural pres-
ence that had, in fact, always been there, though unnoticed. As the poem con-
cludes, with the speaker's insistence on hearing, the details quickly turn tactile,
the speaker "melt[ing]" into the physicality of the other in a way that seems partly
a return to the womb and partly the fulfillment of sexual desire. These lines also
contain another echo, that of Creeley's well-known poem "The Rain," first pub-
lished some thirty years earlier, in *For Love*. "The Rain" also begins with an acous-
tic return, as Creeley describes the rainstorm: "All night the sound had / come
back again, / and again falls / this quiet, persistent rain."[52] The poem concludes
with a plea not unlike that of "Air: Cat-bird Singing," with the speaker asking his
lover to "be wet / with a decent happiness."[53] So, a continuing line of reverber-
ation, then, leading from poem to poem to poem: from the "intent wetness," to
"be wet / with a decent happiness," to "hear me," and back again. Perhaps this is
the chain of events suggested by the poem's title, "Translation." What is certain
is that as Creeley echoes his own earlier poem, the stakes of the return and the
other's testament have risen, as in "Translation" the reverberating sound of the
other provides the lasting register of her presence, whose power dissolves the
boundaries of the speaker's self.

"Translation" suggests the richness of the echo as a figure for Creeley's Or-
phic poetics—sound resounding, making a turn in time and space, and thereby

introducing difference within likeness. As such, it is perhaps not too much to say that the echo is, in fact, Creeley's measure in his later work, which also, not incidentally, becomes intensely elegiac. Not surprisingly, then, several critics have noted the importance of echoes to Creeley's poetics. For instance, Rachel Blau DuPlessis has argued that they reinforce the linkages to Creeley's literary past, which are heard in his frequent citing and alteration of canonical lines and phrases. As DuPlessis demonstrates, this aspect of Creeley's work shapes both the mode of address in his poems and, thereby, the sense of self that is articulated in and through speech: "In dedicating so many poems 'to' dead people, speaking precisely 'to' them, as if they could hear, Creeley is playing with his own liminality (and ours too). He argues that one can easily, even fluently, speak to the dead. The phone lines are being staffed, are being held certainly, perhaps willfully and hopefully, open. Creeley is telling us to keep talking, to him and to each other."[54] DuPlessis's framing of Creeley's appeals to the dead as a means of "playing with . . . liminality" points to one of the most abiding features of Orphic poetics: its persistent expression of an unquenchable Orphic hope that the poet can speak to and bring back the dead. As her discussion continues, DuPlessis makes this link to Orpheus explicit, both directly and rather offhandedly noting its relevance to Creeley's poetics: "The lyric is the poem that continues to sing engaged and thoroughly even while dead—this is, of course, an orphic image, an orphic hope; it means to sing before death as if one were already posthumous, constructing both the song and the echo of oneself. No coincidence that in *Just in Time* there are twenty-one poems with echo/echoes in the title, spurts of memory and afterimages from the past seem to be some meanings of this trope, but it is also proleptic of the posthumous echo."[55] As DuPlessis argues, Creeley's echo poems demonstrate him writing not merely with the memory of others but in anticipation of his own inevitable end, as well. As such, Creeley's Orphic poems further contemplate the power of mortality that Silverman has linked with the myth of Orpheus. Silverman argues that mortality in the Orphic tradition emphasizes commonality over and against the demands of the individual as the basis of subject formation. As she argues, "finitude is the most capacious and enabling of attributes we share with others, because unlike the particular way in which each of us looks, thinks, walks, and speaks, that connects us to a few other beings, it connects us to *every* other being. Since finitude marks the point where we end and others begin, spatially and temporally, it is also what makes room for them."[56] While Silverman argues that finitude may offer a moment of profound connection between individuals, it can also have the opposite effect, when the desire to know the other transforms into fits of aggression. The emotional economy of this scenario is surely consistent with key tensions in Creeley's poetics as he navigates the signature of the self as both given and crafted, as well as his intense interest in and desire for identification with the other that reaches far back into his career. He recollects in his 1968 interview with Lewis MacAdams and

Linda Wagner-Martin, for instance, "My dilemma, so to speak, as a younger man, was that I always came on too strong with people I casually met. I remember one time, well, several times, I tended to go for broke with particular people. As soon as I found access to someone I really was attracted by—not only sexually, but in the way they were—I just wanted to, literally, to be utterly with them. I found myself absorbing their way of speaking. I just wanted to get in them."[57] In the echo poems, which emerged nearly thirty years later, Creeley demonstrates the other side of this equation, as the voices of others have gotten into him, and he explores voice less as a definable quality of one's speaking and more as an ever-inchoate practice of composition by way of echoing the voices of the past.

Arguably the most important of these echoes in Creeley's poetics are the voices of previous poets. He returns to this concern in the preface to his collection *So There* (1998), which reappears as the preface to *The Collected Poems of Robert Creeley: 1975–2005*. The brief essay, titled "Old Poetry," might just as easily have been titled "Old Friends," as it cites voices and circumstances that shaped his practice. Creeley concludes the preface's reminiscences by citing the last two stanzas of Robert Herrick's "To Live Merrily and to Trust to Good Verses," followed by the dedication, "with love, for Herrick and Zukofsky." This pair of allusions signals, among other things, the continued importance of music and musicality in Creeley's poetics. Zukofsky, of course, is a long-standing pillar for Creeley, providing him with the model of poetry as an integral of music and speech, and both Herrick and Zukofsky speak to the persistence of self through the medium of literary form. On this count, in fact, the Herrick citation proves particularly compelling. The poem, one of the most widely anthologized poems from Herrick's only collection, *Hesperides: Or, the Work Both Humane and Divine*, from 1648, provides a catalog of literary precedent, with Herrick naming Homer, Virgil, Ovid, Catullus, Propertius, and Tibullus as he celebrates the immortalizing powers of verse. The book also famously boasts a versified table of contents, and poetry itself is one of the chief themes throughout the collection. Given the book's intense self-reflexivity, it should come as no surprise that Herrick promotes the immortality of verse over and above the fleeting fame of bricks and mortar. To be sure, this is an utterly familiar position for a lyric poet to take, but it is made unusual and compelling by Herrick's joining of it with the poem's other primary theme, drunkenness. As such, the argument of the poem is that it is in the form of revelry, the play of song and dance of language, that poetry acquires its immortality. Interestingly, Creeley leaves aside the stanzas that detail this background for the poem's conclusion, citing instead only the last two stanzas:

> Trust to good verses then;
> They only will aspire,

When pyramids, as men,
Are lost i' thi' funeral fire.

And when all bodies meet,
In Lethe to be drown'ed,
Then only numbers sweet
With endless life are crown'd.[58]

By citing only these last two stanzas, Creeley emphasizes the immortalizing power of language in a way that recalls Silverman's discussion of finitude and subjectivity. In the final stanza, in particular, Herrick enumerates the loss of individuation as the bodies of the dead seem to melt into the river Lethe as if consumed by lava, with only "numbers sweet" providing the coronation of immortality. That is to say, the terms of this conclusion imply that it is in the mathematics of music—the structural, formal organization of language, poetry *as such*—and not the content that carries with it immortality.

In light of Creeley's consistent accounting for his literary heritage, his sense of voice as something given as much as shaped, and the frequency of the term "echo" in his lexicon, the 1994 publication of *Echoes* seems like the culmination of a long-standing project. In a news flash–style commentary midway through the collection, Creeley returns to his ultimate goals for poetry in terms that recall the revelry that underwrites Herrick's poem. Creeley writes, "I interrupt these poems to bring you some lately particular information," including that "writing is a pleasure. So I am not finally building roads or even thinking to persuade the reader of some conviction I myself hold dear. I am trying to practice an art, which has its own insistent authority and needs no other, however much it may, in fact, say. I had not really understood what the lone boy whistling in the graveyard was fact of. Now I listen more intently."[59] In some ways, the note seems a rejoinder to positions that Creeley has prominently taken earlier in his career. The idea that writing poems is not like building roads, for instance, recalls what is surely the most well-known line from his most well-known poem, "I Know a Man"—"well why not, buy a goddamn big car"—as well as his frequent equations of poetry and driving in his earlier essays. For example, in "Notes Regarding Free Verse," Creeley links poetry and driving on the basis of the necessary attention each activity takes. As he describes,

The simplest way I have found to make clear my own sense of writing in this respect is to use the analogy of driving. The road, as it were, is creating itself momently in one's attention to it, there, visibly, in front of the car. There is no reason it should go on forever, and if one does so assume it, it very often disappears all too actually. When Pound says, "we must understand what is happening," one sense of his meaning I take to be is this necessary attention to what is happening in the writing (the road) one is, in the sense suggested, following. In that way there is nothing mindless about the procedure. It is, rather, a respect for the possibilities of such attention that brings Allen Ginsberg to say, "Mind is shapely." Mind, thus engaged, permits experience of "order" far more various and intensive than habituated and programmed limits of its subtleties can recognize.[60]

Some thirty years later, Creeley maintains poetry as a matter of attention, to be sure, but that which is being attended to has shifted so that it is less grounded in the physical experience of his self in the world at the moment of writing and more attuned to those voices that have preceded him. In this sense, the micro vignette with which Creeley ends the "note" speaks to the occasion, mood, and preoccupations of the collection. "The lone boy whistling in the graveyard" is "a fact" of several things, many of them Orphic in nature: the effort of understanding, solitude and song among the dead, and careful listening. Indeed, mortality haunts the collection as Creeley listens intently, hearing, among other things, the voices of Wallace Stevens and Ezra Pound—and, through him, François Villon—as well as his own previous work. In these recollections of good verse, Creeley finds evidence of "all in apparent place, / the resonant design . . . // the way all plays to pattern, / the longed for world / of common facts."[61]

The relationship between the perception of "resonant design" and the sense of self lies at the center of many of Creeley's echo poems. In *Windows*, the collection before *Echoes*, Creeley writes a number of echo poems, including two that are particularly poignant lead-ups to the dynamics and tensions that will shape the subsequent volume. The poems are a pair, "Echoes (1)" and "Echoes (2)." Each written in five couplets, they present a compelling set of contemplations on the tension between stasis and motion in echoes. The first poem reads:

> Patience, a peculiar
> virtue, waits in time,
>
> depends on time to
> make it, thinks it
>
> can have everything
> it wants, wants all
>
> of it and echoes dis-
> appointment, thinks
>
> of what it thought
> it wanted, nothing else.[62]

The ironic tone with which the poem begins becomes darker, even snide, as it goes on. The poem ponders the relationship between patience and time, as this "peculiar virtue" is shown to be, by necessity, delusional (it thinks it can have everything) and, therefore, an echo of disappointment, as it always waits for what it does not have. That is, patience, like desire, can never be satisfied; at the same time, it is in the experience of patience, this ongoing and unquenchable disappointment, that time becomes known. Thematically, the echo in this poem acts as a hinge between patience and virtue: "patience . . . echoes disappointment." What does it mean for patience to echo disappointment? What synonym for echo would satisfy this analogy? The most immediately appealing possibility is "reverberation," such that the noise of disappointment bounces off of something (life's experience) and returns, in a diminished, less harsh, and less clearly defined form, as patience. In this sense, the echo performs an ameliorating function, as if it were a salve. Or, it could seem to perform this function, if patience itself were not seen as such a shoddy prospect in the poem. As such, what had seemed curative in the echo is perhaps better seen as a deadening of the senses. Even as the echo marks the reiteration of life's desires through their reiteration, it is also, in this poem, seen as a static and passive thing.

In "Echoes (2)," this sense of the echo as a temporally static mode in which patience lies trapped within time takes on the characteristics of thought. The poem begins as a contrast; whereas the first lines of the earlier poem had introduced us to patience as a "peculiar virtue," this poem explodes with the first line, "this intensive going in." It might be more accurate to say that the poem implodes, with the line emphasizing the inward motion of an echo into the mind. As the poem continues, though, this echo that had begun with insistent motion now finds residence in the mind and serves as an opportunity to consider, again, desire and, now, both perception and understanding. The poem continues: "to live there, in // the head, to wait / for what it seems // to want, to look / at all the ways // of looking, seeing / things, to always // think of it, think / thinking's going to work."[63] Similar to the ironic presentation of patience in the first poem, this echo poem delineates the process of waiting for satisfaction. Also like the earlier poem, this poem complicates both the object of desire and the ultimate knowability of it, here largely through Creeley's lineation. While the poem is a complete sentence whose paraphraseable sense boils down to a questioning of the efficacy of thought, Creeley's lineation introduces a number of complications into this simple idea. Here, as is so typical of Creeley, lines provide units of meaning that contrast or even conflict with the poem's grammatical sense. Thus, for instance, the phrase that reads, "for what it seems to want, to look at all the ways," is fractured into starkly different units: "for what it seems," "to want, to look," and "at all the ways." Creeley's lineation emphasizes the appearance of desire instead of its reality and, most importantly, equates desire and vision. Creeley similarly breaks the phrasing at the conclusion of the poem, turning the apparently wistful or even despondent lines, "to always think of it, think thinking's going to work," to the imperative, "think of it, think," and the hopeful, "thinking's going to work." As Creeley's lineation thus establishes a self-contradictory quality to the poem, he also foregrounds thought's motion.

How, then, is the second poem an echo of the first? And, further, what does the echoing between them tell us about the development of Creeley's sense of music, his measure and testament, in his Orphic poetics? The answer lies in the formal, thematic, and conceptual relationships between the poems. Their formal consistency invites the pairing of stanzas. And, in fact, placing the poems side by side demonstrates the centrality of the terms "wants" and "all" to both poems; in each poem, these terms make their first, only, and pivotal appearance in the third of five stanzas. The comparison also shows a shift in senses, from the sound of patience echoing disappointment in the first poem to the desire for total visual observation in the second. What's more, the comparison shows that thought is the final term of each poem; and, in each poem, the reliability and efficacy of thought are severely discounted. In this way, it is as if the first poem provides the formal, sonic contours, as well as the thematic material, that is then echoed, repeated with alterations, in the second. That is to say, even as thought and the desire that fuels it are both shown to be suspect in the poems, what persists is the shape. In Creeley's Orphic poetics, form, of the poems on the page and of the progressions of the thinking mind writing them, reverberates.

The poems in *Echoes* go on to contemplate recurrence, repetition, and return as figures for the moment of Orpheus's backward glance. In so doing, Creeley restages the turn of Orpheus as a compulsion filled with both great possibility and tremendous uncertainty. In the collection, echoes are often explored for how they frame the relationship between sound and temporality. As an effect of resonance and return, the echo sonically marks the passage of time, a temporally distinct experience, and it also highlights the fact that recurrence inevitably introduces difference. These concerns are also central to the first poem in *Echoes*, "My New Mexico."[64] As with so many of the song poems from earlier in his career, "My New Mexico" stages a conflict between the senses of sight and sound. The first six of the poem's seven stanzas are dominated by visual details, particularly focusing on the vibrant colors of the American Southwest. However, even in the midst of the poem's panorama, sound enters by way of a figurative use of "echo," when the landscape of "a blue lifting morning" acquires a sense of depth through the echo chamber of the canyons, "miles of spaced echo."[65] As the stanza concludes, the echoing of the canyon walls alters the visual sense perceptions of the speaker, which had so far been illuminated by the increasing clarity of the rising morning sun. As the "echo" comes in, though, at that very moment when sound provides depth perception, it disturbs the chronological order, as "time here [is] plunged / backward, backward." This initial mention of sound in the poem anticipates the speaker's appeal to song in the concluding stanza. The function of the song desired by the speaker would not only construct an identification between him and the landscape based upon the shared (idealized) timelessness of both song and landscape; it would, in doing so, echo the silence of the speaker's desire just as the earlier echoes provide the scale of the landscape, give it shape, demarcate its parameters and contours, and turn it into a resonant chamber. In doing so, the desiring self, like the time reheard in the echo, plunges time backward, recuperating the past and recasting it as the future.

This suggestion of an echo as inverting spatial and temporal order returns in several of the poems in *Echoes*, and it is often similarly framed by a conflict between the senses of sight and hearing. While "My New Mexico" is shaped by a certain hopefulness, many of the echo poems propose echoes, reflection, and recollection as illusions. Thus, for instance, a later poem titled "Echo" begins in exasperation, "Brutish recall / seems useless now / to us all," bemoaning the limitations of memory as we inevitably mis-see what we recollect.[66] The poem concludes: "Fifty years / have passed. / I look back, // while you stand here, / see you there, still / see you there."[67] Characteristically, Creeley here takes a figure of speech (looking back as simply remembering) and considers it as a literal statement; in doing so, he also returns to the moment of Eurydice's second death. Just as Orpheus lost Eurydice because of his backward glance, so, too, does Creeley's speaker lose his companion to a kind of daydream of her previous self; while she stubbornly stands "here," he sees her "there, still . . . there."[68] This sense of echoes as occasions of misconstruing and misunderstanding is extended in the brief poem, "The Cup," which seems to speak for all those, "Who had thought / echo precedent, // shadow the seen / thing" and which goes on to frame the efficacy of reflection in a way that recalls the echo poems from *Windows*. In the poem, the process of reflection also bears upon the notion of "action," turning intellectual inquiry into a primal reflex, "whose thought was // consequential, / itself an act, a // walking round rim / to see what's within."[69] As the poem moves from a statement regarding the temporal and spatial confusion of the echo to the consequentiality of thought, it stakes a claim as to the meaningfulness of such inquiry. As the questioning mind is perhaps inevitably limited to hearing echoes and seeing shadows, mistakenly imagining them to be the originary instances, it cannot recover those instances but only, and importantly, demarcate the perimeters of their absence. For Creeley, the inscription of this turn, whether in poems tightly crafted or openly processual, is the task of the poet, his music and measure.

3

Orpheus in the Garden
John Taggart

As we saw in the preceding chapter, Robert Creeley's Orphic practice is fundamentally shaped by his sense of the relationship between poetry and music. This same concern resonates not only horizontally through the ranks of American poets and writers who came of age in the 1950s but also vertically, down through the next generation of poets working in the Pound-Williams tradition, including Nathaniel Mackey (born in 1947), who is the subject of the last chapter in this book, and John Taggart (born in 1942), whose work interests me here. Taggart's oeuvre can be divided into roughly three periods: his work from the 1970s, which is most clearly grounded in the objectivist poetry of Louis Zukofsky; his development of a signature, chantlike form during the 1980s and 1990s; and an explicit engagement with the pastoral tradition in his collections *Pastorelles* (2004) and *There Are Birds* (2008). His first collections, from the late 1960s to the late 1970s, most strikingly carry the marks of his objectivist predecessors, with him working mostly in short, highly impacted lines, with the focus of what might be called his mathematical imagination evident in many of his book titles from this era: *To Construct a Clock* (1971); *The Pyramid Is Pure Crystal* (1974); *Prism and the Pine Twig* (1977); and *Dodeka* (1979). Even in these early books, music plays an important role, with poems invoking influences ranging from the Baroque to swing, bop, and post-bop jazz. Music becomes most prominent in Taggart's work, though, beginning with his collection *Peace on Earth* (1981), in which he develops a form of chantlike poems that will define his practice through *Standing Wave* (1993). Taggart's work during these two decades acquires its most distinctive voice yet as he develops the form of the chant poems, only to seemingly jettison the form in *Pastorelles* (2004) and *There Are Birds* (2008).

Taggart's explicit invocation of the pastoral in the title of his 2004 collection is actually a return to a long-standing interest of his. As he reflects in a 2002 interview with Brad Haas published in the online journal *Flashpoint*, his original plan for graduate school was "to write a dissertation on the pastoral tradition connected with [Mozart's] *The Magic Flute*. . . . That was about when I figured out that the pastoral tradition was *the* Western Tradition, that the thing looked very large."[1] While Taggart shelved the Mozart dissertation for one on Louis Zukofsky, his interest in the pastoral tradition persisted, and the linking of poetry, music, and order in the natural world is evident even in the cover of his collected poems from 2010. Titled *Is Music*, the book's cover image is a photograph that at first glance appears to be a stylized, iridescent green treble clef. However, the attribution of the photograph clarifies that it is an extreme close-up of a cucumber vine tendril. Just so, Taggart's work is a demonstration of how music links the Orphic and the pastoral as practices of cultivation, practices of attention, and practices of care that uncover, forge, and renew lines of interconnection between objects and beings in the world.

In his linking of the Orphic and the pastoral, Taggart's work returns us to the scene of Virgil's fourth Georgic, which provides the version of the Orpheus myth that most powerfully shapes its role as a model for lyric poetry. In this didactic treatment of rural life, Virgil introduces Aristaeus, the son of Apollo and Cyrene, whose unwanted pursuit of Eurydice results in her being fatally bitten by a serpent. He also introduces the paradigmatic scene of Orpheus's backward glance, consigning his beloved Eurydice to the underworld and configuring the tragic premise of lyric poetry. While these dramatic elements in Virgil's version of the myth become nearly truisms in invocations of Orpheus as the figure of the lyric poet, Virgil's broader framing of the story also suggests other significant, if less commonly acknowledged, elements in Orphic poetics, including, perhaps most powerfully, the link not only between poetry and music but also between poetry, music, and visions of society. The story of Orpheus is a short passage (an epyllion) within the Georgic's broader treatment of the keeping of bees, an allegory for an ideal human society because of their clear organization of labor and their steadfast dedication to their leader. Aristaeus's bees have died, however, a calamity that Proteus tells him is retribution for his role in Eurydice's death. As such, Aristaeus's misdeed—his unwanted sexual advance—is the initial fault that sets off a cascading series of events: Eurydice's first death; the need for Orpheus's doomed descent to the underworld, culminating in her second death; Orpheus's death and dismemberment at the hands of the maenads, signaling the dissolution of an entire mode of unity of knowledge; and, through the allegory of the bees, the loss of order in society itself. In Virgil, the bees can be made to return through the mysterious, somewhat macabre, and ritualistic process of *bugonia*, their spontaneous autogenesis from the rotting carcass of an ox. In this calculus, the task of the Orphic poet is not merely the unification of poetry and music or the celebration of rural leisure typical of the pastoral tradition, but the work of uniting poetry and music and thereby mending rifts in the social order.

The importance of music to this task of mollifying a fragmented world has animated Taggart's poetry since early in his career.[2] In a 1974 interview with Toby Olson published in a special issue of the Gil Ott–edited magazine *Paper Air* dedicated to Taggart, he describes the influence of music on the development of the chant poems from his middle period: "There are analogies in the music of Steve Reich, Philip Glass and the Stimmung piece of Stockhausen, but they're only analogies, I wasn't imitating their work. They gave me a certain encouragement that this sort of rhythm was possible and in fact what could be realized from it was close to this sense of rest, of being at peace."[3] While these poems arise most directly out of Taggart's interest in the repetitions of experimental minimalism, they also give evidence of his broad musical imagination. In addition to Reich, Glass, and Stockhausen, a partial discography of musicians either name-checked in or clearly relevant to his poetry would include: Albert Ayler, James Brown, James Carr, Robert Cline, John Coltrane, Morton Feldman, Aretha Franklin, Marvin Gaye, Olivier Messiaen, and Lester Young, in addition to the traditions of Gregorian chant and medieval and Renaissance music. What's more, like Zukofsky—and like Basil Bunting, Ted Enslin, and other objectivist-rooted poets—Taggart has often taken recourse to musical forms as models for poetic composition.[4] Thus, poems might be derived from the practice of using a cantus firmus or the processes of a ricercar, or they might be carefully modeled on a particular piece of music, as was the case for the poem "Coming Forth by Day," based upon Ornette Coleman's song "Lonely Woman." Taggart describes his process for this poem: "I made a grid from the sheet music for 'Lonely Woman.' The idea was that my lines, shaped in compliance, might take on some of the rhythmic character of the music. Even as I did this, I suspected it would not be enough to transpose already-transposed music into poetry. There would have to be transformation. Not 'jazz poems,' they would have to start from and go away from jazz. They would have to end up somewhere else."[5] Taggart's invocation of music as a model for his poetic practice depends upon a classic understanding of music as the consummate temporal art. For Taggart, music is a form that embodies movement toward rest, the "peace" he heard in the aesthetics of repetition from mid-century miminalism.

Underpinning Taggart's relationship to music is his sense of the task of the poet as being grounded in the twin imperatives of attentiveness and usefulness. Taggart derives this sensibility most directly from the poetry and poetics of Louis Zukofsky, whose work was foundational for him. As he argues in the *Paper Air* interview, "It begins with the attitude of attention. The act of attention is the act of a poem. It must be its first act. Presumably you could bring that act to bear on anything. In my case I chose language because I think it holds all things in a state of potentiality. You use the language in a sense of finding the world; language is a mode of discovery. That constitutes information and possibility of new knowledge."[6] Taggart's terminology frames language as a medium whose truths are processual and contingent, not stable blocks of knowledge that might be passed from writer to reader. What's more, the self is among the discoveries and "new knowledge" afforded by language. He argues in his essay "Songs of Degrees," "The word is spoken, and the self as root is carried, sounded, within our speech. Once this occurs, the word enters an endless branching process, which properly had its beginnings long before our usage, by way of its combination with other words and the speaking of others which continues to carry or recall and yet also deviate from the root. The process is creative in that the root is parent to the branching out to include other words and usages. The self as root, despite the ongoing nature of this process, is not lost but is further manifested. Each time the word is spoken, the root is sounded, carried and displayed."[7] For Taggart, the act of attention that is both prerequisite to and immanent within the poem establishes a rhizomatic sense of self that is connected to all other language, such that the self comes to be a resonant node along these interconnecting roots and branches. Thus, as he argues with respect to Zukofsky, the image toward which a poem aspires "is an image grounded in a shape primarily determined by musical principle and process. It is primarily an acoustic or cadential image."[8] That is to say, for Taggart, music ultimately serves as the model for the poetic image, including that image of the self, for how it gives temporal shape to harmonies, counterpoints, and other modes of buried relation in an otherwise cacophonous and disparate world. His statement on Zukofsky's poem "Mantis" also reads as a statement of his own poetics: "The product of structure, the art object, the poem, assumes its ultimate justification, beyond even the craft satisfactions of an object well made, when the internalized music of the words opens out into a sufficient and available structure; when it offers a path through the space, the landscape of language it composes not merely for our appreciation but also for active use. Care, then use are the lessons to be learned."[9] For Taggart, the summation of this argument is key not only to his reading of Zukofsky but also to his own poetics inasmuch as he is driven by an almost utilitarian desire that his poetry be grounded in a careful attention to language, and that it, thereby, might find usefulness in the hands and ears of the reader. The nature of this usefulness is found in Taggart's discussion of the self and the roots of language; for him, poetry is useful not only insofar as it uncovers and reanimates lost connections among seemingly disparate words but also insofar as such reanimation, such resounding of language, brings different, otherwise disparate selves into sonorous relation.

The fact that Taggart's description of Zukofsky is equally applicable to his own poetry suggests the profound importance Zukofsky has for Taggart. As Taggart's treatments of Zukofsky make clear, he offers more than simply a formal model; his commitment to poetry as an art of temporal form situated at the interval between speech and music speaks to Zukofsky as exemplary of Taggart's own goals and motivations as a poet. Taggart's essay collection *Songs of Degrees* (1994), includes a close reading of Zukofsky's poem "Mantis," as well as two broader considerations of Zukofsky's poetics, both of which develop the idea of music in relation to Zukofsky's critical terms "sincerity" and "objectification." As Zukofsky articulated in his essay "An Objective" (1930), "in sincerity shapes appear concomitants of word combinations, precursors of (if there is continuance) completed sound or structure, melody or form. Writing occurs which is the detail, not mirage, of seeing, of thinking with the things as they exist, and of directing them along a line of melody";[10] the poet's music is a practice of sincerity by which the "rested totality" of the objective might be achieved. As Taggart goes on to demonstrate throughout his readings of Zukofsky, the results of this musical mode of attention, musical sense of structure, and musical ideal of a rested totality ultimately derive from a sense of and responsibility toward love. In Zukofsky's case, this is most often framed in the context of his domestic sphere, in the valentines exchanged between him, Celia, his wife, and Paul, his son, and, ultimately, in Celia's musical score, which Zukofsky adopts as the twenty-fourth and final movement of *"A,"* his "poem of a life." Taggart argues, "The motivation behind Zukofsky's circular end and beginning, the creation of a musical or acoustic/cadential image, is to light up what is loved, to illuminate and to reveal the beloved as substantially as an object held in the mirror of that image. We must hear in order to see. We must hear and see in order to love."[11] For Taggart, Zukofsky's articulation of poetry as a musical form, derived from sincerity and achieved in objectification, is the realization of an ideal of attending to those we love. To love someone is to write about them well, and to write well about them depends upon loving them. That is to say, for Taggart, the Orphic poet is fundamentally a love poet insofar as the musicality of the work—Zukofsky's expanded sense of melody—is an act of love for the world.

This musical mode of attention as a drive toward care is evident in musically inflected poems from early in Taggart's career. One of the earliest examples is his poem "Drum Thing," from 1969. In his essay on jazz, Taggart pays particular attention to the pivotal moment of writing "Drum Thing": "The first jazz that made itself available to me was 'The Drum Thing.' . . . It was a story, a narrative. It had something to do with a journey across a wide expanse. And it was with a journey or simply a straggling procession of musicians in mind that I began the poem. It's tempting to say the music gave me the poem. The contribution of the music, however, was more an instigation, a prompting to begin, than a complete template. . . . It was the first poem which truly pleased me. It seemed to exist apart from me, to have an object existence of its own. And I knew that, without the music of John Coltrane and Elvin Jones, it would have no existence at all."[12] For Taggart, Coltrane's piece has a wide range of specifically Orphic implications: he hears it as articulating a musical and physical quest, as both communal and ceremonial, and, therefore, as the means by which he gains access to the poem that is both within him but not of him. Listening to Coltrane's song is not merely an instance of inspiration; it is an act of initiation through which the Orphic poet gains access to poetic vision. This last turn in his reasoning is curious given his emphasis on the role of the self as a root that is sounded and expanded through the act of the poem. The reconciliation between the drive toward an autonomous work of art and the insistence on an art as grounded within and grounding the self is found in his emphasis on poetry as an act of discovery, as is implied by his insistence on the fundamental role played by Coltrane and Jones. That is to say, in Taggart's poetics, the word of the poem extends from and resonates with the self of the poet; but the poem does not merely reinscribe the self with which it began. Rather, it seeks new interconnective points in language, new selves, not least through the stimulus of other media, including music, which gives voice and provides access to other selves. It is in this way that the processes of reading poems become useful for Taggart, providing readers with the shared knowledge of new temporal, cadential structures, and, thus, new selves.

The role of movement, quest, and reach embedded in the musical instigation that Taggart identifies in "Drum Thing" also inflects his early turns to the tradition of Western European music. For instance, his first collection, *To Construct a Clock*, from 1971, includes the poem "Ricercar," named for a form of Baroque musical composition that translates as "to search out" and is characterized by passages that reach from one key or mode to that of a following piece. As was suggested in the influence of "Drum Thing," "Ricercar" similarly exhibits many of the characteristics that will become central to Taggart's most musically inflected writing: a complex, sometimes dizzying combination of forward movement and return, often in the form of a narrated ritual or a journey, along with the interlacing of song and nature imagery. The poem begins by articulating the sense of an outsider, "The tribe is foreign and / their language you / didn't / know at all," and moves through this traveler's apparent acquisition of a sense of belonging through the practice of manual labor.[13] As, "you put things together," the poem reveals that the alternating "sanded blocks of wood / smooth blond and white / dark / brown wood," appear to be some kind of causeway or bridge, the building of which makes the landscape knowable, as "layers / of the / river / valley, hills appear."[14] Even as the landscape is brought into the visual field through the action of turning it into a road, simultaneously "a fugue appears," linking landscape and song in counterpoint as "all things and / their ornament put in angles

/ that remember themselves."[15] The speaker pauses to consider the parallelism between nature and the human body, "this wood-sorrel / its five petals in your small palm," before returning to the sense of movement derived from the titular song form as the poem concludes.[16] Invoking the truism "all things are a process," the poem problematizes this potentially hackneyed phrase by positioning it as the necessary premise for anything else, from the emergence of human utterance, "procession as the first words," to the joining of voices, "as what comes mutual—a pursuit / of parts / voices / after them . . . in the beginning / in the youngest head."[17] As he had in "Drum Thing," Taggart again finds in music an instigation, a model for his poetics of musical attention, focused on the notion of movement—"process," "procession," "pursuit"—as the precondition for the voice, for language, and for the establishment of communal belonging itself that Orphic poetry enacts.

If Taggart's early work often turns to music as a way of thematizing the essential roles played by movement and temporality, the influence of music on his sense of poetic form becomes most pronounced in his poems written during the mid-1970s and collected in his 1981 book, *Peace on Earth*. The poems in the mode that Taggart develops at this midpoint in his career are defined by their repetition and slight variation and their expanding scale. They consist of blocks of text, the format repeated across sections of the poems, and they repeat lines, phrases, and key words, with their verbs overwhelmingly kept in the infinitive. Perhaps the most well-known of these poems is "Giant Steps,"[18] in which Taggart returns to the influence of John Coltrane. The poem is written in four sections, each on a separate page and each containing a four-line stanza followed by a five-line stanza. This structure effectively presents an upper and lower portion to each section. The formal regularity continues at the level of the line, as the first stanza of each section begins with the line, "to want to be a saint to want to be a saint to want to,"[19] and the second stanza of each section begins with the line, "to go down to raise to go down to raise to go to go down the."[20] The upper stanzas are dominated by surreal imagery of "a snake-tailed saint with wings" and versions of "a horse-headed woman," each accruing shifting details across the four stanzas. Each of the upper stanzas concludes with the phrase, "to wake men from nightmare."[21] The lower stanzas of each section then "go down the ladder" to dance, "as taught by the master."[22] As the poems move through subtle variations on these few key images, it becomes something of an ars poetica for Taggart as he generates an imaginative field of associations based upon his listening to Coltrane's music—for him, this music evokes mysterious and seemingly mythical imagery that unites around the poet's aspiration for a priestly role. It is this role in which the poet finds his greatest use, as Taggart later notes, "if 'things were right' we would all be shamans in our own communities and I would perform this [poem] for people who lived around me and I would perform it as a function of need, that I needed and my community needed."[23] In Coltrane, Taggart hears a man fulfilling this role and filling this need, aspiring to be a saint, performing the gospel work of going low in order to bring high, learning the steps of the master, and dancing his way to everyone's salvation.

This priestly vision of the Orphic poet also underscores the namesake poem from *Peace on Earth*. However, the poem "Peace on Earth" takes its instigation not from a piece of music but from the political, cultural, and social realities of the Vietnam War.[24] As such, the poem is an important moment in Taggart's developing Orphic poetics insofar as it interweaves the spiritual and the political. The poem originally appeared in the 1974 issue of *Paper Air*, and is one of the primary subjects of Gil Ott's interview with Taggart included in the issue. As Toby Olson describes in his introductory essay on the poem, "Peace on Earth" is "far enough away from restricting anger to be able to mourn those dead and damaged souls from Viet Nam with the proper dignity. . . . [It] is . . . a poem whose movement is able to cleanse the dead of the politics that caused their death, resurrect their clean bones, and celebrate their passing. Both its method and its narrative content are transformative."[25] As Olson's comment suggests, the process of "Peace on Earth" shares the structural logic of "Giant Steps," with a defining form repeated over the course of the poem's three sections. However, the scale for "Peace on Earth" is larger, with the poem spanning thirty-eight pages. Taggart's mathematical imagination is again on display as the three sections consist of three, nine, and twenty-seven pages, respectively, an exponential logic that lends the poem a sense of potentially endless accumulation. The poem's expanding framework is held together by Taggart's use of the space of the page: each page consists of one eight-line stanza, a single line, and a four-line stanza. The standalone line that divides each page functions as an evolving refrain with subtle changes from one section to the next. Thus, in section one, it reads, "care touches the face, untwists the face";[26] in section two, it becomes, "Carry torches, carry each other";[27] and, in the final section, it transforms into, "Carol heart's ease ring of flower's thought."[28] As Ott's observation suggests, these changes in the central line of each section, with "care" becoming "carry" becoming "carol," and "touches" becoming "torches" becoming "heart's ease," mark the poem's movement toward a cleansing resolution by way of song.

The shifts in the refrain in "Peace on Earth" are triggered by the poem's central image, the Nick Ut photograph of Phan Thi Kim Phuc, widely known as "Napalm Girl."[29] The poem begins with an admonition "to love those as children as the / valiant children who have gone into hiding / children who hide in a house from the roaring."[30] The figure of frightened and hiding children recurs in several of Taggart's poems, often as an analog to the condition of the poet and, as here, emblematic of the way the innocent can be so easily violated by the machinery of politics and capitalism. On the third page of the first section, the generalized image of "the children" becomes specific when Taggart turns to "the roaring of ones marching in confusion / bones marching in napalm in napalm."[31] Against this backdrop, the refrain, "Care touches the face, untwists the face," shifts from merely suggesting the calming effect of a compassionate caress to the role of the poet working in response to the atrocities of war. The "care then use" at stake in "Peace on Earth," then, is nothing less than the question of the Orphic poet's task in the face of such personal and social suffering. As the references to napalm proliferate in the poem, the refrain as written in the second section—"carry torches, carry each other"—becomes more haunting and more suggestive. On the one hand, the line seems to invoke the torches associated with mob violence; on the other hand, it seems to ask for enlightenment and mutual assistance. Even the latter suggestion, though, is now underwritten by the flames of the napalm, such that the poem now seems to ask what or how we can learn from the horrors of war. In the final iteration of the refrain, the answer is song: "Carol heart's ease ring of flower's thought." The image of the flower here resonates with Taggart's repeated usage throughout this section of phrases from a healing ceremony as recorded by Antonin Artaud in his explorations of the Tarahumara people of Mexico and aligns the imagery of the bleached bones with that of the leaves and petals of the flower. The atomization of language in this final version of the refrain points, too, to the songlike state toward which Taggart moves the poem. The locked hands of carolers, easing the heart's pain and ushering in an impossible blossom after the war: these are the task of the poem, as it concludes, "to lift up bones in curled leaves and petals / to intend the greatest gifts / to hold the shining / ring that is an ardor and a blossoming."[32]

As admirable as Taggart's project surely is in "Peace on Earth," it is not without problems. As Taggart reflects upon the poem in his later essay "The Poem as a Woven Scarf," he notes, "I found my voice tired and hardened because of a very deliberate cadence and the poem's length. . . . Saturation was obtained at the cost of my becoming a drone."[33] He goes on, "I had thought density was the true goal. . . . Complete saturation leaves no room to move . . . the model ought not to be the ecstatically still saint, but the moved dancer."[34] Taggart finds just such a model in another of the chant poems included in *Peace on Earth*, "Slow Song for Mark Rothko," the first of two poems he has written in response to the work of the iconic mid-century American painter.

As with the earlier chant poems, Rothko's paintings provide "an instigation, a prompting to begin," for Taggart rather than a template to be followed.[35] In the special issue of *Paper Air*, he discusses the influence of Rothko's paintings on "Slow Song for Mark Rothko," emphasizing "the quality of the light. It's a quality of light you could identify with certain stained-glass windows, and which I identify particularly with the work of Mark Rothko, in which you get very pure, radiant, complex light, which gives one a sense—when you're looking at one of his paintings—of radiating, of hovering slightly off the canvas."³⁶ Taggart is drawn, here, to a feature of the paintings that is at once perhaps the most fundamentally tied to their identity as works of visual art and, at the same time, the most ephemeral and difficult to quantify: the sense that they radiate light. Taggart finds his solution to this challenge in verbs. As he explains, "I chose those infinitives as a kind of hovering quality that would allow at the same time to bear down in an unremitting way. It's always in process, so with the infinitives it's always happening. The light is always going on. This is why there is so much repetition."³⁷ As Taggart focuses the ekphrastic energies of this poem on the peculiar illumination of Rothko's paintings, the cross-media analogs proliferate, as he describes in a later preface to the poem:

> My first interest was neither Rothko nor his paintings, but stained glass. I came to feel almost a hunger for the dense, complexly luminous colors shining within the giant black boxes of cathedrals. This hunger was for the colors themselves. It may also have been for the basic properties of stained glass as laid down by Suger, the abbot of St. Denis in the twelfth century: a bearer of holy images, intrinsically rich material resembling precious stones, a mystery because it glows without fire or heat. Like the composer Messiaen, I was dazzled by the colors of stained glass and moved by the presence of mystery, by—to combine Messiaen and Grosseteste—the power of the light residing in and shining through the glass as embodied spirit.³⁸

As Taggart elaborates upon the parallels he sees between medieval stained glass making, the quality of light in Rothko's paintings, and the overlapping musical analogies from Messiaen to Steven Reich, he also turns to Rothko's own reflections on art: "As I continued to think about the relation between glass and painting, I was further encouraged by Rothko's own statements. One of the most important of these is: 'the people who weep before my pictures are having the same religious experience I had when I painted them. If you . . . are moved only by their color relationships, then you miss the point.' And one other that is made use of in my poem: 'I do not believe that there was ever a question of being abstract or representational. It is really a matter of ending this silence and solitude, of breathing and stretching one's arms again.'"³⁹ Across these seemingly ever-expanding lines of association and inspiration, Taggart's practice in this poem recalls his sense of the Orphic poet as a shaman or a priest, and his allusion to Rothko's spiritual aspirations sets the bar very high for his poetic response to Rothko's work. What's more, his turn to Rothko's well-known summation from his essay "The Romantics Were Prompted" (1947) signals his attention to art as a practice of sound, of communication, and of bodily movement. That is to say, in the stained glass windows and the Rothko canvasses, Taggart sees a dynamic quality of light that exhibits the same capturing of potentiality that draws him to language.

As Taggart suggests, Rothko's statement provides the action at the center of this poem. The first stanza takes Rothko's heroic depiction of the artist, in which the artist seems to be reborn through his own act of creation, and situates this autogenesis in the act of breathing, which he turns to the Orphic production of song. The poem begins, "To breathe and stretch one's arms again / to breathe through the mouth to breathe to / breathe through the mouth," and concludes, "breathe to sing to breathe to sing to breathe / to sing the most quiet way."[40] As the poem continues, this description of the act of singing evolves through the development of the refrain that concludes each page. It begins as, "to sing as the host sings in his house,"[41] shifts to, "to give as the host gives in his house,"[42] and ultimately becomes, "to take as the host takes into his house."[43] As song becomes first a gift and then a means of welcoming into the house, the poem adopts a strongly ritualistic tone with echoes of the Eucharist. As such, the poem becomes a field of spiritual aspiration animated by the interweaving and interdependence of the somatic, the gestural, and the incantatory.

Over the course of the poem, the bodily production of the Orphic song, the singing poet's breath and gesture, take on associations that powerfully evoke the pastoral tradition as it articulates a process that both integrates song and the natural world, and, through this integration, seeks to establish a new communal order. This process can be identified most clearly in the poem's linkage between the aesthetic production of song and the growing of a garden. The first section of the poem celebrates the enlightening qualities of song in terms that resonate with Taggart's affinity for Rothko, as both song and light are shown to radiate: "to sing to light the most quiet light in darkness / radiantia radiantia / singing light in darkness."[44] As the first section continues, the image recurs as "radiant light of *seeds in earth*,"[45] developing the imagery of song as a variety of seed-sewing that occurs throughout the section. In section two, these "radiant seeds" transform into "fiery saxifrage . . . self-lighted flowers in darkness."[46] Taggart's description of saxifrage clearly invokes William Carlos William's poem-manifesto "A Sort of a Song," in which he famously prescribes, "no ideas but in things," and proclaims "saxifrage is [the] flower that splits / the rocks."[47] Williams drove inward into the etymology of the word to reveal the paradox of unity and fragmentation embedded within it—a fragile flower that splits rocks; a metaphor that can thus "reconcile the people and the stones."[48] So, too, does Taggart, although his turn to the botanical links saxifrage to the poem's earlier "radiantia," as the *saxifraga radianta* becomes "self-lighted flowers in the darkness / perfect and fiery hope / to hold out lighted flowers in the darkness."[49] The peculiar illumination of the lines suggests the next step in this evolution, as the "self-lighted flowers" turn to "excited phosphor," the "light in the darkness."[50] From radiantia, to saxifrage, to phosphorus, the flower that blooms from the seeds sewn in the song that is articulated throughout "Slow Song for Mark Rothko" illuminates the poem's hope for a newfound intimacy—with one another, with "the poor," especially—and thereby "To take into the light in the darkness / into star-flowers before sunrise / to be in light in the darkness. / / To take as the host takes into his house."[51] For Taggart, the ritualistic, incantatory quality of these poems works as a means of establishing a community in and through the performance of the poem. As such, this poem performs the crucial Orphic work of forging and voicing unities between poetry and music, between words and things, among people, and between people and the natural world. The poem enacts an Orphic process of reconciliation and redemption, the possibility for which is contained within the initial breath and gesture of Rothko's artist.

The form that Taggart develops throughout the poems in *Peace on Earth* reaches its apex in his masterpiece, "The Rothko Chapel Poem," published in *Loop* (1991). While "Slow Song for Mark Rothko" engaged with ideas about embodiment and the aesthetics of repetition in Rothko's paintings as seemingly condensed within and emanating from Rothko's own reflections on art, turning to the installation of the Rothko Chapel is to wade into some very deep waters of mid-century American modernism. Located in Houston, Texas, the chapel was originally commissioned by Dominique de Menil, who called for a building to be designed by Philip Johnson with paintings by Rothko. Johnson left the project due to differences of opinion with Rothko (his work to be carried on by Howard Barnstone and Eugene Aubry), and the location of the chapel was moved from the original plan for the campus of the University of St. Thomas to an independent site nearby. Upon the chapel's completion (after Rothko's suicide), the American composer Morton Feldman composed one of his most well-known works, also called "Rothko Chapel," in honor of the chapel and his friend.[52] Open since 1971, the chapel is described in its mission as "a sacred space, open to all, every day, to inspire people to action through art and contemplation, to nurture reverence for the highest aspirations of humanity, and to provide a forum for global concerns."[53] The interior of the chapel is octagonal, with four primary opposing sides and four connecting sides somewhat shorter in length, capped with a translucent skylight. The interior of the chapel is lined by fourteen massive Rothko canvases, each roughly fifteen feet tall and ten feet wide, arranged on the eight walls as three triptychs (on the north, east, and west walls), and five single-panel paintings (on the south wall and the angled walls), and each featuring a somber palette of deep red and black. Evincing the same technique that had caught Taggart's attention during his writing of "Slow Song for Mark Rothko," the Rothko Chapel paintings similarly bring to mind stained glass, with their multiple, thin layers of color taking on remarkable depth and luminosity.

The interior of the Rothko Chapel provides an intense viewing experience.

The scale and proximity of the paintings, the lighting of the chapel, and the starkness of the interior combine such that the viewer is almost inevitably over-whelmed by Rothko's canvasses and the interplay between them. As Sheldon Nodelman has described in his masterful analysis of the chapel installation, Rothko designed the chapel as a complete work, and the paintings present numerous, sometimes competing groupings and relationships. As Nodelman describes, the chapel aspires to a condition of aesthetic unity that clearly resonates with Tag-gart's interest in repetition and his desire to produce an art of suspended, main-tained potentiality:

> A first condition of the chapel installation, following from its nature as an interactive system, is that its content is a collective one, enunciated by the whole, and that its individual members cannot be evaluated independently of their place in this whole and of the patterns that assert themselves within it. A second condition, following from the chapel installation's status as a cycli-cal and simultaneous system patterned by repetition and mirroring, is that it can ultimately contain no linear progression from beginning to end . . . the installation appears perfectly suited to manifest not a succession of events but a unified and constant state of affairs, even if this state is complex and dynamic rather than passive or static in its internal structure.[54]

Perhaps the most obvious tension in the chapel is in the relationships between the paintings on the two primary axes, north-south and east-west. The south entrance wall features a single canvas with a background field of oxblood red on which is superimposed a black square. The opposing north wall is a recessed apse on which is mounted a triptych of black canvasses through which occasional strokes and streaks of an underlying red can be seen. The stark contrast between the canvasses on the north-south axis is contrary to the canvasses on the east-west axis, which are characterized by similarities insofar as both of these walls present triptychs that also bear further compositional and technical affinities. What's more, the shorter, connecting walls on the angles of the octagon each have what are described as "monochromes," the largest canvasses in the group that are the most purely dominated by black and deep purple hues. As Nodelman demonstrates, the relationships between the paintings based upon their compo-sition and placement proliferate to a dizzying extent. He frames the viewer's in-teraction with the chapel space as proceeding through three moments: the ob-servation and appreciation of the individual canvasses; an analytical exploration of the interrelationships between them; and, finally, the disintegration of the dis-tinction between the canvasses and the self of the viewer.[55] This three-fold pro-cess of engagement with the interior of the chapel thus establishes the conditions of possibility for the transformation of the self that Rothko saw as the goal of his art, and it is in just this mode of engagement with the paintings, at the point where the self of the viewer is undergoing radical transformation, that Taggart's speaker operates.

Given the experiential and interpretive richness of the Rothko Chapel, "The Rothko Chapel Poem" is a massive undertaking. The nature of Taggart's project in this poem is best understood by reading it as originally published in *Loop*, because although it is included in his new and collected poems, *Is Music*, its preceding poem, which serves as a preface, is not. This poem, titled "Eight Headnotes" and dedicated to Robert Creeley, is made up of four short prose paragraphs about the paintings in Rothko Chapel and four quotations on the weaning of the child from the "Exordium" of Søren Kierkegaard's *Fear and Trembling*. The headnotes to Creeley attend to the formal details of the paintings from Rothko Chapel, focusing in particular on how Rothko multiplies space within the paintings, such that "the entire painting at the center of the triptych contains several smaller Rothko's within itself and creates, in the process, several cross shapes. . . . It is, indeed, a center from which there can be 'slippage' as the eye travels, but no evasion."[56] This sense of the paintings as both incorporating abstracted versions of the Christian cross and ensnaring the viewer continues as Taggart imagines them as three-dimensional art, being folded upon their vertical lines such that they become, "a constant cross, crucifixion," from noun to verb, the artworks no longer objects but processes suspended in time.[57] The four brief passages from Kierkegaard that follow focus on the narrative of a young mother blackening and then hiding her breast so as to wean her child, with the mother and child first mourning together their lost period of intimacy, and then the mother providing "stronger food" for the child.[58] In addition to their allegorical quality, these passages also anticipate "The Rothko Chapel Poem" for how the blackening of the breast resonates with the play between black and red that is at the heart of the Rothko Chapel paintings themselves. That is, in their color play, the paintings seem to embody or even enact the traumatic scene from Kierkegaard, as well as its resolution in providing the necessary heartier nourishment to the child as it matures beyond infancy.

While Kierkegaard's *Fear and Trembling* is the source for the "Eight Headnotes" that precede "The Rothko Chapel Poem," his volume, *Repetition*, is even more important to the work of the poem.[59] Rothko was a devoted reader of Kierkegaard, and, as Nodelman has demonstrated, *Repetition* is key to the complex interrelationships between the paintings established by Rothko's meticulous composition of the entire chapel space.[60] Kierkegaard distinguishes repetition from recollection, arguing that they "are the same movement, except in opposite directions, for what is recollected has been, is repeated backward, whereas genuine repetition is recollected forward. Repetition, therefore, if it is possible, makes a person happy, whereas recollection makes him unhappy."[61] In this framework, recollection is a melancholy desire, characterized by the hope that what has been lost will return in its previous form; repetition, on the other hand, is the reappearance of what has come before, reanimated and made new again. To recall Taggart's terminology from his description of Zukofsky, it is "re-vivified." Furthermore, whereas recollection is backward looking, Kierkegaard construes repetition as a forward-looking receptivity to the possibility of an as-yet-unknown future good, an opening outward to the possibility of the good that may be bestowed upon us from elsewhere. As such, repetition depends upon a certain renunciation of will since it cannot be brought forth from within oneself; rather, one must forego the self and even, ultimately, renounce the self so as to be in the condition in which to receive the repetition that may be bestowed upon them. This is why, not surprisingly, Kierkegaard's models are Abraham and Job, biblical figures who suffer unanticipated tragedies that test their faith and who regain all they had lost from the same power that had taken it.

This renunciation of the self as precedent for repetition is the basis for the merging of the experiences of the artist and the viewer that lies at the core of both Rothko's and Taggart's aspirations. Tellingly, the Kierkegaard commentator, Edward Mooney, takes recourse to music as a way of conceptualizing Kierke-gaard's sense of repetition. Mooney bases his analogy on the effect of a musical repeat as experienced by both the performer and the audience. As Mooney ar-gues, individuals "are both 'performers' and 'audience' in the music of creation and self development," and, "as one moves toward the religious or wondrous, one becomes less an actor than an alert receptor. Here the job of freedom is sus-taining receptivity. A nondespairing self is ready at every instant both to resign the world (as target of one's interventions) and get it back again (as gift) . . . Self and world become reciprocally articulate."[62] Mooney's use of the musical anal-ogy is an apt link to the practical instances of repetition that exemplify the prac-tice as Taggart hears it in the music of Gregorian chant, American minimalism, and jazz. In his poem, "Were You," which began as a letter to the poet Michael Palmer, Taggart also invokes St. Augustine to make the point, noting that repe-tition is "a mode of assuring the seeker that he is on his way, and is not merely wandering blindly through the chaos from which all form arises."[63] Uncannily echoing Mooney's discussion of the relationship between performer and audi-ence, Taggart continues, "through song the singer & the listener become iden-tical."[64] Taggart's comments suggest the importance of poetry as a performed art,[65] one in which the Orphic poet and the reader become immersed in the artwork at the time of its reading, giving voice to and taking on new selves, and thereby communing with the broader world around them. In this Orphic calcu-lus, both self and world are mutually constitutive and contingent upon their own earlier histories, endlessly finding and forging new identities in and through their process of being open to one another.

This notion of repetition as a creative, life-giving, and soul-nourishing mode of receptivity is at the heart of "The Rothko Chapel Poem." As the poem's title indicates, it is, in the first instance, a matter of attending to the particular place and space of the chapel, and Taggart translates the intensely visual experience of the chapel into the song-based mode of his chant poems. Ultimately, the poem is an extended and immersive Orphic meditation on the space of the chapel. Thirty-four pages long, the poem consists of unnumbered blocks of text that invite grouping into a wide range of possible sections based upon number of lines per page, repetition of words, and the use of page space. If the pages are organized based upon the number of lines and their placement on the page, then there are twenty-three sections to the poem. However, more precise categorization is possible based purely on the structural qualities of the text. For instance, the first section of the poem, spanning the first three pages, stands out as the only section that contains nineteen lines; and there are two sections, each two pages long, in which the entire page is filled with twenty-three lines of text, each repeatedly urging that it's "time for some passion in this language it's time to move."[66] Further, there are six sections that begin with the word "doorway," equal to the number of doorways in the chapel. As Nodelman discusses, these doorways without doors echo the shape of Rothko's images, an effect magnified by the lighting of the chapel such that the rectangular shape of the shadow-crossed doorways echoes and frames the paintings. In the poem, these brief doorway sections are each placed on the bottom center of their respective pages, recalling the visual effect of seeing the doorways alongside the massive canvasses on the adjoining walls. The "doorway" sections also indicate the passage of time and space as the speaker passes through them, as do sounds heard by the speaker. Aside from these sections, which frame both the viewing experience and the reading process, the majority of the poem consists of fourteen tightly patterned sections, alternating between a two-page section of thirteen lines per page, followed by a one-page section of fifteen lines, and then one of the "doorway" sections. Finally, the last section of the poem, its final page, is the only section that is centered at the bottom of the page with text the width of the margins; it is also the section in which the speaker emerges from the chapel into the courtyard outside. While it is tempting to align the sections of the poem with particular canvasses on the walls of the chapel, in most instances, the text is simply not descriptive enough to make any such associations definitive. Instead, the poem is a linguistic experience analogous to the visual one of standing before the paintings and being absorbed by the kind of engagement that Nodelman describes.

The one section of "The Rothko Chapel Poem" that clearly corresponds to a particular painting in the chapel is the opening section. In addition to its unique length, the poem begins with imagery deeply imbued with the specifics of the painting on the south entrance wall, thus adhering to the logic of the chapel's layout. The painting on this wall is singular in two striking ways: it is the only painting in the chapel that so prominently features red as a framing field for the black inner square; and, it is the only painting on one of the four primary walls (north, south, east, or west) that is a singular painting instead of a triptych. As Nodelman notes, "despite—or better, because of—its lonely eminence, the entrance-wall panel is the point of departure for the discursive system of the installation."[67] Appropriately enough, then, the poem begins:

> Red deepened by black red made deep by black
>
> prolation of deep red like stairs of lava
>
> deep red like stairs of lava to gather us in
>
> gather us before the movements are to be made
>
> red stairs lead us lead us to three red rooms[68]

As with his reference to Kierkegaard, Taggart here seems partly to follow the associations of the colors red and black, in addition to the shape of the painting. In this instance, the link is to the medieval musical notational practice of prolation, which is a symbolic representation of time similar to modern key signatures. While modern music uses a base of two to indicate the duration of notes, medieval and Renaissance practice also included a base of three, and the use of prolation indicates shifts from one to the other, often with the use of red ink for notes that diverge from the norm (in black). With the introduction of this term, then, it's as if Taggart sees the black square framed by the red rectangle on Rothko's canvas as a massive musical note of unusual temporal duration, thus shifting the rich sensory experience of looking at the painting into a musical one. As such, this term, from the poem's second line, immediately registers the temporal dynamics of Rothko's installation at the level of the interplay between the colors within the individual painting on the south entrance wall, as well as how that dynamic echoes across the installation as a whole. What's more, inasmuch as prolation is a device found in polyphonic music, this allusion also suggests the multiplicity of voices: the multiple voices within the poet's one voice, as well as the joining of the poet's voice and that of the reader.

As a linguistic analog to the experience of the chapel, Taggart's poem is an immersive experience in which the repetition and variation of lines, images, and words becomes similarly overwhelming. The effect toward which Taggart strives is evident in his prefatory remarks to a 2012 reading of the poem in the Rothko Chapel, in which he distinguishes the manner of attention it calls for from that required by "more lyric poems." Whereas shorter lyrics invite or even demand that the audience "really bear down" on individual words, he instructs the audience that the structure, scale, and simple duration of "The Rothko Chapel Poem" require that the listener "let it wash over you," a claim that clearly picks up on the sense of receptivity that is so important to Kierkegaard's notion of repetition. In these same remarks, Taggart further qualifies how the poem relates to the audience by citing Walter Ong's *Presence of the Word*: "My voice really goes out of me. It calls not to something outside, but to the inwardness of another. It is a call from one interior, through an exterior, to another interior."[69] This phrase from Ong is central to Taggart's understanding of the poem's task, and he refers to it twice, including by saying that it is the link between the day of the reading and the poem as it was written two decades earlier. The charge for the poem, then, is this communication between interiors: between the poet and the reader, between the performer and the audience, between Taggart's current self and former self. Ultimately, what is communicated is not a description of the paintings but a linguistic experience that is an instantiation of the experience of attending them.

The occasion of "The Rothko Chapel Poem" is a wedding to which the speaker has been invited, but the poem goes to great lengths to distinguish its work from the communal act of marriage. The opening section of the poem tells us that "there is to be a wedding / we are the guests the welcome wedding guests / the groom welcomes us the bride welcomes us," but this setting is complicated by the images of "the red like stairs of lava," "three red rooms," the "room full of deep red light," and the ominous black of the paintings.[70] When reading the poem as published in *Loop*, this repetition of red against black not only introduces a striking color contrast to conventional wedding imagery but also recalls the imagery of the mother "blackening" her breast in order to ween the child. This unexpected sense of the wedding as a ritual of separation is reinforced as the poem continues, particularly in the second section, which breaks from the form of the first section and spans the entire width of the page. The speaker chides, "did you think we'd move as a gathering of wedding guests / did you think it'd be let's waltz like wedding guests time," and instructs the listener to "make the move by yourself / first movement of infinite resignation by yourself alone . . . away from warm welcome."[71] As the poem continues, this emphasis on the circumstance of the individual intensifies, such that the wedding comes to be not so much the occasion of the poem as the backdrop against which it takes place.

This framing of the poem's occasion happens most prominently in its two self-reflexive sections. In addition to cautioning the reader against the expectations of a formal dance—a waltz—these sections also reflect upon the language of the poem itself, as well as its directionality. Formally, both of these sections are dramatic departures from the rest of the poem insofar as they both fill the entire page with text. The first of these sections deploys elongated phonemic phrasing, emphasizing the reading of the poem as an oral and aural performance:

"Time for some passion in this language it's time to move / it's time to move to make a move ma—mah—moo-euve-veh / move out of deep red light move of this purple light."[72] The beginning of the second of the self-reflexive sections shuffles the order of the same text and describes "the second movement" as "the movement of rosy transparency."[73] Throughout the two pages of each of these two sections, the poem reiterates and shuffles these phrases, with the combined effect of emphasizing the singularity of the individual even in the context of the social situation of the wedding and the need for movement. Insofar as the other sections of the poem seem to emanate from the speaker's engagement with Rothko's canvasses, these sections serve as supplements to the more direct ekphrastic response in those passages, framing, conditioning, and directing both the speaker's and the reader's progress through both the Rothko Chapel and "The Rothko Chapel Poem."

In addition to the directionality of the sections that insist on the necessity of movement, the speaker's progress through the poem is punctuated by the six "doorway" sections. These sections are formally identical to each other, each eleven lines long and centered at the bottom of their respective pages; their diction is nearly identical, too, and the changes indicate the passage through space and time. Each of these sections begins, "doorway without a door / the doorway always open," a depiction of both the physical characteristics of the doorways inside the chapel and their spiritual significance as the chapel welcomes all-comers.[74] While the doorway sections, like the rest of the poem, are unnumbered, their repetition implies both return and change in the process of the poem. The repeated first lines present doorways that are, at first glance, the same; if reading the poem without reference to the chapel, for instance, a reader might well take these passages as returns to an archetypal doorway. In their difference, however, they accede to the condition of repetition as Kierkegaard would have it, providing an unfolding sense of newness. In fact, this sense of the doorways as simultaneously static and dynamic is contained within their recurring line, "one at a time inside," which partly describes the passage of the guests into the room but also takes on a wide range of other associations throughout the course of the poem, including the movement into a room (perhaps the same room) filled with echoing screams and the speaker's conflict within himself. This sequentiality in the doorway sections is most clearly indicative of the passage of time in their last two instances, which read "almost the last doorway"[75] and "the last without a door,"[76] respectively. As such, while the doorway sections reiterate the superimposition of static and dynamic senses of time that lie at the heart of the poem, they present the reader with directionality through the chapel, through the poem, and ultimately into the courtyard outside.

One of the most powerful ways in which Taggart translates this intense visual play of the chapel into the Orphic realm of the aural and the musical is through his treatment of the voice. In the first doorway section, the speaker observes, "inside one hears screams / begins to hear screaming / screams within screams / screams in collision / turbulence of collision / turbulence in the rooms / screams in black rooms."[77] The speaker's cognition of the screams is complicated in much the same way as the viewer's visual comprehension of Rothko's paintings. In this first instance, the speaker hears multiple screams, signifying conflicting voices in the unseen rooms. However, on the following page, in a section of the poem distinct from the "doorway," the speaker realizes that "it is really only one scream / echoes of only one scream in / of one scream within itself / screams within the one scream / within one passionate scream / one scream has been sustained / one scream is being sustained . . . the one scream will not decay / not decay in one black room."[78] As the speaker realizes that what he had taken to be multiple screams is really the echoes of one scream, time is stopped as the sound of the scream does not decay. As such, Taggart introduces yet another layer of the movement-stasis, dynamic-static tension that lies at the heart of both Rothko's paintings and his interaction with them. Insofar as the language continues, the poem will always project itself forward; and yet, in its repetition of words and phrases, it also invokes a time that is held fast.

The depiction of the screams signifies broader tensions at the heart of the poem. The setting is both communal, as a wedding, and insistently individual, through its focus not on the events of the wedding but on the speaker's engagement with the paintings. The poem is both visual, fixated on the red and black of Rothko's paintings, and adamantly musical in its treatment of time as a malleable medium. Ultimately, these internal aesthetic tensions point toward the effects of the speaker's engagement with the paintings and, in turn, the reader's engagement with the poem. As Nodelman observes, as the viewer's self is immersed within the paintings and transformed through the self's interaction with them, "the chapel becomes a theater of the self."[79] The poem is a dynamic inscription of this process as it occurred to the speaker, transmitted to the reader. Even as the poem consistently reiterates the singularity of the scream that had been taken for many screams, it similarly frames the speaker's sense of self. In the third "doorway," for instance, just as we had heard the scream in the earlier doorway, we now find the speaker insisting on the indivisibility of his self: "Doorway without a door / the doorway always open / one at a time inside / one at a time I am one / no third person is one / one is one is I me / the one primitive I me."[80] In this repetition of the doorway, the place of the scream is taken by that of the speaker's self, and it undergoes the similar process of seeking clarifying unification. Where the earlier process had been to distinguish the single voice, it is now to assert the singularity of the self. Yet, this singularity is, at the very least, elusive. The poem has previously identified the speaker with the apparent source of the scream in the chapel, "the one child is the poet the child of pain."[81] As such, the assertion of singularity in the third "doorway" is deeply problematized, more so as the section continues, "I me the child of pain / the primitive I inside / inside the turbulence / inside the black rooms."[82] Even as the speaker asserts that there is only one "I," that I is also identified with the child, with its "primitive," that is to say, previous self, and, perhaps, even distinguished between the "I" and the "me," the subject and object, both observing and being absorbed by the black (and red) rooms of the paintings. As such, the drama of selfhood that unfolds in "The Rothko Chapel Poem" is that of experiencing the multiplicity within one-self, a self that is both static and dynamic, both imbued with the primal associations of red and black and practiced in the social ceremony of a wedding, both a screaming child and a singing man.

The transformation or awakening of the self that is realized by the speaker of "The Rothko Chapel Poem" finds its bearing on the broader social world on the final page of the poem in which the setting dramatically shifts to the midday light of the courtyard outside the chapel. This final page of the poem contains twelve lines of text; the first six address social groups engaged with the chapel and its paintings. In sharp contrast to the contemplative and ritualistic mood of the sacred space inside this chapel, the courtyard is bustling with chatter:

> Tourists leave Chapel explosion of their talk
>
> giggles of college girls "could you paint that?"
>
> someone doubts Passion of Christ is the theme
>
> someone dislikes hearing about "blood paintings"
>
> I know a woman who was married in the Chapel
>
> the paintings turned out black in her pictures[83]

The groups of people in these lines are defined by institutions: the tourists participating in the institution of commodified travel; the college girls attending the chapel because of their belonging to an educational institution; and the wedding guests, perhaps the same ones that have been at the center of the poem, gathered through the institution of marriage. None of these groups—or, rather, none of these individuals insofar as they are defined by their identity with these institutions—seems capable of engaging with the paintings. In fact, the description of the "blood paintings" presages a comment Taggart makes in his introduction to his 2012 reading of the poem: "It is a long poem; it is a passion poem; it is a long and passionate poem." Unfortunately, instead of engaging with the passion of the paintings, or with the possibility of considering them as a minimalist take on the Passion of Christ, the tourists chatter, the college students joke, and the wedding guest bemoans not being able to get a good picture.

While the conclusion to "The Rothko Chapel Poem" is somewhat biting insofar as the other figures do not seem to have had a transformative experience in the chapel, the poem proposes that the transformation has been an internal one for the speaker. Instead of reshaping the speaker's relationship to social institutions such as the university, the church, or consumption-tourism, his experience of the chapel reorients his awareness of the natural world. The poem concludes:

> blue sky humid afternoon it's Spring in Houston
>
> underneath the peeling blue sky I see this red sky
>
> there are swallows darting over a shallow pool
>
> flower beside pool tiny florets like bow ties
>
> ground where the flower grows turns deep red
>
> this ground that keeps turning deep red ground.[84]

Even as he leaves the chapel, the speaker's vision of the world is marked by the color play of the chapel's paintings. The deep purple of the monochromes is recalled in the blue humidity of the Houston springtime sky, and the oxblood red now finds its echoes in the tiny flowers of the courtyard's trees as they color both the branches and the ground underneath. As such, the conclusion of "The Rothko Chapel Poem" records the extension of repetition into the speaker's perception of the world around him, to which he returns and which is returned to him, revivified.

The conclusion of "The Rothko Chapel Poem" suggests the importance of exterior spaces to Taggart's work. Toby Olson notes as much in his 1979 *Paper Air* musings on Taggart, recalling a scene from the mid-1960s, when he and Taggart were together at the Aspen Writers Workshop. Listening to Taggart read Robert Creeley's poem "A Song," next to the aptly named Roaring Fork River, Ott realized, "John was listening to the poem *and* the river, the river a kind of baseline for the poem."[85] This sense of communion between the natural world and the performance of a poem continues throughout Taggart's career, with his attention sharpened as he focuses on the cultivation and naming of plants and how the landscape is made knowable through traces of human movement, such as roads, bridges, and even tractor furrows. This commitment to exploring poetry as a means of knowing the world underwrites Taggart's stark shift in form, beginning with *Pastorelles*, his 2004 collection, in which he jettisons the large-scale, chant-based poems in favor of more descriptive poems that work in a more identifiable lyric mode. In spite of this formal shift, however, Taggart's work continues to be animated by the charge of the Orphic poet to not merely unite words and music in song but, through singing, to imbue places and things with meaning and to both find and forge links between them. As we might expect from their title, the fifteen "Pastorelles" treat the life of the land, and the poems are shot through with history and the marks of humanity upon the landscape. The collection is framed by poems that contemplate the task of the poet: lest we forget, "Pastorelle 2" reminds us, "the object is a song."[86] These are, that is, songs of place, and, as such, they are effectively a return to his interest in the pastoral that he cited from his graduate school days.

The link between the Orphic disposition and the pastoral mode is heard throughout *Pastorelles*, which focuses primarily on rural life in South Central Pennsylvania's Cumberland Valley, where Taggart has lived since he began teaching at Shippensburg University in 1969. Thematically, the poems mostly focus on the contours of the landscape and the daily events of rural life. In this landscape, Taggart trains his attention on movement, much as he had done in "Drum Thing" decades earlier. The poems are dominated by imagery of transit, the physical marks of humanity making its way across the land—by stagecoach, by bridge, by highway, by roller skate. Thus, the first *Pastorelle* begins the series with a "glance" of the countryside along Pennsylvania Route 641. The poem begins:

> Glance to the right all that's possible
> Driving south
> On 641 what was the old stage coach route
> Curve on 641 curve and descent[87]

As the stage coach route has become the modern highway, it has inscribed its movement, its curve and descent, onto the landscape itself. The land is knowable insofar as it is demarcated by the accumulated tracks of history. What's more, the movement through this scene recalls Orpheus's glancing gaze and his descent to the underworld, as if the speaker's drive through the Pennsylvania countryside is a repetition of the lyric poet's paradigmatic search for his lost love. However, instead of Orphic trials, Taggart encounters the land and its signs of human engagement with it. Thus, one of the glances the speaker gets is of a "wide field / brown green brown / where the farmer plowed where the farmer didn't where he did," the furrows of a cultivated field delineating the contours of the landscape like relief lines on a map, or like the lines of a sentence, or those of a musical staff.[88] Taggart's reading of the marked landscape again deploys the sense of music he articulates in his poem-essay "Were You." As Taggart frames his goal to Michael Palmer, "the idea is to conceive the music as an arrangement or system of gaps and not as a dense pattern of sound."[89] The lines in the field frame just such a system of gaps, a system that is observable only in the fleeting instant of the glance. As such, the task of the Orphic poet is to capture these fleeting moments in language and in a form that will allow them to be repeatable and shared in their resounding. In the final poem in the collection, "Plinth," Taggart explicitly points to the communal and pedagogical drive of the poet, as he draws a parallel between the writing of poems and the reconstruction of shattered monuments, shoring up their fragments on a "foundation of stones from the old school house," addressing the challenge: "what can be done / that music may enter as through a welcoming portal may enter this // air / among these pines."[90] Much as the poet driving across the landscape repeats the history that lies beneath the present-day highway, the wind blowing through the shards of this reconstituted monument forms a link between it, all that it carries with it, and the surrounding trees.

This sense that the song of the Orphic poet serves a communal and even pedagogical function also underscores "*Pastorelles* 14," which focuses on Ramp Bridge. Listed on the National Register of Historic Places as the last remaining authentic covered bridge in the Cumberland Valley, the bridge dates from 1882 and spans the Conodoguinet Creek, "the creek or / small river also named after Jacob."[91] The first of the poem's nine sections sparsely thematizes the life of its namesake, Jacob Ramp, the son of a prominent family from Cumberland County who slowly made his way west, a "migrant in the great migration Indiana Kansas Missouri finally Oregon."[92] As the poem has it, his life is "proof you can leave your mark / if you leave / and if you're remembered."[93] The remaining eight sections of the poem focus on the bridge's construction—its use of the truss and arch principle—and, above all, questions of "use" that resonate powerfully with the importance of that term in Taggart's poetics. The poem again displays the importance of enumeration to Taggart, with the fifth of its ten sections being both the longest and that which connects the geometrical attributes of the bridge, its usefulness, and its embodiment of wonder to the idea of music. The section begins in the declarative, "the structure = the truss principle / which = all parts / of the bridge connected by a series of triangles // one post leaning against / another series of one against another each connected at the top and / the bottom by beams the beams are called chords."[94] Taggart's Orphic drive for unity animates these lines, as the interconnectedness and interdependence of the parts of the bridge articulate a geometry of mutual reliance. Conveniently, the architectural term for the connecting beams, the "chords," bears a powerful musical homonym. As Taggart's description of the bridge continues, it is first concrete and mathematical, with "the structure = the truss principle + arch / the arch in sections / pinned / bolted to the posts upright posts of the triangles," and then, finally, spiritual, with the repeated and simple assertion that "this is marvelous this is the mystery what really matters / the structure is / what matters the flower the music of it."[95] In his treatment of Ramp's Bridge, Taggart displays the range of commitments that animate his Orphic poetics and the use toward which he aspires. The mathematical principles evident in the construction of the bridge are important insofar as they demonstrate the strength and durability of interconnected parts; the name of the bridge resounds the personal history of its namesake, including everything from his link to this small creek to his trip west; and the point of it all is its music, the ways in which it captures time and continuously blossoms with meaning.

Taggart's invocation of music as the final arbiter of why the bridge "matters" draws attention to the other ways the music of the bridge is active in the poem. Taggart builds from the commonplace pun between this piece of public works architecture and the musical bridge, each getting from one piece of continuous, ongoing line of development to another—bringing us across the gap, whether temporal, spatial, or melodic. Just as the bridge spans the creek, in its very structure and its name, it similarly reaches across time, serving not merely as a monument to Jacob Ramp but also as an active and living connection to him. Spatially, the bridge's continued practical usefulness keeps it a living part of the landscape, "saved from quaintness from the antique the 'collectible' / by use still in use the plank runners worn smooth / by traffic."[96] In this traffic, Taggart identifies perhaps the most important signature of the bridge's continued vitality: "use = noise / cars burning rubber squeals and shouting of passengers horns honking / how to know a covered bridge is still in use = noise."[97] As the connecting beams of the bridge, its chords, reverberate with traffic noise, the bridge is transformed into a resonant chamber. Tellingly, Taggart's description of these acoustic signs of life focus not on the grind of engines but on the sounds of wheels playfully spinning across the boards, the voices of passengers, and the percussive blasts of horns. That is, what starts as noise becomes a kind of musical performance.

The pastoral mode of Taggart's *Pastorelles* is not that of an idyllic landscape dotted with the occasional shepherds and their flocks. Rather, it is a landscape that is known and knowable by way of human interaction with it. As such, the task of the Orphic poet in this landscape is to identify and reactivate in song the affinities that lay buried beneath the veneer of everyday life. This concern with the embedded histories of a place continues in Taggart's subsequent collection, *There Are Birds*, published in 2008. The centerpiece of the collection is the long poem "Unveiling / Marianne Moore." Over the span of sixty pages and eighty-nine numbered sections, the poem contemplates the scientific and vernacular naming of trees, the geography of South Central Pennsylvania, the continued vitality of literary traditions, and the fate of European explorers in America, among other topics. Underpinning the poem's thematic range is another variety of repetition for Taggart, the fact that he lives in the same locale as that to which Marianne Moore relocated as a child. The relation here is an imagined and projected one. By the time Taggart moved to the area to take his teaching position at Shippensburg University in 1969, Moore had lived elsewhere for nearly fifty years. In his turn to Moore, Taggart reminds us of her (rather tenuous) association with the objectivist poets, her collection *Observations* having been cited by

Zukofsky as exemplary in the 1931 objectivist issue of *Poetry* magazine. However, his relationship to Moore in this piece is not merely or even primarily one of literary lineage; rather, the drive for this poem is their shared locality across time. As the third section of the poem tells us, "surroundings answer questions,"[98] and the work of this poem is largely to consider the questions of how the poet's work relates to those surroundings. He sets the standard of his task early by rejecting traditional literary uses of nature, noting that his goal is "neither *eiresione* nor *daphnephoria*," that is, neither the personification of nature nor the ritual and ceremonial deployment of nature.[99] Instead, this poem is "not any kind of bringing in the tree story rather the reverse / bringing oneself to the tree."[100] That is, for Taggart, the goal of this poem is an Orphic and pastoral one, a matter of giving oneself over to the material and linguistic traces of landscape, etymology, and history so as to sing their unities. Later, in section fourteen, Taggart enumerates the key terms: "local girl bark of a tree skin of a snake,"[101] and in Moore he presents a model of how we might proceed, "she read in her own way with propriety not for the point for the picture the / truer identity."[102] Following her lead, Taggart similarly sets about writing a poem whose primary task is not to prove a point but to demonstrate a larger, more suggestive picture of the ways in which the landscape of the Cumberland Valley resonates with hidden linkages and affinities. Setting aside the chantlike mode of his middle period, Taggart nonetheless turns to this landscape with the same Orphic drive that animated his attentions to the Rothko Chapel.

When Taggart surveys this landscape, he associates it with both poetry and music. Early in the poem, Taggart reflects upon Moore's early life in the valley, noting that she "grew up around here in this valley in the / space between north and south mountains two blue mountains / long waveforms/ridgelines of two blue mountains // in this valley between forms/lines."[103] As Taggart notes the parameters of the valley, the ridgelines of the mountains to the north and south give the valley form, much as the lines of the poem are the substance of its form. Taggart's process in his survey of the landscape carries the mark of his predecessors Ezra Pound and Charles Olson, in that he finds other versions of this form throughout Moore's physical surroundings. Thus, he reads Moore's surroundings after she and her mother had moved to a row house, "some of the houses all in a / row are stuck together no space between them // between 343 and 345 a narrow passage leading to a narrow back yard."[104] The crests of the mountains are translated into the peaks of the houses, and the valley below, in which life resides, becomes the alleyway. This framing of the space becomes fundamental to Taggart's image of Moore, as it "was what she was / between."[105] As the poem continues, the essential betweenness of Moore is also identified with her reading practices as a child. Taggart notes that she snuck the tales of La Fontaine (whom she would later translate) into church and slipped them between the pages of the Bible: "a classics illustrated comic book the classically animated fables of / La Fontaine / will fit in a narrow/thin space between the thin / pages of a bible or of a hymnal between the brotherhood / and service tunes."[106] In the logic of Taggart's associations, while the poet might appear to be attending to the conventions of a church service, the real object of study is hidden between the pages: the tales of La Fontaine between the songs of the Bible, the truth of the alleyway between the walls of the row houses, and the ground of the Cumberland Valley between the form-giving lines of the mountain ridgetops.

As Taggart explores the features of his local landscape, he pays particular attention to the conventions of naming objects in the world. His most poignant example, that with which he begins and which serves as a touchstone throughout the poem, is the naming of trees, in particular, the maple variety *Acer tegmentosum*, which he notes is "snake bark maple" in common usage. The poem begins with an extended contemplation on the scientific name of the tree, with Taggart delineating the logic of scientific nomenclature, "combination of noun and adjective / binomial // substantive and modifier of the substantive . . . two Latin words noun and adjective for one thing the tree / and its covering leaves // noun for genus for family adjective for species one particular member of the family."[107] As Taggart considers the practice of scientific naming, he demonstrates that it is not so much a matter of greater precision, but, rather, a richer range of context and association for objects in the world. It is, in this estimation, a "system for naming and for classifying / bringing things into relation with other things other plants and / animals // multiplying contact // no system no / understanding of the world sum total set of names and things the world the / total set 'the larger beauty' // a system an effort to tell the truth."[108]

Taggart's consideration of scientific naming runs parallel to a similar contemplation of the vernacular. As he describes it, "another / other" effort at the truth, "the no system apparently no system of the vernacular the common / names," including that of the tree, "snake-barked."[109] While we might assume that the vernacular is less rule bound than the process of scientific naming, Taggart proposes an underlying similarity between the two systems. Much like scientific nomenclature proliferates the interconnectedness of things, the vernacular, building from the example of this "snake-barked tree," is fundamentally both metaphorical and metonymical. As the poem describes, the vernacular is a process of "saying one thing is another / overstatement of identity not A=A the nonstatement/ pseudostatement of / 'true identity' but A=B saying one thing is another / truer statement of identity when it is truer."[110] Thus, "snake-barked tree" is a "truer statement of identity" for the tree because it avoids the false precision of tautology and instead embraces the fundamentally associative nature of metaphor.

Later in the poem, we learn that Taggart has turned his attention to this particular variety of maple because it, like Moore and like him, has been transplanted to Pennsylvania. The tree is one of the specimens found in Taggart's own tree garden, and he notes that the planting of the tree on his property is an answer to one of the poem's challenges, "if the tree's home is China / then how to come to the tree when my home is in this valley between / two blue mountains // plant the tree in this/my own valley."[111] This importing of the tree is not without reservations, though, and Taggart pauses to consider the possibility of it becoming an invasive species. He wonders, "isn't this wrong / to plant a tree from one valley in another," but he finds comfort in the vast expanse of geological time in which his "own valley" was connected with the tree's home in China, "the one the other were once / long ago the very same / connected valley."[112] Ultimately, for Taggart the tree is no more an invasive species than is Marianne Moore or himself. While this sense of fundamental connectedness might be unpersuasive to wildlife management professionals, it signals Taggart's Orphic disposition and charge. For Taggart, nothing is static, everything is dynamic, and the challenge is to find the connections that persist across this range of movement. As such, the planting of the tree so that he might bring himself to it rekindles a unity of place that has been hidden through the shifting of continents.

Although the mechanisms of scientific nomenclature and vernacular naming are different, they both belie the process of veiling that resonates in the poem's title. Recalling Taggart's emphasis on attention, in "Unveiling / Marianne Moore," he tells us, "the principal verb is think,"[113] its conjugation a notable shift from the insistent infinitives that characterize his chant poems. Thinking as the basis of the poet's work and song is the process at work here, and it yields a kind of etymological clarity as Taggart repeatedly describes the process of "unveiling." As the poet thinks about the associations embedded within the names of the tree, that tree is "made truer/more vivid unveiled A having been veiled however momentarily by B / which is another rule the veiling to be unveiled rule // the veiling taking place in the fusion" of the snake and the tree in the snake-bark tree.[114] This process of continuously and simultaneously revealing and concealing knowledge is the source of an underlying Orphic unity for Taggart, since "to know one thing . . . another thing/other things must be / known paid attention to known and brought together hyphenated fused / A-B which is / another rule the intense fusion however momentary so that the / first is the last thing that gets your attention."[115] Taggart again returns to his key term, "attention," and frequently contemplates throughout the poem the ways in which the term "snake-bark" gets a person's attention because, quite simply, snakes get people's attention.

In this sense, the poet's primary task is to attend to, to think about, naming conventions and, in so doing, to bring to light the hidden and interlocking truths of the objects named. The poem enumerates the mechanisms at work: "identification / of one thing through another thing // and attention precedes the painting of identification."[116] Later, this invocation of metaphor becomes even more pointed, as Taggart observes that "what holds me . . . a tree in the total set the world in the larger / beauty of the landscape";[117] and he explicitly invokes metonymy: "metonymy // a tone a little tune / coming from interior of the body identifying / what's truly mine/me."[118] The play of metaphor and metonymy in this process of "unveiling" resembles nothing so much as Jacques Derrida's description of the Orphic movement of the veil in his essay "A Silkworm of One's Own": "un-veiling, unveiling oneself, reaffirming the veil in the unveiling. It finishes with itself in unveiling, does the veil, and always with a view to finish off in self-unveiling. Finishing the veil is finishing with self."[119] Similarly, for Taggart, attending to the interconnectivity that underwrites both metaphor and metonymy does not shed the veil and expose a hidden truth; rather, it draws our attention to the threads of the veil of language.

As the poem concludes, Taggart's Orphic quest for the linguistic threads that link him to the tree, to the valley, and, ultimately, to Marianne Moore becomes a quest for liberation of the self through an awareness of oneself as enmeshed in the patterns of interconnectivity embedded in the names we give to trees and in the collocation of poets across time. As the poem builds this interconnected field of association, the speaker's desire is ultimately to go beyond the tree line, and he cautions, "nymph with/within the tree not / end or final aim / not the end of my story but an effort to tell the truth of what's / further/beyond far into the woods."[120] He continues, "the woods which = memory," and concludes the poem with literary memories: passages from Chaucer's *Troilus and Criseyde* and "The Dream" from *The Book of the Duchess*. The first of these reflects upon Taggart's poetic practice, which he describes as "a meander a mirror," recalling Chaucer's "make a mirror of his mind."[121] The allusion continues, as Taggart quotes *Troilus's* description of his site of Cressida, "al hoolly her figure," apparently aligning Moore and Cressida. This invocation of female literary figures continues in the allusion to "The Dream": "I see a face of sorrow a young man's face 'of sorwe so great woon."[122] In these passages, Taggart does more than simply invoke tragic female figures from the literary canon; he invokes the canonicity of that canon, in that both of these passages are also featured by Ezra Pound in his 1934 *ABC of Reading* as examples of early poetry that is untranslatable for the perfection of its song in the original language. As such, the conclusion of the poem is a final release into the web of associations: "the truth // this is far into the woods and this is / liberation."[123] Far into the woods by way of a single tree whose associations sound a vast linguistic web of interconnected threads that are sought out and sounded by the Orphic poet.

The linkage between song and place that animates the Orphic work of "Unveiling / Marianne Moore" runs throughout *There Are Birds* and is starkly foregrounded in the book's final poems. In "Show and Tell / Robert Creeley," Taggart returns to the same scene as that described by Toby Olson in the special issue of *Paper Air* some four decades earlier: he, Olson, and other poets and friends reading poetry alongside the Roaring Fork Creek. In Olson's recollection, he suggests that Taggart was listening to the creek even as he read from Creeley's collection *For Love*, interweaving the sonorities of the landscape and those of the poem. In this poem, Taggart confirms Ott's earlier suggestion and makes a summative statement that could just as well serve for the book and, in fact, his career as a whole: "this poem is a song an / act / a work of love."[124] Song, act, and work of love: the animating concerns of Taggart's Orphic poetics. The collection concludes with two cadenzas further reflecting upon his practice, "song against song and other songs in a blending of wavy pitches // there are birds there is birdsong / unmourning and unmournful having come through // like the light like / like love never for sale."[125] The reference to song as being unmourning and unmournful brings the collection full circle as it recalls the book's first poem, "Refrains for Robert Quine," in which birdsong is invoked as a curative for the trap of melancholy in the wake of the death of Quine, an influential punk rock guitar player who was also Taggart's classmate as an undergraduate at Earlham College. The final cadenza consists of three repetitions of the title phrase, "there are birds," signaling a certain faith in the perpetuity of the natural world, that same natural world of trees to which the poet brings himself in order to find his self, his song.[126]

Taggart's invocation of song in the final lines of *There Are Birds* reinforces the importance of the art of music to his poetics much as did the cover of *Is Music*. In spite of the striking formal shifts that characterize his career, his work is consistently underwritten by its bringing together of an Orphic disposition that seeks to unify words and music and a pastoral mode of attention. In Taggart, the Orphic is evident in his unwavering commitment to exploring the linkage between the temporal arts of poetry and music. From early in his career, Taggart seeks to create poems that take time as their material, forging language into a distinctive temporal experience that diverges from the wash of the quotidian in search of contemplative peace. And it is in this contemplation that his pastoralism operates. Whether in the company of the visual field of the Rothko Chapel—its own kind of pastoral space—or among the trees and local histories of rural Pennsylvania, Taggart trains his Orphic ear on how the environment is imbued with meaning through acts of cultivation: in paint, in the alluvial histories that undergird highways and bridges, in the naming of trees. For Taggart, music is both an identifiable, sonic art form and a very real and very figurative ideal for the possibility of achieving active and ongoing unity.

4

Eurydice Takes the Mic

Improvisation and Ensemble in the Work of Tracie Morris

Blackness, which is to say black femininity, which is to say black
performance, will have turned out to be the name of the invaginative,
the theatrical, the dissonant, the atonal, the atotal, the sentimental,
the experimental, the criminal, the melodramatic, the ordinary. It
is and bears an aesthetic of the trebled (troubled, doubled) seer's
voice disturbed by being seen and seeing up ahead where escape,
crossing over, translation will have meant the continual reanimative
giving—unto the very idea of freedom—of the *material*.
—Fred Moten, *Black and Blur*

"Eurydice": derived from *eurys* (wide) and *dike* (justice)

Throughout classical versions of the Orpheus myth, Eurydice is with-
out voice or volition. She is the object of Orpheus's love and the cause of his
agony; she is the foil in what is most definitely his story. As discussed in chapter
2, this conceptualization of Eurydice as the traumatic source at the heart of lyric
sets in motion a calculus in which the darkness of her absence is the fuel for Or-
pheus's creative potential. As such, this traditional framing of the story mobilizes
a set of assumptions about language and expressivity, passivity and action, gen-
der, and the grounding of the self that revolve around the notion of blackness.
Eurydice occupies this space of blackness, and, as such, her condition resonates
with Moten's work on the relationship between the concept of blackness and
the lived experiences of persons who are called "Black." As Moten argues, the

performance of blackness is a fundamental refutation of dominant social conventions even as access to those conventions has been made unavailable, a fugitive swerve away from the controlling confines of the normative. Moten's suggestive, associative, vatic framing of blackness suggests one way we might envision an alternative to the silencing of Eurydice. Exercising her namesake "wide justice," Eurydice would wrest the mic from Orpheus's death grip and speak from her silence and doubled darkness, claim the power of the music of language, and perform a self that is forged in and through the endless task of crossing over from the land of the dead into that of the living. She would perform a contingent self that is not simply a refutation of Orpheus's model but a claim to the power of music and poetry that works otherwise.[1]

This Eurydicean poetics of performativity is powerfully demonstrated by the poet and sound artist Tracie Morris. As with Orphic poets, Morris's practice has long been influenced by music and the power of the performed word. She first came to prominence as a slam poet during the 1990s at the Nuyorican Poets Café, winning the 1993 Nuyorican Grand Slam and competing in the National Poetry Slam, and she has performed as a singer throughout her career. Beginning in the late 1990s, Morris increasingly began to work in avant-garde sound art, and she soon came to be associated with Language poets, including Charles Bernstein, with whom she has collaborated and on whose radio show, "Close Listening," she has appeared; Bernstein would write the introduction to her *Handholding: 5 Kinds* (2018), which I treat in detail below.[2] Throughout her varied career, Morris has explored the expressive possibilities and conceptual implications of the performed voice.

In her graduate work on J. L. Austin, Morris expands his notion of performativity beyond his focus on the practical efficacy of turns of phrase to incorporate how human utterance itself can be understood as performative. As Austin defines the performative in his 1955 William James Lectures at Harvard University, published in 1962 as *How to Do Things with Words*, the performative "indicates that the issuing of the utterance is the performing of an action—it is not normally thought of as just saying something."[3] While Austin focuses on complete words and phrases, he also repeatedly invokes the openness of his method and invites subsequent readers to expand upon or refine his project. Morris takes him up on the offer in her book *Who Do with Words* (2018), based upon her dissertation, and trains her attention on the elemental and impromptu nature of utterance itself, including of the most basic building block of verbalized language, the phoneme.[4] As she writes, jousting with Austin: "*Say what?* / *Says Who?*: The beginning of language isn't utilitarian, as Austin states (but does not *perform*). It's exclamatory, onomatopoetic, divine. The first compulsion to 'say'—whether a baby's cry or the gasp at the new one's arrival, an utterance that began as an urge that often releases as coming too (the body explicating in two ways through two portals) is not *planned* speech. It is the speaking that *must* come. It is as fundamental a human need as the inhalation and exhalation of breath. Even in solitary confinement, one utters, not to describe a word but to do, to make one, to make one's *self*."[5] For Morris, even the merest utterance bears the world and self-making potential of performativity. The newborn child and the expressions of wonder at the sight of that child are both indicative of the insurmountable need to be heard, which exists before and separate from the intentionality of the forming of words or sentences. As Morris shifts her frame of reference from the vocalizations of a newborn child to those of an inmate, the stakes of her project become clear: the voice itself, the speaking voice per se performs an action in and through which a self is formed and maintained, even (perhaps, especially) in such dire conditions as imprisonment.

Morris frames utterance itself as a performative, emphasizing the creative and communal nature of the expressive human voice. As Morris argues, while utterances precede the formation of words, phrases, and sentences that perform the actions that are the subject of Austin's attention, she identifies categories of Austin's speech acts in utterances themselves. For instance, she identifies elements of utterances as "behabitives," verbalizations that Austin describes as "includ[ing] the notion of reaction to other people's behavior and fortunes and of attitudes and expressions of attitudes to someone else's past conduct or imminent conduct."[6] Austin notes that "behabitives" are similar to descriptions or expressions of feeling but are distinct partly insofar as they involve reactions to a social context. Therefore, as Morris argues by extension, "the *behabitive* aspect of utterances is for generating rapport, social relationships and not for specific meaning."[7] With this emphasis on utterance as both communally situated and communally constative, Morris reframes Austin's description of "phatic acts," language use that Austin describes as "the uttering of vocables *as* belonging to a certain vocabulary."[8] Austin's examples of phatic acts emphasize the use of inverted commas to denote in print those moments when a speaker reports the language use of someone else. This structure distances the speaker from the language they cite even as they use that language. For Morris, this gesture provides a critical lever for the recycling, redefining, and redeployment of given vocabularies. As she argues, *"Phatic acts* (expressions that primarily communicate social ideas through vocabulary) allow meaning to be created and recreated over time. African diaspora communities have generated phatic expressions from the *beginning* of human concepts of time."[9] Taken together, Morris's exploration of the behabitive and phatic nature of utterance situates utterance as an essential part of performative self-formation that both takes into account the language in which it is given to operate and provides new modes of selfhood made available through innovations in language use.

Throughout Morris's consideration of the performative capacities of the utterance, she balances her awareness that language users exist alongside other users of the same language with a commitment to recognizing the unique, defining features that distinguish any given user's individual use of that language. Thus, as she argues, "knowing that the sources of utterances are creative (and utilitarian *because* they are creative, poetic) as well as that we have a specific lens in understanding how to generate re-humanizing value from them despite all odds, is showing 'doing' and 'being' with words. How to create, recreate, remix utterances foundational for human understanding of ourselves (including non-language based utterances that are onomatopoetic and glossolalic), reaches toward something beyond Austin's humane utilitarianism and into a state of consciousness, of *grace*, that can be an even more brilliant 'light of the world.'"[10] For Morris, this redemptive possibility of utterance extends from an elemental factor of humanness that both registers the singularity of that individual and their relationship(s) with broader communities, histories, and identities. As she argues, utterances register the "human *need* to embody, reflect the extraordinary, sacred, profound, scary, resistive restive through speech / song / poetry / articulation / expression that is at the crux of the need to understand and to be understood. This perception-intonation is at the heart of why and how we utter, as well as the world-building this drive for uttering does. These are the fundamental tools we have always used to assert our particular ways of being and doing with words."[11] For Morris, our utterances are performatives that bear the marks of our individuality, signal our participation in a larger community, and bring new selves into being.

As Morris argues in the introduction to *Who Do with Words*, her interest in the performative qualities of the basest elements of language makes her project a distinctly political one. She poignantly notes, "For those whose *humanness has been questioned*, (my focus is on people of the African diaspora), our understanding of, and reconfiguration of, utterances as performative have often been used *by us* to make ourselves *free*" (15).[12] As Morris takes up the political performativity of the utterance, she thus develops an Eurydicean poetics that is both critical and creative as it mobilizes the noise of a human body claiming its right to be and to be expressive. As she describes in a 2008 interview on Charles Bernstein's "Close Listening" radio show, experimental art that foregrounds the expressive potential of the human body therefore plays a complementary role to more concrete, issue-based political advocacy: "It's complicated, because on the one hand you have the overt 'save this thing' that's political, and makes us feel better or makes us feel mad . . . and that's important and I am committed to doing that and like to think that's helpful. But, there's almost a metaphysical import and impact to making art, too. . . . I think about people like Jimi Hendrix and Miles Davis and many others who sometimes might say something that's overtly political, but just the fact that they're continuing to experiment, to push the envelope, to take things to another place, reconfigures people's concept of what kind of world they can exist in."[13] For Morris, while political action that is based upon identifiable content and achievable goals is clearly an important element to both her worldview and her art, she is also deeply committed to the visionary value of experimentation itself.

Morris's belief in the ability of experimentation to conjure up endlessly new possible worlds and modes of being in those worlds, coupled with her background in music and live vocal performance, draw her to a poetic practice that is grounded in improvisation. She emphasizes this aspect of her work in her introduction to a performance of her sound poem "The Mrs. Gets Her Ass Kicked" at the University of Arizona Poetry Center in 2009, noting, "All of my sound poems are improvised." As I will discuss in detail below, even her text-based poems often derive from improvisation.[14] Whether in her sound or print-based art, Morris embraces the forward-looking, probing, contingent, propositional nature of improvisation as a means of fashioning a self. In her sound poems, Morris often begins with recognizable speech and then atomizes that speech into the phonemic blocks out of which it is made, exploring alliterative and rhyming associations, as well as possible differences in pronunciation or intonation. When reading her own print-based poetry, she also routinely incorporates incidental mistakes or misreadings, capturing her own missteps as performative opportunities and integrating them into her vocal performance. As Christine Hume has argued, Morris's performance practice thus extends her reconfiguration of "illocutionary performatives," Austin's fundamental term, which he defines as statements through which "the issuing of the utterance is the performance of an action."[15] As Hume argues, "by inhabiting and improvising within one sentence, Morris releases the physicality of words, plays with sonic associations, and funnels the referential residue of language into more visceral, more estranging and ethical functions. Familiar speech sets in motion something close to glossolalia by way of accent, slur, stutter, backtracking, striation, and telescoping tempo."[16] That is to say, in her improvisational play, Morris shifts the frame of Austin's concept from that of the word to that of the phoneme and demonstrates the performativity of the self in the act of the vocal, human performance of utterance prior to language.

The performative self that emerges through Morris's sound poetry thus demonstrates the link between improvisation as artistic practice and improvisation as self-formation. In doing so, Morris's work demonstrates the vitality of improvisation that Fred Moten explores in his book, *Black and Blur*: "Composition is imagining improvisation. . . . Improvisation is the animative, electric, hieroglyphic-seismographic tension that cuts the pose while also being its condition of possibility, even as the pose is the condition of possibility of the whole in its unavoidably narrative, unavoidably fantastic theatricality."[17] Similarly, in Morris, improvisation is the method that brings selves onstage in a continuous process of proposition, disruption, superimposition, and cross-cutting.

This performative self, which Morris brings into being through improvisation, is thus consistent with how Walton Muyumba characterizes improvisation in the jazz tradition. In Muyumba's framework, "the construction of an improvised solo is designed to articulate the music's openness to renewal and revision while also enabling the public expression of the self as performative—both are oth-ered in the play. When musicians improvise they are detailing some elements of their individual and/or ensemble musical educations and jazz performances, as well as creating spontaneous, new compositions."[18] Thus, as Muyumba demon-strates, in improvisation, the player (or poet) is both immersed in the tradition of their musical background and thrown forward as they seek new means of ex-pression. Referencing Amiri Baraka's writing from his transitional period of the mid-1960s, Muyumba explicitly links improvisation as an artistic practice and improvisation as a condition of black identity. Citing "blackness's foundation in improvisation," Muyumba elaborates, "in other words the black self is, in fact, not foundational because the imperatives of improvisation actually force one to interrogate and subvert the search for essence."[19] As does Moten, Muyumba ar-gues that improvisation lies at the core of black identity, foregrounding the fact of identity as performative rather than foundational in ways that frame Morris's own extension of Austin's work.

The importance of improvisation to Morris's Eurydicean poetics is equaled by that of the ensemble. The traditional framing of the Orpheus myth values the singular will of the heroic artist while disparaging images of feminine multiplic-ity, as in the figures of the maenads, who tear Orpheus limb from limb in their lust-driven rage. In sharp contrast, Eurydicean poetics embraces multiplicity, whether in the form of multiple individuals within the group or ensemble or of the multiplicities contained within any ostensibly singular self. As Moten de-scribes the relationship between the ensemble and improvisation, "ensemble is the improvisation of . . . singular identities . . . and the totality generated by lingering in the music that airily fills the space between them. They speak in en-semble and are written there in a moment at which we are given, through the mediation of improvisation, the whole of the history of the whole and the whole of the history of singularist (and differentiated) totalizations of the whole."[20] As Moten argues, the work of the ensemble is a conceptual space and an improvisa-tory practice in which artists establish their singularity in and through the con-text of the other members of the ensemble, a critical and creative performance that is especially poignant for black artists and others who engage with and are shaped by cultural histories of marginalization and oppression.

The importance of the ensemble as a means of establishing the counter-normativism that Moten identifies as at the core of Black performance under-writes Morris's penchant for inclusion as a conspicuous characteristic of her Eurydicean poetics. Describing herself as a "blerd" (a "black nerd"), Morris's frame of reference includes science fiction, from the mainstream of the Marvel Cinematic Universe to the Afrofuturism of Samuel Delany; canonical literary figures, from Shakespeare to Edgar Allen Poe; the modernist avant-gardism of Gertrude Stein and the surrealists; monumental figures in black writing, from Amiri Baraka to Harryette Mullen; and, of course, music, including rap, hip-hop, jazz, blues, and afro-punk. In Morris's work, this range of influences fuels her performative self as it eschews stasis and predictability in favor of fluidity and contingency. As such, one of her primary practices as a poet is to bring artistic and cultural traditions into unexpected contact with one another. Thus, for instance, she turns to Poe's famous poem, "Dream within a Dream," and sings it as a slow, smoky jazz ballad. Morris's author page at PennSound features several performances of the piece, including one from the 2008 Conceptual Poetry and Its Others Conference at the University of Arizona. At this reading, Morris introduces Poe's poem by noting, "It's a poem, but I'm making it a found poem. I hear this poem as lyric."[21] Hearing Poe's pre–Civil War poem as a song lyric, Morris places it into the musical idiom of jazz in a style most reminiscent of vocal performers such as Billie Holiday, Ella Fitzgerald, and Sarah Vaughan.

Morris's treatment of the "dream within a dream" of Poe's poem thus transplants it across time, notably across the unresolved racial divide of the Civil War, providing historical associations unknowable to Poe and unavoidable to Morris. Morris's singing style also registers a readily identifiable historical period, one that is largely defined by the struggles of the civil rights movement. As such, the Romanticism of Poe's "dream" is made to literally resonate with the political dreams of Langston Hughes's 1951 experimental book-length poem, *Montage of a Dream Deferred* and Martin Luther King's famous address, "I Have a Dream," delivered at the 1963 March on Washington for Jobs and Freedom. As such, it might be tempting to say that Morris's performance of "Dream within a Dream" sutures the wound of the Civil War insofar as it brings Poe into contact with the later work of Hughes and King. However, as Moten has argued, such a reconciliatory vision for black art misconstrues the legacy of racial violence. Discussing the role of systemic material violence that underscores Aunt Hester's scream in Frederick Douglass's autobiography, Moten argues, "Black art neither sutures nor is sutured to trauma. There's no remembering, no healing. There is, rather, a perpetual cutting, a constancy of expansive and enfolding rupture and wound, a rewind that tends to exhaust the metaphysics upon which the idea of redress is grounded."[22] Similarly, Morris's performance aligns the existential futility of Poe's poem with both the political disillusionment of Hughes and the optimism of King, as a means not of reconciliation or healing but, rather, of articulating the persistence of racial injustice, reframing and reminding us of the persistent *incivility* in American society; the wounds of racial injustice are not healed through Morris's singing of Poe's poem but rather are made a dehiscent fecundity.

The juxtaposition of cultural references that animates Morris's performance of "Dream within a Dream" is also at the center of her sound poem "Mahalia Theremin." At a performance of the poem at the University of Pennsylvania's Kelly Writers House in 2013, she introduces it as an "Afro-futurist piece" that combines the historical figures of the African American gospel singer Mahalia Jackson and the Russian engineer and musical inventor Leon Theremin, both of whom she describes as visionaries who were "looking towards another kind of future. Theremin was looking towards a speculative future, and she towards a concrete one during the Civil Rights era."[23] In Jackson, Morris turns to one of the most prominent examples of the relationship between African American music and the civil rights movement. Achieving tremendous success and renown as a gospel singer, Jackson was deeply involved in the cause of civil rights, often performing at marches and gatherings, including the 1963 March on Washington that featured King's speech. In Theremin, meanwhile, Morris finds another, if very different, powerful link between art and politics, with Theremin's musical inventiveness often mobilized on the behalf of his native Russia and later the Soviet Union as demonstrative of Soviet technological superiority.[24] In spite of the cultural, historical, and aesthetic differences between Jackson and Theremin, Morris sees them both as imbuing their art with a certain performativity, an ability to imagine and therefore make a new world.

In "Mahalia Theremin," this performativity is heard in her use of her voice as an instrument. The content of the piece is based on the spiritual "Joshua Fit the Battle of Jericho," with Morris improvising on the line, "Joshua fit the battle of Jericho and the walls came tumbling down" over a span of just over two minutes. Her first performance of the line is in a fairly straight gospel style, and subsequent repetitions become increasingly distorted such that her voice takes on the qualities of Theremin's eponymous instrument. By halfway through the piece, the words of the lyric are no longer distinguishable, as the performance has become entirely the stylized articulation of phonemes, recalling Morris's discussion of "utterance" in *Who Do with Words*: "Through imagination, through utterances of sound, by saying we are doing: making meaning for / of ourselves and remaking as the desire arises."[25] In the case of "Mahalia Theremin," Morris reimagines the musical victory at the heart of the original gospel tune through the lens of Theremin's futuristic invention. In the biblical story, Joshua conquers Canaan by surrounding the city with his soldiers, who then bring the walls down with the sound of their trumpets. In "Mahalia Theramin," as Morris's voice shifts from that of a gospel singer to that of Theremin's ethereal, mechanized instrument, language itself falls, clearing the ground for the future.

Even as Morris invokes ensembles between herself and other poets, artists, and visionaries, living and dead, in her Eurydicean poetics, her commitment to improvisation lends her sound poems a quality of contingency and openness. As improvisations, no two performances are ever identical; she describes them as having a guiding narrative framework, but every performance is shaped by its conditions, including her mood and that of the audience, ongoing political or cultural events, the location of the performance, and the response of the audience. This improvisational approach to sound poems is perhaps most dramatically demonstrated in a 2013 performance of her poem "The Mrs. Gets Her Ass Kicked," also during her visit to the University of Pennsylvania's Kelly Writer's House. At the performance, Morris politely declines the audience's request that she perform her poem "Africa(n)," and she asks that they make another request. In response, she performs "The Mrs. Gets Her Ass Kicked," which she describes as being inspired by Doris Day. Morris begins the piece by rhythmically tapping on her chest, literalizing the opening lines of the poem's song source, Irving Berlin's "Pennies from Heaven," which includes the early line, "my heart beats so that I can hardly speak." Her percussive use of her body becomes increasingly frenetic, loud, and constrictive as she continues, to the point that by the end of the piece her voice sounds as if she is being strangled. This progression of her bodily performance creates a disturbing, violent juxtaposition with the text, thus highlighting the restrictive violence of gender roles and standards of beauty.[26] With roughly a minute remaining in the performance, at a point when Morris's vocalizations have again been reduced to their phonemic base, she unexpectedly shifts into the opening lines of "Africa(n)," the piece she had originally declined to perform, whose central line is "it all started in Africa." As she notes in the question and answer period following the performance, she had never before experienced such crossover from one piece to another, and she understands it as stemming from a shared concern with "articulating what it means to dehumanize someone . . . so, whiteness did not save women from being made inhuman . . . so the same physicalized abuse just spreads out, it's not controlled."[27] As Morris's improvisation thrusts her from the context of transatlantic slavery to the domestic violence hidden beneath the veneer of 1950s conventional gender roles, the performative of her sound poetry lays bare dominant structures of social power.

As Morris's early forays into sound poetry demonstrate, her Eurydicean poetics of ensemble and improvisation is a musical mode of responsiveness to both her predecessors and contemporary artistic, social, and political circumstances. The possibilities for this Eurydicean poetics are poignantly demonstrated in her 2016 collection, *Handholding: 5 Kinds: Sonic, Textual Engagements*, a collection of responses to the work of five other artists. As was the case with John Taggart's *Is Music*, the importance of music to Morris's project is evident from the cover of the book: a background of blank sheet music, upon which is superimposed a collage that depicts the five fingers of a hand, a cropped eye, and a mouth with a button held between its open teeth. The subjects of the handholdings are named in the collage in ways that suggest their cultural or aesthetic significance. In place of the palm of the hand is a white circle with the book's title around the inner perimeter and a smaller black circle at the center, like a vinyl 45, with the name "CAGE" at the center. In the image of the eye, the name "KUBRICK" similarly follows the curvature of the iris. The pinky finger has been replaced above the first knuckle by a prayer candle bearing the name "AKOMFRAH." The image of the mouth with the button in the teeth is on what appears to be a rectangular strip of a page torn from a magazine, placed as the arm descending beneath the open hand. Curving away from the left-hand side of this arm-mouth is the name "STEIN," while "SCHWITTERS" is near its base and aligned such that the tops of the letters in the name touch the last line of the staff, as if the name were a musical note. Thus, Morris's partners in *Handholding* are introduced: John Akomfrah, John Cage, Stanley Kubrick, Kurt Schwitters, and Gertrude Stein.

Morris's title for the collection indicates the practice she develops in the book, what she calls "handholding." As she describes both in the preface and in the prefatory comments for the individual pieces, "handholding" is closely related to surrealist automatic writing. Although the specifics of each work vary in ways that I will address in more detail below, Morris's general principle was to write in response to the texts at hand, producing in the "handholdings" works that are primarily the result of her associative imagination.[28] As with her earlier sound poems, and as signaled by the subtitle of *Handholding*, Morris's associations in the "handholdings" are both sonic and textual. Extending from her earlier sound poetry, here, too, sound, rhyme, rhythm, puns, and echo words often lead the way in her responses to the source texts, as does her abiding concern with issues of race and gender. What's more, in naming this self-performance as a "handholding," Morris emphasizes her connectedness as an artist, again developing a poetics of the ensemble that is in stark contrast to claims of heroic singularity or individuality. As she notes in her preface to the Schwitters "handholding," the collection presents "a template of what it can mean to handhold, what it will continue to mean for [her] to walk with these masters."[29] As the image of handholding suggests, and as is reinforced by her choice of words in calling these works "engagements," this improvisatory ensemble is a practice born of affection, though not uncomplicated, and carried forward as an ongoing relationship.

Echoing the breadth of Morris's influences and the openness of her performances, *Handholding* is a multiple text. Not only does she respond to a wide range of predecessors, but she also does so in ways that problematize the boundaries of the text. The printed text of the book is accompanied by a link to sound files of Morris's performances of the five pieces, hosted at the music website, Bandcamp.com, performances that she frames in the introductions as being variously more or less necessary to the printed versions of the pieces. What's more, these performances are augmented by her extensive catalogue at PennSound, which is an indispensable resource for experiencing her art. As Morris notes in the preface, in spite of the shared elements of her practice, "each of these pieces here has its own story, its own reason for its presence in this collection."[30] Morris's open framing of *Handholding* is another instance of her recasting Austin's concept of the performative. As she argues in *Who Do with Words*, with respect to the creative and re-creative act of utterance, "This re-creating is another way of understanding Austin's idea of locutionary acts in speech. Our range of utterances, overlays, foundations, and innovations can be dovetailed into these categories of 'making' as a form of meaning, 'remaking' as a form of intent to make. The affect is to make fresh, through the engagement with another (or oneself) in the effect of making."[31] In *Handholding*, Morris turns to works that are formative for both her aesthetics and her politics as the members of her ensemble and creates an open, multimedia, multidimensional, improvisatory text.

The first two members of Morris's ensemble are the filmmakers Stanley Kubrick and John Akomfrah. Both of these pieces respond to the visual and auditory experiences of their films: Kubrick's *Eyes Wide Shut* (1999) and Akomfrah's *Songs and Other Sevens* (1993), a treatment of Malcolm X that Morris describes as "a hybrid documentary and mythology . . . a beautiful creation."[32] In her prefatory comments, Morris notes that the entire collection came out of her interest in Kubrick, dating from her youthful appreciation of *2001: A Space Odyssey*. After having admired and thought about *Eyes Wide Shut* for years, Morris was serendipitously provided with an opportunity to formalize her interest in the film for a panel titled "Feminism Meets Neo-Benshi: Movietelling Talks Back," at the 2013 Associated Writing Programs conference. Morris dropped the reference to Benshi, the practice of live performers providing narration for silent films with roots in Japan, because of her sensitivity to cultural appropriation, and reframed the "talk-back" of her work in the context of the call-and-response that is so important to African American music, religious worship, and, as she notes, moviegoing: "The idea of talking back as the movie is playing, often with extensive commentary, is a well-known signifier of Black audiences watching films, both in public and in private. It's part of our call and response tradition from antiquity and applies to a Black presence through speech acts."[33] In the Kubrick "handholding," Morris's back talk is driven largely by questions of race and power in the film, including, as she notes, a conspicuous lack of black characters for a film set in New York, as well as the role of the colors black and white in other aspects of the film. For instance, black as the backdrop for the white letters in the film's opening credits and the color of Nicole Kidman's character's dress in the opening scene, and the whiteness of interior space coupled with the white privilege enjoyed by the central characters. The resulting interweaving of the source text and Morris's "handholding" with Kubrick is contrasted by her work with Akomfrah's film. While this piece similarly "rel[ies] on the words and images (including images of words)," it purposefully stands more on its own as a series of what Morris describes as "chants," "an erasure poem" whose dominant drive is to monumentalize Malcolm X and link the tragedy of his death with ongoing racial injustice in the United States.[34] Much as we are led to expect from the book's cover image, the Akomfrah "handholding" amounts to an ongoing artistic vigil in honor of Malcolm X.

Whereas the "talk-back" in the Kubrick and Akomfrah "handholdings" is driven by the visual experience of film, Morris's sonic imagination is brought most sharply to the foreground in her engagements with Stein and Schwitters. The Stein "handholding," "If I Re-viewed Her," consists of three sections: "Objectively," "Consumption," and "Enclosed," corresponding to the "Objects," "Food," and "Rooms" structure of *Tender Buttons*. Not unlike the Kubrick "handholding," the Stein piece was also facilitated by serendipity: an invitation to write a review of Stein's landmark work on its centennial for the poetry website *Jacket2*. Morris's preface to the Stein "handholding" foregrounds her interest in the performance of voice. Her first step in writing the piece was to watch a YouTube video of Stein reading her poem-portrait, "If I Told Him: A Completed Portrait of Picasso," whom Morris interestingly identifies as "a friend of hers."[35] Morris notes that she "liked the idea of hearing [Stein] speculate on telling in her own voice. Her voice was telling . . . It was also *telling*. I thought about the speculation of me presuming to review Stein. I liked the 'if.' Stein's voice was rather controlled, contained. It was a container."[36] As Stein's reading projects her own voice into the conditional, it opens a space between the telling and the voice itself, turning that voice into an object both related to Stein and yet removed from her.

For Morris, the contents of the voice—those objects in the container that is the voice—are fundamentally related to a person's geography. This focus on the specificity of an individual is consistent for Morris, such as, for instance, in *Who Do with Words*, when she reflects upon the particular perspective she brings to her reading of Austin: "The lens I use, however, is the one *I* see through as a Black woman from Brooklyn, a grown woman, on this earth now, part of a people. A people who have found ways where there were none and who also managed to make paths meaningful when they weren't designed to be."[37] As Morris notes, the individual features that define her and make her unique also link her to various communities, including those of grown, black women from Brooklyn who are currently living as a part of the global human family. In her introduction to the Stein "handholding," Morris notes these specificities and recalls that at her first reading of the poem, she was introduced by Bernstein, whom she identifies as "a dear friend," in a gesture that echoes her framing of Picasso's relationship to Stein. She goes on to describe that Bernstein had recently relocated to Brooklyn, where she grew up and where his mother was from, and that there is an inside joke between her and Bernstein about her "tenuous cultural and religious connection to Judaism."[38] Emerging from Morris's biographical sketches is an emphasis on her and Bernstein's voices as being distinctly New Yorkers' voices: "We both have heavy New York accents which, during a particular point in NY history, irrespective of one's race/ethnicity/religion, is an amalgam of African, African-American (southern), African-American (immigrant), Puerto Rican, Irish and Yiddish Jewish. The permutations and emphases depend upon where you grew up."[39] Discussing both the shared cosmopolitanism and the local differences between her and Bernstein's New York accents, Morris notes that they "sound more like each other, irrespective of our racial differences than, say, a Black person born in Paris or an Eastern European Jewish person born in Michigan. It's how we sound here."[40] Morris's interest in the specificities of voice and accent as shaped by geography raises larger questions about "the voice and performative utterances of text and how we embody it. I've listened to Stein's recording many times, so it's in my body to a certain extent."[41] As Stein's voice takes up residence alongside Morris's identity as a black, female, Brooklynite, these contrasting selves "handhold" in the amalgamated performative voice of the text, in what is not always a comfortable cohabitation.

As Morris describes in the prefatory remarks to the Stein "handholding," her approach varied in the three sections of the piece. She "detected the change of mood in each portion of *Tender Buttons*" and adjusted her compositional process accordingly.[42] She describes the first section as "playful, exploratory, the commentary of the items of this one woman. Even if parts were not happy, they were engaged in a playful way."[43] The mood is strikingly different in the second section, however, as it is written with the foreknowledge of Stein's infamous racist epithet in "Food." In a section titled "Dinner," Stein writes: "It was a time when in the acres in late there was a wheel a shot a burst of land and needless are niggers."[44] Knowing that this passage was a part of the work before her in writing the second section of the Stein "handholding," Morris notes that "this section was much more difficult to write. It continued to pull at me, pull parts of me away from other parts. Her racist epithet is also jarring and pulled me away. I was disappointed in her. (My muse was right to be pissed off at the outset. She knew what was coming . . .) I had more to say."[45] In addition to talking back to this aspect of Stein's text, Morris also addresses the question of space as raised by the final section of *Tender Buttons*, "Rooms." As Morris notes, "one can't talk about *Tender Buttons* and not talk about place. The objects are placed, the foodstuffs are placed, in the rooms, everything is in place. The room is a place where things are placed."[46] These changes in mood and topic across the three sections of the Stein "handholding" are powerfully registered in Morris's alterations to her performing voice.

As a trained performer and experienced singer, Morris has developed a voice that is extremely agile, perhaps most markedly so in her ability to finely modulate her articulation of words or even phonemes. As such, the tone she senses in Stein is manifest in the vocalizations of her text written in response to Stein. Thus, for instance, the measured clarity of "Objectively" is in stark contrast to the beginning of "Consumption," which is strikingly sharper, harsher, and faster, with her voice often sounding angry, registering that "pissed off" attitude she noted of her muse when working on her response to Stein's "Food" section. Within sections, too, Morris often adjusts her voice, sometimes shifting into patterns of Black English or into her New Yorker, Brooklynite accent. Part of the point, of course, is that the signifying possibilities register with a range of aspects of her identity: she is an African American New Yorker from what she frequently describes as a rough neighborhood, her musical imagination is shaped by a wide range of influences, she is a "blerd" with a PhD from NYU, and so on. In addition to these purposeful shifts in pronunciation, Morris also continues her performance practice of often pausing to capture mistakes or misreads and integrate them into the recorded performance. The combined effect of Morris's performance practice is to foreground her voice as an artistic medium of its own, a voice that, while not sung, is similarly an aesthetic, expressive, performative thing.

Morris's engagement with *Tender Buttons* is in line with an important tradition of feminist and African American investigations of this text. Although not framed in terms of the gender dynamics of *Tender Buttons*, Marjorie Perloff's classic reading of the text as an example of modernist "indeterminacy" lays the conceptual groundwork for many subsequent critics and artists. As Perloff argues in *The Poetics of Indeterminacy*, "to read a text like *Tender Buttons* can be exasperating or boring if one expects to find actual descriptions of the objects denoted in the titles—a carafe, a cloak, eyeglasses, a cutlet, cranberries. But Stein's are by no means Imagist poems. Rather, the author offers us certain threads that take us into her verbal labyrinth, threads that never quite lead us out on the other side but that recreate what [John] Ashbery calls 'a way of happening.' Gertrude Stein's linguistic codes are tentative and buried; her Surrealist transformations of events must be taken literally as vivid if indefinable presences."[47] Building upon Perloff's identification of "certain threads" that suggest passages into Stein's "verbal labyrinths," Juliana Spahr has focused on the polyglot nature of Stein's writing, grounded as it is, she argues, in Stein's personal experience with language acquisition. As Spahr argues, "Stein abandons her authorship and turns it over to readers, who, when reading the work actively, participate by constructing their own readings. Her work does not deny authority but instead advocates its dispersal (decentralization), a dispersal that relies on the multiple possibilities and interpretations distributed among different readers, and one that has, literally, to do with not knowing the language."[48] Elizabeth Frost similarly focuses on how Stein's experimental practice invites readerly participation, and she raises the frame of Stein's importance to subsequent writers. As Frost argues, "Stein disassembles existing systems of language, yet she does so without sacrificing the pleasures and functionality of the symbolic. Stein's practice offers not only a joyful multiplicity but also a model for the feminist avant-garde text. Embracing language as thing and symbol at the same time, with a sense of both the signifying function of language and the disruptive release of prelinguistic pleasure, *Tender Buttons* shows us a poetics of fetishism, an eroticized, liberated objective world."[49] For each of these critics, Stein's work develops a model of experimental literary practice in which the thingness of language coexists with its symbolic function, a model that is taken up and advanced by later writers, including Morris.

One of the key touchstones both for Stein and for Morris's "handholding" with her is the practice of stream of consciousness. Morris describes her process in *Handholding* as stream of consciousness, and, as Priscilla Wald has demonstrated, Stein's work with the psychologist William James while she was a student at Johns Hopkins University deeply shaped her sense of the relationship between language and identity formation, particularly as found in *The Making of Americans*. Wald writes, "By demonstrating the influence of character on how and what a person sees, Stein prepares for a conclusion that forms the basis of *The Making of Americans*: cultural factors determine perceptions that shape the experience of the self."[50] In her psychology experiments, in which subjects were asked to read aloud while being read to, Stein identifies an avenue to the truth of a person's identity as being grounded not in the content of what they say but in their manner of speaking. For Stein, reading in this distracted state allowed a hidden self to emerge from the subjects. Wald describes, "The reading [Stein] advocates will lead . . . to an experience of estrangement, but that estrangement in turn will take the reader past the words of a text to an awareness of a story beneath the story. Like Freud, Stein advocates a different kind of attending, a suspended listening in which 'the bottom nature of people' emerges in the rhythms and cadences, the repetitions and patterns, rather than the content of their conversations. 'Bottom nature' is an untold and conventionally untellable story."[51] For Stein, uncovering this "bottom nature" of people and releasing it by putting the literally unthinkable in contact with the imagination was the fulfillment of art's greatest potential. Morris's surrealistic turn to Stein, her automatic writing in response to Stein's text similarly depends upon and animates not only her own "bottom nature" but that embedded within both Stein's texts and her own reader. As such, Morris's sonic, textual engagements with Stein perform a sounding of her work that resonates with the points of contact and tension between Stein, Morris, and the reader.

While Morris's engagement with Stein is a continuation of the critical and creative conversation about Stein and feminist avant-gardism, it is even more powerfully driven by Morris's concern with race. As such, the Stein "handholding" is inevitably in conversation with Harryette Mullen's books *Trimmings* (1991) and *S*PeRM**K*T* (1992), which are responses to the "Objects" and "Food" sections of *Tender Buttons*, respectively. Like Morris's "handholding," Mullen's earlier works are inspired by and explore the prospect of extending Stein's innovative practices. As Mullen describes in the preface to her 2006 book, *RECYCLOPEDIA*, "*Trimmings* and *S*PeRM**K*T* correspond to the 'Objects' and 'Food' sections of Stein's *Tender Buttons*. I share her love of puns, her interest in the stuff of life, and her synthesis of innovative poetics with cultural critique. However, my own prose poems depart from her cryptic code to recycle and reconfigure language from a public sphere that includes mass media and political discourse as well as literature and folklore. Although I've been inspired by Stein, I'm also interested in the collision of contemporary poetry with the language of advertising and marketing, the class of fine art aesthetics with mass consumption and globalization, and the interaction of literacy and identity."[52] Taking her inspiration from Stein's avant-garde practice, Mullen produces texts that similarly torque the referentiality of language, although what Perloff would call their "referential traces" are more evident in her texts because of her interest in the language of the postmodern mediascape. As such, as Robin Tremblay-McGaw has argued, Mullen's texts carry a didactic and performative responsibility that prefigures Morris's practice. Mullen "invites the reader to participate in this educative process of conservation and production, enclosure and fugitive run. Her work articulates a need for a more equitable ecology, one of acknowledgment and memory, conservation and reuse; she and we as readers are caught up in her recyclopedia, an ongoing poetics of reuse that benefits from the multiple perspectives of a heterogeneous community."[53]

Much like Mullen, Morris's work is also engaged with the challenges of literary heritage. While there are certainly a wide range of African American poets, artists, and musicians whose work is influential for both Mullen and Morris, they both also confront the fact that many of their most important predecessors are white avant-gardists, including writers such as Stein, who had deeply troubling understandings of race. As Deborah Mix has argued with respect to Mullen, the challenge for critics of her work, then, is to understand her engagement with Stein as a critical and creative response to both the possibilities and the limitations embedded within the historical avant-garde. As she argues, while the basic facts of chronology place Mullen "in a kind of subordinate position" with respect to Stein, "Mullen's work cannot be read as simply an experiment in remaking Stein's work, 'passing' as a kind of deracinated experimental writer. . . . The significance of recognizing what lies behind the mask [of minstrelsy] cannot obscure the ugliness of the mask itself. It is imperative that we not visit upon Mullen's work the fate so often conferred on black creativity: we cannot erase Mullen's work or misread it as derivative of Stein's."[54] Similarly, with Morris, the critical

challenge is to understand that even though in coming after Stein, Morris is inev-
itably in the position of responding to her work, she is no less derivative of Stein
than Eurydice is of Orpheus. The legacy of avant-garde literary history is as the
telling of Orpheus's story: it is the context in which Morris and Eurydice speak,
and it sets the stage on which they and other members of the ensemble impro-
vise their back talk.

As Morris takes in hand the question of her position with respect to her pre-
decessors, she is also deftly attuned to how her performance affects her reader/
listener. In her instructions on how to approach the Stein "handholding," Morris
advises "reading *Tender Buttons* and listening and/or reading both texts simulta-
neously as legal proofreaders do."[55] Morris calls for a divided attention on the
part of her reader in a way that powerfully recalls the structure of the automatic
writing experiments that Wald identifies as an important precursor to the writ-
ing of *The Making of Americans*. Asking for her audience to read and/or listen si-
multaneously, Morris puts her reader/listener in a nearly irresolvable state of
confusion, particularly since her texts in the Stein "handholding" do not closely
correlate or correspond with the Stein material. The reader/listener is im-
mersed in two separate but related linguistic experiences. What's more, Morris
calls for the reader to adjudicate the relationship between these texts, much like
a "legal proofreader": looking for consistency across two texts and reconciling
differences between them, with the consequences of legality attached. Morris's
reference to this professionalized reading also resonates with a similar gesture
in Moten's discussion in *Stolen Life*. In a characteristic rhetorical move, Moten
invokes Herman Melville's "Bartleby the Scrivener" with just the slightest men-
tion: "To refuse what has been refused is a combination of disavowing, of not
wanting, of withholding consent to be a subject and also of refusing the work, of
withholding consent to do the work, that is supposed to bring the would-be sub-
ject online. It is to prefer not to."[56] Moten invokes Bartleby, here, as a figure for
black subjectivity. Moten argues that a disavowal of the demands of normative
subjectivity is the condition in which Black people find themselves. That is, be-
cause Blackness is seen as antithetical to the subject, their path to subjectivity is
a Bartleby-esque casting of desire into the negative, "to prefer not to" participate
in the drama of normative subject formation, to which they have always already
been denied access. By explicitly positioning her reader in a similar condition,
Morris also asks that the reader "prefer not to," that they resist the work of the
teleology of subject formation and reside, instead, in the irresolvable improvisa-
tory space between the two texts.[57]

Immersed in this interstitial space, the reader/listener of the Stein "hand-
holding" is forced to parse the relationships between Stein's text, Morris's print
text, and her oral performance of that text. While Morris focused on the appeal
of the conditional "if," in her preface to the piece, its opening lines focus most

prominently on the "I" of "If I Re-viewed Her, Objectively." In the first short paragraph, Morris riffs on the prospect of reviewing Stein. The piece begins, "If I reviewed her, if I reviewed her. I reviewed her."[58] The Steinian repetition is partly a grammar game that encourages us to think about how the same four words can mean differently when used in different constructions, a sense that is reinforced in Morris's recorded performance of the lines. Just as each of the phrases means slightly differently because of its shifting grammatical context, they also mean differently because of the ways in which she voices them. Her voicing is consistent with the sense of these constructions. The first iteration sounds as a declarative statement; the second sounds as a qualification of that statement; and the third sounds as an assertive resolution to this miniature drama, shifting from the conditional to the past tense with the elimination of "if." Morris then muses on the object of her review, Stein's collection: "Her her button. Her boutonnier. Herbal. Her boobeleh. Her boo. Her Too. Her tuchas. Her view. Her book."[59] Morris's word associations emphasize Stein's domestic world, with the matrimonial "boutonnier" invoking her relationship with her partner, Alice B. Toklas, followed by terms of endearment, including the Yiddish "boobeleh," and a capitalization of "Too," emphasizing the importance of the relationship between Stein and Toklas.

As the piece continues, Morris turns her attention from Stein's text to her own predicament of not merely writing a review of *Tender Buttons* but of re-viewing it, seeing it anew. The first brief passage hinges upon distinctions between past and present: "If I viewed her like I used to. I talked to. I teased her. I teach her. I reach. I rearview."[60] Having previously engaged with the text as, among other things, a teacher, the poem announces the challenge to Morris of moving beyond merely seeing Stein in a retrospective way, which would reduce her to a static object of study and pedagogy. Since Morris feels Stein as an ongoing, lively presence in her poetics imagination, her challenge is to somehow move beyond the retroactive seeing characterized by these lines and, instead, both reach back into the literary past and project forward a relationship with Stein.

Morris's improvisation in response to Stein intertwines elements of her own biography and associations with *Tender Buttons* in ways that are consistent with her emphasis on specificity in her introduction to the piece. Thus, for instance, an early paragraph reads: "'If 'if' was a fifth . . .' Black lettres. Black pov. 'res' onate, Ur-words. Sona. Salon. If I revved up, I could view her through another glass. Toklas, another poem. W(h)atts a smatter-shattering. That piece of bright bling attached to a cloth with sharp edges, rounded o'er time, a button. A carafe."[61] The link of associations in this passage moves from the 2010 cut "If if was a Fifth," by the hip-hop duo Webbie & Lil Phat, to the French spelling "lettres," invoking Stein's longtime residence in France, a reference reinforced by "salon," to Morris's own "black p(oint) o(f) v(iew)," and on to her "handholding" with Kurt

Schwitters, published in the same volume.[62] Recalling Wald's description of the mode of reading advocated for by Stein in *The Making of Americans*, Morris's work, here, eschews ahistorical generalities or abstractions in favor of concrete particulars of her historical moment and her lived life. That is to say, this is an improvisation that tells us about both the improviser and the text upon which she plays: the cultural references, diction, and even the speech cues (such as the abbreviation "o'er"), signal the importance of race in Stein's text. Her improvisation, too, recalls critical assessments of Stein that focus on the relationship between the domesticity of *Tender Buttons* and Stein's own domestic world with Alice B. Toklas. Morris concludes this passage, the third paragraph of the piece, by coming to rest on the first of Stein's "objects," "a carafe." As such, the early work of "If I Re-viewed Her: Objectively" troubles the very proposition of objectivity, much as Stein's playful text both invokes and withdraws the object-hood of the items she enumerates. In doing so, Morris creates the space for her improvisational ensemble, both continuing and altering the trajectory of Stein's original work.

As Morris continues in "If I Re-viewed Her," the "carafe" of Stein's piece is transformed into the stereotypical melting pot of the United States. The paragraph reads: "What patterns clash? What suits ya? What cymbals? What Sabians, Armenians, Jews, Germans, Blacks, Latins, Americans? Euro-detritus? Explights' us? I wonder."[63] Morris's vocalization of this passage emphasizes the near-rhyme between the "carafe" that concludes the preceding paragraph and the "clash" of the first sentence here. As she moves from the opening question, which seems at first to indicate visual patterns, she shifts to auditory associations. The "patterns" that may clash in the first question are turned into an auditory phenomenon by her invocation of "Sabians," one of the largest contemporary manufacturers of cymbals. And yet, these cymbals are also "symbols," especially when the passage is heard rather than read. As such, the religious associations of Sabians, a Gnostic religious group described in the Quran as a people of the book, along with Christians and Jews, are brought to the fore, and the sounds of the clashing/crashing Sabian cymbals is transformed into the uncomfortable clashing of religious, ethnic, and racial communities within the United States. With the suggestive neologism "explights,'" Morris suggests the commonality of the "expatriate" immigrant, their "plight," and their susceptibility to "exploitation"; and as to the hope that these commonalities might lead to a sort of mutual understanding or compassion, she and we are left to wonder.

As this passage suggests, the openness of Morris's engagement with Stein is reinforced by her vocal performance of the "handholding." Among her performance strategies is the repetition of words, sentences, or even sections of the printed text, often with alterations to the pronunciation of words that draw out their latent signifying possibilities. One of the most poignant examples of this practice is found in "Consumption," her engagement with Stein's section "Food."

Throughout the Stein "handholding," Morris foregrounds issues of race, perhaps nowhere more so than in "Consumption," as is to be expected given Stein's use of a racist epithet.[64] While Morris most explicitly responds to the racism in the passage containing Stein's racist language, the entirety of "Consumption" resonates with how race conditions Morris's engagement with Stein, including her treatment of Stein's section "Roast Beef." The first item in Stein's "Food," "Roast Beef" is also the longest, and it is replete with images in which race and color play powerful roles. For instance, Stein poses the question, "why is there a shadow in a kitchen," to which she replies, "there is a shadow in a kitchen because every little thing is bigger";[65] yet, the image also can't help but bring to mind race and kitchen staffing.[66] As Morris responds, "When we brought food, despite our emaciation, despite emancipation, we brought foods. Black foods. They had foods, Red foods. I wonder. I wonder. I wonder what they'd do without our colored foods: watermelon and tomatoes. Red fruits full of water, spilling. / break over."[67] Morris's improvisation in this passage plays with the issue of color as being at once a mere descriptor of a food ("red") and also a descriptor laden with cultural significance ("Black foods" that are red). In her reading of it, her enunciation of the last two words reinforces the connection to the job of a domestic servant, as she quickly notes "break over" in a tone that sounds like a worker's matter-of-fact recognition that it's time to go back to the kitchen.

As Morris continues in her response to "Roast Beef," her vocal performance includes one of the most compelling instances of her recursive use of her own text. To capture the development of Morris's chain of associations, I will quote her piece at length:

> Two points joined, make a joint. Make a shadow. It looks 3 dimensional, loosely. A loosening of a dimension, of light. What is a sculpture? How do we know it when we see it? Because of the light play. Because of the way light shines off of it. Because of the shadow. Because of the shadow this loose playing of the "facts" of the matter. The way it shatters a prism. That's what it's loosely based on. So when they call us shadows, when they call us spooks, spooky what they're saying is, what they're saying is that we are what is reflected off them. They are *repleat* [sic] with reflections. Everyone else is just a mirror, a mole. A collection of melanin, potential melanoma. Sambo is samo. They say simian = Indian = Black. In the dark who knows, among the grey, who cares? In a colonial, a colony is a colony. And so the same stories are. It's what is killing but can be unseen. On the underside of people. Which we are not. In which way we are not.[68]

Morris begins this passage by making the word association between "roast beef" to a "joint" of beef, proposes a conceptual link between our visual perception of that object and the dimensionality of sculpture, and continues through a series of further associations that center on the role of Blackness as that which absorbs and includes all colors, itself thus becoming the colorless outline that, unseeable itself, defines what we do see. Morris's improvisatory engagement with Stein, here, carries an analytical edge again consistent with Moten's framing of blackness. As he argues, "Blackness names what is not (there); even its thingliness is nil in relation to something, some point, some pure, abstract and ascendant singularity the possibility of whose presence we continue to assume against the grain of natural social history's constantly lived assertion of and insistence upon its absence."[69] Both Morris and Moten track the relationship between the color black and the experiences of African Americans, probing the ways in which casual conceptualizations of one influence the social and philosophical implications of the other. In this sense, Morris's improvisation on Stein's "roast beef" starts with a seemingly simple substitution of one term for another, "joint" for "roast beef"; but, in doing so, she triggers a rich chain of associative thinking that draws together the aesthetic, the social, and the political.

As poignant as Morris's textual response to Stein is in this passage, she complicates it in verbal performance. On the recording, Morris returns to this passage three times, each time reading more of the passage. The first time, she only reads through "two points joined, make a joint. Make a shadow," after which she pauses for several seconds, giving the effect of a title to what is to follow. However, instead of continuing, she returns to this opening line and then continues almost halfway through the paragraph, stopping after the line, "They say simian = Indian = Black." This second time through, her reading is measured and even, without any striking pronunciation or altering of words. The third time through, however, Morris adopts a very different reading voice at several points in the passage. For instance, when she reads, "Because of the shadow this loose playing of the 'facts' of the matter," she sets off "facts" with a marked pause both before and after the word and changes the register of her voice in a way that signals the quotation marks around the word in the printed text. As she continues, she also adopts a higher, more conversational voice as she comes to the words "spooks" and "spooky," in mild disbelief at the casual use of racist language. Her tone abruptly shifts as the sentence continues. She reads the next clause, "what they're saying is" in the same conversational tone but then adopts an aggressive, lower tone with an urban inflection as she continues, "what they're saying is," giving the impression that the second iteration of the phrase is a rejoinder to the first. As Morris shifts her voice throughout her returns to this passage, she proliferates its possibilities of meaning and registers a range of speaking identities. This Eurydicean drive for a performative justice comes to a point in her final pronunciation of the passage's closing lines. Her vocal performance is a stern rejection of racialized invocations of Blackness as that against which society is defined: "which we are not. In which way we are not."

The multiplicity and performativity of the self that Morris demonstrates in "Consumption" continues as she engages with questions of space in the final section of the Stein "handholding," "Enclosed." Responding to "Rooms," Morris similarly improvises on the suggestiveness of Stein's text and explores questions and implications of containment, compartmentalization, and spatiality. Thus, she begins the piece by contemplating, "what's a room? What's an heirloom? // To contain something. To define its size by the perimeter, parameter. A room is an act. A performer, a room does. A room is vowels, consonants, a constriction, a making, a formulation."[70] As the "handholding" continues, Morris muses that "we have all been led to believe that rooms are actual rooms when rooms are not. There are no rooms. Cells are the way we define matter but we also say cells are porous. Rooms are cells, yes even in prison."[71] In this passage, as Morris asserts the fictitiousness of rooms by way of the analogy to "cell" as a biological term, she inevitably confronts the usage "prison cell" and acknowledges, "prison is real, don't get me wrong but what are cells? Cells are structures of selfishness. Cells are shellfish. They mean different things depending on the person but they are not things in and of themselves."[72] On the audio recording, Morris's intonation and cadence shift over the course of this passage, with the reference to the reality of prison cells sounding more markedly urban, while she adopts a questioning, speculative tone as she notes that the meaning of the terms depends upon the context and the speaker. That is to say, much as Wald identified in Stein's psychological experiments, Morris performs the contingency and contextuality of identity and meaning throughout this "handholding."

Throughout the Stein "handholdings," Morris develops a poetics of performativity in which Eurydice's "wide justice" is brought to bear upon literary history. In reaching to Stein, Morris's handholding grapples with the legacy of race in the modernist avant-garde; it is a legacy that can be neither ignored nor simply corrected. Rather, critics and creative workers must explore how questions of race underscore even those aspects of modernism that we might wish to retain. As Morris demonstrates in the Stein "handholding," one way to go about this process is to sound the contours of the racial imaginary in precursor texts and take those limitations as the very material for a way forward. In doing so, Morris develops an improvisatory ensemble with the past, one that does not resolve the problems of the past but, rather, in integrating them and making them part of the material of her engagement with that past, performs a way forward. This, ultimately, is the mode of justice embedded in her Eurydicean poetics.

While Morris's Stein "handholding" gains a great deal of its energy through the interplay between Stein's printed text, Morris's written response to that text, and her verbalization of that response, her engagement with Kurt Schwitters is purely sonic and, thus, performative in a very different way. Titled "Resonatæ," this "handholding" is an audio recording of her verbal response to Kurt Schwitters's landmark sound poem "Ursonata," which he first performed in 1922 and continued to revise for the following decade. Tracking the relationship between Schwitters's piece and Morris's response is made tremendously easier by the publication on PennSound of a two-track recording that aligns Morris's performance with that of Schwitters's son, Ernst.[73] In her preface to "Resonatæ," Morris describes her improvisation in response to Schwitters's piece: "What I did with 'Resonatæ' (the title being somewhat impossible to pronounce and has a strong phonemic character to it) is to let Schwitters's poem affect me. I wanted to respond to his call in real time. Unlike the handholding with Stein, I didn't allow myself time to veer, I had to stick with Schwitters' time frame. It is also improvised and unedited unlike the other pieces."[74] Whereas her "handholding" with Stein is the product of a multivalent associative logic in which sound leads sense, with a resulting richness of denotative and connotative meaning, the process of "Resonatæ" follows Schwitters's lead in using the granular elements of language as we speak as its material. In "Ursonata," Schwitters treats phonemes with a musical logic, grouping, decoupling, and regrouping them in ways that mirror the problem-solving nature of sonata composition. Responding to Schwitters in real time, Morris similarly foregrounds the materiality and performativity of utterance in such a way as to approach her discussion of onomatopoeia in *Who Do with Words*. As she argues, "Saying the unsayable, the failure of utterance is the beginning of what would become language and poetics of/as language. Onomatopoeia is the approximation of the performance, the performativity of sound through the human mechanism of the voice. It is as close as we can get to that sound [the unsayable]. The phonemic source of utterance is in onomatopoeia. The clusters and revisions of these approximations beginning with the attempts to articulate the unutterable are the atoms of poetry that make the molecules of language."[75] Although neither Schwitters's original piece nor Morris's response to it are onomatopoetic, their shared attention to the performativity of sound by the human voice enacts the drama she describes here. Returning to the logic of lyric as the attempt to put into language that which cannot be said, Morris emphasizes the fact that doing so demonstrates the fundamental human will to expressivity.

One of the most striking features of Morris's improvisation in response to Schwitters is her performing voice. While Schwitters invokes the song form of the sonata in the title of his piece and uses that form as a model for the permutations through which he puts the phonemes, the physical performance of Ernst's voice is, with a few notable exceptions, reserved and almost uniformly even in tone, timbre, and volume. The effect is a kind of clinical precision in his voice, which allows the play of patterns within the phonemes to come to the fore. By contrast, Morris frequently exploits a broad range of expressive potential in her voice, including in ways that carry clear cultural and historical connotations. Thus, for instance, she will sometimes harmonize with Schwitters and then slowly bend the note out of tune; at other times, she scats, trills, and uses vibrato in her voice. In contrast to the tonal constancy of Schwitters, she also climbs scales and shifts her voice across registers; and, finally, she intones rhythms and syncopation of those rhythms on top of Schwitters's piece. In moments such as these, Morris's voice is a singing voice with a specific and readily identifiable background in jazz, much as is heard in "Mahalia Theramin."

The songlike elements of Morris's voice signal the ways her response to Schwitters is specific to her experience and her grounding in Black music. This emphasis on specificity, much as she discussed in her introduction to the Stein "handholding," also shapes her use of echo words in her response to Schwitters. Since Schwitters takes the base building blocks of western European languages as the material for "Ursonata," any listener who speaks one of these languages will inevitably hear echo words, phonemic combinations that the listener hears as words even though they are not words in Schwitters's text or performance. In this way, a listener's response to "Ursonata" is strikingly situational, cultural, and personal, demonstrating their defining linguistic self, much as Stein identified in the automatic writing of the participants in her psychology experiments. Similarly, Morris's response is animated by those concerns most central to her relationship with language. Perhaps not surprisingly, then, among the most prominent ghost words in her reply are "free," "forgive," "obey," and "ok"; at one point about midway through the performance, she also seems to ask, in French, "tu es ou" (where are you)? The effect of Morris's Eurydicean improvisation in response to Schwitters is partly the performance of an identity that is both grounded in Morris's biography before the Schwitters acoustic performance and contingent upon that performance for its own identity formation. That is to say, the identity that we hear performed in Morris's vocal performance is a self that is brought into being by her engagement with the preceding text. What's more, even though Schwitters's text avoids the racially charged history of Stein's, the ghost words in Morris's performance and her interweaving of recognizable voices reminds us that the self that is brought forth through the act of engaging with her predecessor is not devoid of prior identity or history but, rather, an articulation of that history with the text at hand.

As is true throughout *Handholding*, one of the most crucial elements of Morris's cultural background in her response to Schwitters is the tradition of call-and-response in African American art and culture. As she notes in her preface to the piece, she "wanted to respond to his call in real time." This framing of the "handholding" with Schwitters brings his "Ursonata" from its grounding in the white European avant-garde into the context of jazz and gospel. In the performance, this turns Schwitters's sonata into a musical conversation, as Morris's response to him reframes and rephrases his utterances, responds to them in ways that imply conversation or dialogue, and occasionally anticipates him. Residing on the cusp of language, Morris's performance transforms Schwitters's text into an opportunity for social formation; taking the most elemental, purely sonic elements of language and deploying them as a dialogue, "Resonatæ" performs the conditions of possibility on which a self is grounded, in the sounding and resounding between two speaking voices.

Ultimately, *Handholding: 5 Kinds* is a companion text to *Who Do with Words*. Together, they demonstrate a Eurydicean poetics of performativity that foregoes the conventions of the Orphic disposition and, instead, claims the power of the ensemble and the practice of improvisation as central to both poetic practice and the formation of the self in and through that practice. As Eurydice talks back, her voice reaches across the threshold of social exile and death, gathers the voices of her predecessors, and sings a self onto the stage.

5

"Orphic Bend"

Music and Meaning in the Work of Nathaniel Mackey

Music encourages us to see that the symbolic is the realm of the
orphic, that the symbolic realm is the realm of the orphan.
—Nathaniel Mackey, "Sound and Sentiment, Sound and Symbol"

He showed up at the door carrying a record and said there was
something he wanted me to hear, something on the record which if
I hadn't already heard I had to hear and which if I had I had to hear
again, something I needed to listen to, something I would learn from.
—Nathaniel Mackey, *Bass Cathedral*

At its core, the myth of Orpheus makes a claim that is both simple and
astonishing: poetry and music are significantly the same. As a simple claim, this
is a descriptive one that traditionally leads to the truism that musicality is central
to poetic language and, from there, to interpretive practices such as scansion as a
way to engage with the music of poetry, whether in closed verse forms or in the
broader, looser patterning of open-form or field poetics. This aspect of poetry
is, in fact, so elemental that poets with very different, even competing aesthetic
commitments, affiliations, and projects seem to agree on it. The astonishing
claim, however, is a Gnostic[1] and speculative one that proposes that music and
the musicality of poetic language embody and enact a distinct order of knowl-
edge, uniting the temporal arts in a zone of meaning that is based upon trauma
and loss, that is mysteriously powerful, and that is only ever imperfectly accessi-
ble to nonpoetic language. This claim proposes that music and poetry can move

the immovable and bring back the dead, and that, in and through their tempo-
rality, they enact a mode of knowing that values heterogeneity, contingency, and
propositional richness over uniformity, stability, and certainty.

Working along this radical Orphic bend, Nathaniel Mackey has forged a sin-
gular career that limns the relationship between poetry and music, establishing
an oeuvre of critical and creative work that variously explores and enacts the
epistemological claims of Orphic poetics. For Mackey, even as the relation be-
tween poetry and music is forever an asymptotic one, the act of teasing at their
limits opens us to orders of knowledge not otherwise available.[2] In criticism, in
creative prose, and in poetry, Mackey explores how attentiveness to resonances
of sound, image, and idea can propose experiences of meaning and orders of
meaningfulness beyond the constraints of the given regime of knowledge. This
musical disposition toward language and thinking animates Mackey's two collec-
tions of critical essays, *Discrepant Engagement* (1993; 2000) and *Paracritical Hinge*
(2005; 2018), and lies at the heart of his creative work, the epistolary fiction
titled *From a Broken Bottle Traces of Perfume Still Emanate*, and the serial poems "mu"
and "Song of the Andoumboulou." The contours of this epistemological field can
be seen by juxtaposing a passage from *Atet A. D.*, the third volume of the fiction,[3]
with one from his oft-cited essay, "Sound and Sentiment, Sound and Symbol."
At the conclusion of the last letter in *Atet A. D.*, the narrator, N., and his band-
mates decide to name their long-awaited debut album, *Orphic Bend* (the event
that gives the present study its title). Pleased with the band's ability to antici-
pate the return of their drummer, Drennette, N. tells his correspondent, Angel
of Dust, that "no-look obliquity blessed [them] with a prescient, post-optic apti-
tude in Orphic disguise, Orphic bind borne as roundabout reprieve."[4] Mackey's
allusion to Orpheus at this key point in the history of both the band (they've cut
their first record) and the novel (the last lines of its twenty-nine letters) signals
the importance of the mythical poet and resonates with a similar invocation in
"Sound and Sentiment, Sound and Symbol." The essay considers the role of music
and song in instances ranging from the mythology of Papua New Guinea to the
poetry and prose of Jean Toomer, William Carlos Williams, and Wilson Harris.
In the course of his argument, Mackey deploys sound as a means to suggest like-
ness between otherwise unlike concepts, the phoneme shared by "Orphic" and
"orphan." Mackey suggests, "Music encourages us to see that the symbolic is the
Orphic, that the symbolic realm is the realm of the orphan. . . . Poetic language
is language owning up to being an orphan, to its tenuous kinship with the things
it ostensibly refers to."[5] These two passages, one from Mackey's fiction and the
other from his criticism, are paradigmatic of his Orphic bend, a poetics in which
content and practice are constantly intertwined as he both describes and demon-
strates musicality as a variety of knowledge in which meaning, like the self, is

unrooted, such that it becomes a dynamic process of endlessly searching for resonance, even though any such echo will inevitably be fleeting or flawed.

Mackey's invocations of Orpheus embody his interest in the spiritual and mystical traditions related to poetic practice. The most conspicuous of these in his oeuvre is, to be sure, the mythology of the Dogon, from which he derives the title of one of his two serial poems, "Song of the Andoumboulou," as well as the subtitle for his serial fiction-within-a-fiction, *The Creaking of the Word*. His spiritual breadth is just as impressive as his musical one, as he draws upon Haitian vodou, Cuban Santería, the Christian Gnostics, Rastafarianism, and Sufi Islam.[6] As Norman Finkelstein has demonstrated in his crucial reading of Mackey's work, Mackey's disposition as a poet can thus be usefully framed as a variety of shamanism. Attending to the roles of violence, sexuality, and trauma, movement through time and space, and the relationship between esotericism and initiation in Mackey's work, Finkelstein addresses its utopian underpinnings, arguing, "The disturbing but revealing paradox of Mackey's poetry, a paradox of which he is quite aware, is that this utopian vision, this vision of cosmic order and wholeness, can be realized only through an arduous process of initiation, a seemingly interminable crossing, a mystical, erotic longing for gnosis that cannot be fulfilled."[7] In the Orphic epistemology articulated in and through Mackey's poetics, music and musicality are the primary mechanisms in this endless search, by turns locating and constructing orders of expression and truth that are in sharp contrast to the given elements of daily life. In his poem "Alphabet of Ahtt," Mackey speaks to this "anagrammatic / ythm, anagrammatic myth," where the absent but implied "rh" sounds the relation between rhythm and myth, those procedures that keep the time of human lives.[8]

Mackey's investment in musically inflected modes of knowledge and expression powerfully shapes his notion of the poet's voice. For Mackey, the precondition of the Orphic voice of the poet is irrecoverable loss, and the aesthetics of that voice are therefore identifiable in the ways in which it manifests absence, imperfection, and lack. In his essay "Cante Moro," for instance, Mackey notes the significance of Federico García Lorca's inclusion in Donald Allen's 1960 *New American Poetry* anthology, providing, as Mackey notes, the lone non-Anglophone voice to that seminal anthology and introducing the notion of *duende*. As Mackey argues, "Lorca does not so much define *duende* as grope after it, wrestle with it, evoke it through strain, insist on struggle."[9] This sense of a critical term as tantalizingly sought after rather than argumentatively presented resonates with Mackey's own frequent etymological play and his broader interest in the heterodox, the ambiguous, and the profoundly imprecise. That is, *duende* is poignant not simply for what it means but also for the Orphic manner in which it means. Slippery and suggestive, *duende* indicates at its most literal level the gravelly graininess in a flamenco singer's voice, that capacity for expression that resides at "the far side of skill."[10] More broadly, this quality of the voice serves as a mode of critical remove, a kind of acoustic leverage against the homogenized vocalizations of speech, as well as those of harmony and melody in song, and thus the epistemological orders they actuate. *Duende* is also inherently tied to the ache of irrecoverably lost origins, and Mackey frequently invokes the term as a way of charting the generally under-recognized but influential role of African-rooted music and culture in the West. As his discussion in the essay "Limbo, Dislocation, Phantom Limb" makes clear, *duende* is a critical term that insists on the Orphic work of the poet as both aesthetic and historical: "The *duende* is both an omen and a goad. It insists upon the insufficiency, the essential silence of mere technical eloquence, stretching the singer's voice to the breaking point. This pursuit of a meta-voice, of an acknowledged and thus more authentic 'silence' beyond where conventional elocution leaves off, this impoverishment or tearing of the voice, corresponds to what Harris, quoting the Barbadian poet Edward Kamau Brathwaite, refers to as 'tunelessness,' the essential condition of the Caribbean's 'orchestra of deprivation.'"[11] It is in this sense of the singer's voice stretching to include that which exceeds mere technical skill, striving toward a metaphysical yet emotively powerful beyond, that we can locate Mackey's Orphic aesthetic and an epistemology deeply tied to the cultural circumstances of diasporic peoples. That is, the extramusical scratch of *duende* gives voice to the "tunelessness" and is the Orphic voice as instrument in excess of the "orchestra of deprivation" described by Brathwaite, making that deprivation knowable. As such, *duende* functions as an Orphic reminder that "you have to root your voice in fabulous origins, find your voice in the dark amongst the dead."[12]

For Mackey, *duende* makes the musically or poetically performed Orphic voice powerful by multiplying it. Noting *duende*'s denotative significance, Mackey quickly shifts into looser, more connotatively rich implications of the term: "The word *duende* means spirit, a kind of gremlin, a gremlinlike, troubling spirit. One of the things that marks the arrival of *duende* in flamenco singing is a sound of trouble in the voice. The voice becomes troubled. Its eloquence becomes eloquence of another order, a broken, problematic, self-problematizing eloquence."[13] Functioning as an other-voiced eloquence, *duende* comes about by the singer's and the poet's "reaching for another voice."[14] As Mackey describes, this reaching amounts to "a taking over of one's voice by another voice. . . . This wooing of another voice, an alternate voice, that is so important to *duende* has as one of its aspects or analogs in poetry that state of entering the language in such a way that one is into an area of implication, resonance, and connotation that is manifold, many-meaninged, polysemous. One has worked beyond oneself. It is as if the language itself takes over. . . . Bound reference, univocal meaning, is no solution to the riddle of language."[15] Recalling the vatic tradition of the poet as seer,

Mackey here also thereby articulates the multiplicity of registers in which poetry operates. While his discussion is richly suggestive of his poetic lineage, music is also a powerful frame of reference. That is, Mackey here connects "aspects or analogs in poetry" to something that is at its core a musical phenomenon, a quality associated with the voice as sung. As such, his consistent exploration of *duende* should always remind us not simply of poetry's troubled voice but, more specifically, of how it is musicality that thus problematizes and characterizes the Orphic voice; it is in its excesses of sound, structure, and organization, its associative and indexical logic, that the Orphic poem differentiates itself from the wash of everyday language and thus makes other orders of knowledge available.

The emphasis on trouble, incompletion, and loss in this discussion of *duende* as a defining feature of the Orphic voice intimately links lyric expression with the experience of desire. As Mackey cites Lorca, "*duende* often has to do with a kind of longing that has no remedy, not simply loss, unrequited love and so forth, but what Lorca calls 'a longing without object.'"[16] The emotional logic in Lorca's phrase here not only echoes Orpheus's loss of Eurydice but also almost exactly replicates the mechanism of desire as articulated in psychoanalytic theory. As Bruce Fink so clearly paraphrases the effects of the split between the appetite for satisfaction and the demand for love, "desire, strictly speaking, has no object";[17] it is the relentless, definitionally insatiable condition of wanting. In this configuration, any object of desire is only a stand-in, a substitute for some primordially lost object. However, the mechanism of desire at work is not one of acquisition or even recuperation but one of retroaction. Fink explains, "There never was such an object in the first place: the 'lost object' never *was*; it is only constituted as lost after the fact, in that the subject is unable to find it anywhere other than in fantasy or dream life."[18] The economy of desire here recalls the casting of the Orpheus myth by Maurice Blanchot and Gerald Bruns, as discussed with respect to Robert Creeley's poetry in chapter 2 of this study: it is Eurydice's absence, per se, which gives rise to Orpheus's voice even as that voice both names her absence and instantiates substitute objects of desire in her stead. Mackey's Orphic disposition often thematizes just such a sense of a fictional primordial loss and proposes music and the musicality of poetic language as mechanisms not so much for retrieving what may have been lost as for making seem both real and knowable a lost object or time that may never have actually been.

As this discussion suggests, one of the key features of the epistemological circumstance of Mackey's Orphic bend is its sense of temporality. As Devin Johnston has argued with respect to Mackey's chapbook *Septet for the End of Time* (1983), Mackey often references music as offering an alternative to the regimented, normalizing pulse of clock-time imposed by the industrial revolution. Thus, Johnston argues, "through music, Mackey's writing often suggests, one recaptures the true heterogeneity of time in a most palpable form."[19] In an interview with Paul Naylor, Mackey seems to partly confirm this recuperative capacity of music that Johnston identifies in his work. Responding to Naylor's question about "the correspondences and dissonances" that Mackey finds "in representing the kinds of temporality that distinguish music and writing," Mackey alludes to Charles Olson's discussion of alchemy in "Against Wisdom as Such." Mackey remarks upon Olson's idea "that we invoke other times when we master the flow of time, that we take time and heat it, bend it to serve ourselves and to serve form, that a song is heat and so on. . . . We persist in believing in the promise of consummation or disclosure proffered by time on a smaller scale, persist in believing time will tell."[20] In this discussion, Mackey identifies more in the way of "correspondences" than he does of "dissonances," as both poetry and music are described as heating time, accelerating it, and making it malleable. What's more, as this fire "takes time where it was already headed, only faster," poetry and music achieve their identities as structural allegories for human desire, human lives, and history.[21]

What's striking in Mackey's invocation of alchemy, however, is the amount and sort of labor implied. The poet's work in these lines is certainly not that of channeling a lost time but that of constituting time anew; this is now the poet as *poietes*, not as *vates*. In Mackey's Orphic poetics, poetry and music operate on the same aesthetic plane; music is no more proximate to a lost time than is poetry. What's more, the entire body of Mackey's poetry, criticism, and fiction suggests that the notion of an "originary experience" is perhaps the foundational irresolvable haunting. As such, the time we hear in music and the musicality of poetry is not so much a recuperated time as it is a time retroactively constituted in the interaction between the poem and the reader—that alchemical relation. That is, there is no time brought back in the song or the poem; it cannot be recuperated any more than Eurydice can be reclaimed. There is only time created, time made knowable. What makes it seem like recuperated time is the nostalgic quality of desire, the fact that having heard the song or read the poem, we look back and remark its temporal disjuncture from the telos of our everyday lives.

The primacy of musicality in this lyric machinery of desire comes to the fore in "Sound and Sentiment, Sound and Symbol." In the essay, Mackey synthesizes the musical-anthropology of Steven Feld's *Sound and Sentiment* and the metaphysics of music found in Victor Zuckerkandl's *Sound and Symbol* to analyze the way Black music has served as a mode of cultural critique for American literature. Invoking Legba as well as Orpheus as primary figures of the poet, Mackey identifies literary manifestations of the central absence that Zuckerkandl identifies in music. Thus, in this discussion of literary texts, Mackey cites Zuckerkandl's argument that musical tone is meaningful not because it is resplendent or lush but, rather, because of its inherent lack of completion and the resulting "dynamic quality . . . its will to completion."[22] Mackey sees music as signifying for these poets not simply because it symbolizes cultural legacies of inequality but also because it activates that insufficiency as the core of lyric. Reaching beyond itself, lyric does so by way of its acoustic materiality. As Mackey argues, this sense of will in the lyric constitutes its relation to temporality. Listening to the absence activated in the dynamics of the tone, the listener is drawn into a temporal relation with the music: "To hear a tone as dynamic quality, as a direction, a pointing, means hearing at the same time beyond it, beyond it in the direction of its will, and going toward the expected next tone."[23] For Mackey, the traditions of Black music similarly signify the ways they articulate "limbo, liminality, lift," those absences of place and phantoms of limb that are the Orphic poet's sense of "animate incompleteness" in the world.[24]

Although Mackey cites only Zuckerkandl's discussion of tone, Zuckerkandl similarly reconfigures our common understanding of directionality in musical rhythm. Zuckerkandl argues that music is the temporal art not in the pedestrian sense that it takes place in time but in the concrete sense that it takes time as its material and makes it meaningful. As such, music means not by way of the demarcating beats of rhythm but in the desire-laden moments between those beats. Susan Stewart picks up on Zuckerkandl's reading of musical temporality in her "Letter on Sound" and notes that "rhythm is described after the fact as the particular structure or order of tones in time," arguing that the distinction between rhythm and meter "helps us see the tension between the organic and experiential unfolding of rhythm and the 'time' of meter—that fixed and ideal measurement by which we say we are keeping time."[25] For Stewart, "the sound of the poem emerges from this dynamic tension between the unfolding temporality of the utterance and the recursive temporality of the fixed aspects of the form."[26] As readers, we are drawn into the poem by its oscillation between the energies of speaker and those of form. Thus, Stewart argues, the poem takes on the nature of a perpetual promise, always made and made again and always deferred. As Mackey's work reminds us, it is in this deferral, coupled with the retroactive quality of desire, that we can locate the work of lyric.

Emerging from this overview of Mackey's critical relationship to music is the sense of an Orphic poetics deeply grounded in music as a variety of knowledge. That is to say, the Orphic bend of Mackey's poetics is an epistemological condition in which poetry and music provide poets, musicians, and initiates to their works access to modes of knowledge that are both privileged and contingent. This poetics is further developed in his analyses of Amiri Baraka, particularly in the essay "The Changing Same: Black Music in the Poetry of Amiri Baraka." In this essay, Mackey explores how Baraka's relationship to music is a matter of both concrete reference and abstract metaphysics. As he observes, "Black music is the meeting ground for two contending forces in Baraka's thought. An acknowledgment, on the one hand, of the importance to life and art of the contingent manifests itself in the sociological orientation of *Blues People* and much of *Black Music*. On the other hand, something like a mystic's respect for the other-worldly aspirations the music so often expresses both informs many of the essays in *Black Music* and accounts for a drive toward indeterminacy in Baraka's poems."[27] Suggestively linking the "poetics of outside" with the practice of jazz musicians who play "outside," Mackey argues that Baraka's poems similarly "seek to circumvent stasis, to be true to the mobility of thought, perception, and the play of unconscious forces. Their 'tendency toward obliquity' is a gesture that pushes the limits of what we take to be meaningful."[28] Mackey identifies in Baraka a feature of music that is also central to his own project. If anything, his own writing, in both poetry and prose, even further stretches the limits of what is available to be known, what counts as knowledge, and what role music as a feature of poetic language might play in this expansion of the epistemological field.

Mackey explores the Orphic zone of meaning occupied by music and musically inflected language in his serial fiction *From a Broken Bottle Traces of Perfume Still Emanate*. The fiction comprises letters from N. to a character named Angel of Dust. Beginning in Los Angeles during the late 1970s and extending into the 1980s,[29] the letters recount N.'s life as a member of a band whose music derives from the traditions of post-bop experimental jazz and African-rooted world music. Mackey's choice of the epistolary form stands out as the first mechanism by which he foregrounds the relationship between text and music. Not only is the form insistently textual[30] even as it is devoted largely to the depiction of musical performances, but its presentation of one side of a verbal exchange foregrounds the role that communication plays in the construction and dissemination of knowledge. That is, the epistolary structure pricks our ears to the fact of discourse as a communal act between individuals. That we get only one side of the conversation emphasizes the struggle to complete the meaning of the conversation. The effect is that reading the letters sent from N. to Angel of Dust is not unlike listening to one track of a recording session; we are drawn in to interpolate the voice of the missing instrument(s) and must surmise what could have been played/said by the other performer(s).

As this use of the epistolary form suggests, the books literalize and radicalize one of the most powerful truisms of jazz and improvised music: that the musical performance is a conversation. Throughout *Broken Bottle*, Mackey exploits this prospect as N., without framing commentary, describes the performances of the band in the terms of a conversation. To be clear, the performances are not described as analogous to conversation; N. does not present the exchanges between the musicians as being *like* discourse. The exchanges are, without fail, presented *as* discourse, with instruments taking on the capacity of linguistic expression. That is to say, one of the methods by which Mackey explores an Orphic order of knowledge is to ascribe to music the discursive powers of language. For instance, early in *Bedouin Hornbook*, the first novel in the series, N. recounts to Angel of Dust the experience and aftereffects of a particularly powerful performance during which N. introduced a new piece to his bandmates. The relationship between this performance and language is evident in the way N. both introduces and concludes his description of the piece. As he tells Angel of Dust, "I gave a debut performance of 'Opposable Thumb at the Water's Edge' for the other members of the band, not saying much about the piece other than announcing its title";[31] after their performance, Aunt Nancy, the violinist, exclaimed, "Whew! What was *that* all about?" By verbalizing of the question, she alleviates confusion in the room: "We all laughed, a little bit more at ease, but the specter of our collective swoon had introduced an at once congratulatory and cautionary air which was so intense it precluded any talk of what had taken place. I find it hard to put words around it even now—but equally hard to rid my mind of what occurred."[32] This reluctance to describe the emotionally powerful musical event indicates the limited ability words have to describe the experience of music. What's more, the nature of Aunt Nancy's response is specifically to question the *meaning* of that experience, the epistemological status of the experience they all just shared. That is to say, while the experience defies both conventional description and explanation in language, it was held in common by the members of the band in the experience of their musical performance. Thus, the limitations to which Mackey alludes in this passage are not so much limitations of language per se but, rather, the limitations of language in the mode of conventional narrative description. There was, N. tells us, a particularly meaningful experience in the performance, and Mackey, through N.'s pen, has rendered it in the language of the novel. The nature of the language, though, is not that of description. It is, instead, that of enaction; that is to say, N.'s recounting of the band's performance, here and elsewhere, is not descriptive but demonstrative of a mode of knowledge grounded in music.

Indeed, throughout the fiction, whenever N. recounts a musical performance, he does so by way of a content-rich instrumental conversation between the members of the band. It is as if Orpheus's legendary ability to move inanimate objects with his words set to music is reframed such that music acquires the capacity for intellectual debate. In the example of "Opposable Thumb at Water's Edge," for instance, five pages of text portray the musical performance in language that ascribes remarkable discursive abilities to the music. The central event of this episode is an "extraordinary experience," which we eventually learn is the band members having been knocked unconscious during (and perhaps by) their performance of N.'s new piece. After N. provides an introductory model of the composition, the others take it up, and the conversation begins. The first two musician-conversants are the reed players, Penguin and Lambert. Both male, their contributions to the conversation are concerned with origin stories. Penguin enacts an Egyptology lecture, as "by way of a flurry of 16th and 32nd notes, [he] made it known that the Papyrus of Nesi-Amsu, repeated a legend reputed to be 'older than the pyramids,' reports that Temu 'had union with himself' and thus produced the gods Shu and Tufnut ('air' and 'moisture')."[33] In response, Lambert, the tenor player, shifts to a humorous subject rhyme from his childhood in Texas, a practical joke in which "one of [his friends] would say in a matter-of-fact way, 'I've heard that jackin' off leaves whelps on your hand.' Anyone caught looking at the palm of his hand, as everyone who didn't know the trick immediately did . . . was loudly laughed at."[34] Lambert's joke is both sophomoric and apt. Its mechanism relies upon a policing of insiders and outsiders, such that being the butt of the joke is a kind of initiation into the knowledge of this story about masturbation in a way that parallels the structure of becoming an initiate into the kind of knowledge that lies at the heart of Penguin's lecture. As such, the performance between the two male reed players becomes a learned musical inside joke.

The joke is also phallocentric, though, and it earns the opprobrium of the band's female members, Aunt Nancy and Djamilaa. As Aunt Nancy's violin and Djamilaa's harmonium chide the male performers for "having lapsed into locker-room humor," Mackey's assigning of instruments to the characters engages with traditional associations of wind and stringed instruments with notions of expressivity and reason, respectively.[35] It is the male performers who play the wind instruments, their expressive saxophones, while Aunt Nancy's stringed violin is closest to Apollo's lyre, and Djamilaa's harmonium seems an embodiment of both wind and strings in its combination of bellows and keys. What's more, whereas the male performers had each taken their individual turn in performance, the women respond if not in unison, then in profound, mutually reinforcing harmony, with "Aunt Nancy's bowing, embroidering the hem of Djamilaa's threadbare drone."[36] As the women play, they turn the conversation back to more serious matters, focusing on the image of the hand at the core of both Penguin's and Lambert's stories, first through Aunt Nancy's use of tremolo and then through "Djamilaa's harmonium [which] spoke to us of an amulet known in Brazil as a *figa*, a fist carved of wood, metal, or stone," the figure that would ultimately strike the bandmates unconscious.[37] N. explains the event: "What occurred, I think, is that a symbiosis from which every horizon had fallen away sought to extend itself. Falling short of this, the horns undertook a role of deceptive bottom or unsecured buttress, an illusory 'base' in relation to which Aunt Nancy's persistence (the undulant tenacity of her central assertion) inhabited the hollow she'd eternally resent, an 'opportune' exposure to every grasp ever sown by grief—an elusive anchor, if you will. This left us free, I believe, to forage in whatever ways we might, which is what we did."[38] Through this episode, Mackey casts music as a mode of knowledge capable of encompassing in instrumental performance topics typically seen as the purview of discursive language. He also explicitly frames it in ways consistent with the expansiveness he saw in Baraka's turn to music: as both individual and communal, as both rational and emotive, as both abstract and material, as both hypotactic and paratactic. The result is an Orphic event of such power that it can literally knock us senseless and, thereby, open us to new orders of sense.

Passages such as these present a discursive capacity in music that is further thematized throughout subsequent installments of the fiction as Mackey introduces the device of cartoon-like balloons that periodically emerge from the band members' instruments. On its face, the prospect of speech-bearing balloons emerging from the bells of musical instruments can sound simply silly; and, in fact, there is a charming self-awareness to these episodes, which read partly like farcical extensions of the logic that underwrites Mackey's exploration of the discursive possibilities of music. The episodes are also seriously meaningful, though, as even in their self-awareness, they again demonstrate the ways Mackey probes the limits of what is knowable. The balloons first emerge during a performance during which N. and Djamilaa reach a unique level of intimacy and mutual understanding, as "she fingered the valves and blew into the horn, matching what I played note for note, flurry for flurry—miming what I played, to be more exact, for though she fingered and blew not a sound came out."[39] As this half-mimed duet continues, a balloon emerges from the bell of her horn, bearing the following words: "Bottle cap suzerainty lifted its magic wand, a conductor's baton it tapped me on the shoulders with as if dubbing me a knight. A page, a prompter-in-waiting, arose with each tap, one on my left shoulder, one on my right."[40] The order of events in this passage bears consideration: Djamilaa stops playing her trumpet, and N. begins playing his; as he plays, she begins to sing a wordless and soothing song; her physical actions then replicate his on the same instrument; the result of this duet is a speech balloon emerging from her horn that recalls a previous encounter between the two of them. In fact, this performance suggests a particular kind of intimacy between Djamilaa and N., a merging of her self and his that brings forth a textual voice that is grounded upon yet distinct from theirs. That is, in this performance, N. and Djamilaa achieve an "other-voicedness" and are, in turn, be-knighted by it.

As we might expect, this event and subsequent ones when the balloons reappear become the focus of a great deal of speculation, with N. proposing several readings of their significance and meaning. In the next letter to Angel of Dust, for instance, each of the first three paragraphs propose a possibility: "the balloons are words taken out of our mouths"; "the balloons are love's exponential debris"; "the balloons are thrown-away baggage, oddly sonic survival, sound and sight rolled into one."[41] As the story continues, we learn that there had been a photographer at one of the performances at which the balloons appeared. But, as N. tells Angel of Dust, "he says he took photos of them or at least thought he had until he developed the film. He says he could find no trace of them on either the negatives or the prints. Everything else—the band, the instruments, the stage and so forth—came out fine, but the balloons were nowhere to be seen. He doesn't question that they were actually there that night—he saw them, no doubt about that, he insists—but this new revelation . . . has added to the controversy surrounding the balloons."[42] The logic of this passage is not unlike the description of "the extraordinary event" earlier in the book. The photographer does not dispute the reality of the balloons or even their significance; but, just as the performance eluded narrative description, so, too, do the balloons evade the visual capture, and stasis, of photography. As such, the fact that the balloons prove unrecordable to the visual apparatus of the photograph reinforces the primacy of music and aurality in Orphic poetics that recurs throughout *Broken Bottle*, as when N. describes the band's proficiency on their debut album as demonstrating their having acquired a "post-optic aptitude."

If Mackey's Orphic project in his fiction is partly to develop the proximity of music and language by textualizing music, he also works to musicalize text.[43] This is perhaps best demonstrated by an etymological debate that runs through several letters in *Atet A. D.*, as the band searches for a new name.[44] As the discussions of music in his critical prose make clear, Mackey probes and proposes music as an epistemological mode that proffers as meaningful those associations that we conventionally deem accidental, incidental, or transitory, such as in the leap from "Orphic" to "orphan" in "Sound and Sentiment, Sound and Symbol." A similar playfulness of meaning is demonstrated in the fiction in the context of an etymological debate. Early in *Atet A. D.*, N. describes the genesis of a new work as being grounded in linguistics and etymology, his interest piqued by a confluence of events. After visiting an old schoolmate who was researching "stories the Juaneño Indians told regarding a black rock known as Tosaut," N. was also reading C. L. R. James's classic text, *The Black Jacobins*, which he reminds us is "on Toussaint L'Ouverture and the Haitian Revolution."[45] A third stream of influence comes from Lydia Parrish's *Slave Songs of the Georgia Sea Islands*, which suggests an Arabic provenance for the word "shout." As N. summarizes his train of thought, "One black rock had led me to another. The Juanaño had led me to Mecca by way of Haiti and the Georgia coast."[46] Sounding for all the world like his author, N. proclaims, "'Tosaut L'Ouverture,' I now knew, was a piece I *had* to write. It would demand all the syncretic salt I could muster. Exactly the sort of work I like most."[47] Drawing together three unrelated streams of influence based upon the meaningfulness of an incidental rhyme, N. turns to compose a work that, even in its title, links the history of the black diaspora and musical form—"Toussaint L'Ouverture" and "Tosaut L'Ouverture."

As compelling as this playful yet serious punning is, N. is confronted with a problem when he describes the genesis of the piece to his bandmates. He begins his letter of August 4, 1982, "Djamilaa says Turner was wrong. . . . When I got to Turner's idea that the use of the word 'shout' to refer to circumambular movement derives from the Arabic word *saut*, Djamilaa said no, that couldn't be, that *saut* isn't pronounced like 'shout' and that it doesn't mean to walk around the Ka'aba, it means voice, sound."[48] Notably, Djamilaa's correction points to a mistake in which N. had confounded ritual movement with "voice, sound." Undaunted, N. reframes his thinking about the piece and urges his bandmates, "Rather than take shout literally . . . treat it like a mistake that's bound to be made and that one both wants and doesn't want to make. Remember that the 'shout'—the *saut*—in [the song] has to do with a detour thru relativizing salt. Remember that salt gives its grain of truth a renunciative spin. Remember that shout posed as movement rather than sound is a way of dancing by another name."[49] This reconfiguration of "shout" and "*saut*" doesn't hold either, though, as only two days later N. writes back to Angel of Dust to inform him, "Turner was right. . . . The problem turns out to be that the word rendered *Saut* in Parrish's book doesn't appear that way in his. Parrish uses an *S* instead of the phonetic symbol ʃ that Turner uses. . . . There is in fact an Arabic *saut*, which, as Djamilaa pointed out, means voice, sound, but we now see that's not the word Turner meant."[50] N. goes on to integrate his further correction and clarification into the background for his piece and concludes this etymological drama by noting, "It was incorrect but not a mistake, a mistake but a fertile mistake, to read the '-saut' in 'Tosaut' as though it was Turner's ʃ*aut*. 'The accuracy of the bow is judged by its curve,' Ibn 'Arabī says."[51] This exploratory etymological debate is paradigmatic of Mackey's Orphic epistemology. He, through the figure of N., treats the meaning of the word much as post-bop jazz musicians often treat squeaks, squawks, and other nontonal sounds as valid components of a performance, to be integrated and elaborated upon just like any other expressive possibility of their instrument. As N. and Djamilaa pursue the possibilities embedded within false starts and miscues, their give-and-take is that of two language researchers for whom meaning extends in unpredictable directions. The assertion behind these passages is that it is the process of this search for meaning, the curve of this particular Orphic bend, not the final resolution, that is the most meaningful, truest outcome of the endeavor.

Mackey's fiction thus proposes the Orphic as a mode in which knowledge is only ever temporarily or partially known and therefore endlessly pursued. In this framework, the task of Orpheus is to deploy music and musicality as exploratory instruments for sounding and resounding possible, propositional, contingent truths. This sense that music and musicality are the conditions in which the

Orphic poet operates also profoundly shapes both the content and practice of Mackey's poetry. Mackey's poetic work has focused on two ongoing serial poems, "Song of the Andoumboulou," taking the name from Dogon cosmology, and, "mu," deriving more directly from avant-garde jazz aesthetics. Mackey developed the two serial poems separately for the better part of three decades, before interweaving them in his collection *Splay Anthem* (2002), a process that continues in subsequent collections, *Nod House* (2007) and *Blue Fasa* (2015). Mackey's serial poetics is a major extension of this line of experimentation in American poetry, particularly in the example of Robert Duncan's serial poem "Passages." Joseph Conte's summation of the relationship between individual poems and the work as a whole in Duncan's poem can just as accurately be applied to Mackey: "Each poem is complete in itself, an event enacted; but in the context of the series, each is but a part of the ongoing process, and thus incomplete."[52] In Mackey, this sense of a form that is both internally coherent and open-ended is also deeply influenced by post-bop jazz, with the first three "mu" poems collected in the 1986 volume *Eroding Witness*, dedicated to the musician Don Cherry. The issue of titles, numbers, sequences, and sets becomes increasingly complex as the series goes on, and the series immediately demonstrates a sense of fluidity to its boundaries similar to that of the letters in *Broken Bottle*. The first two sections of the "mu" series are included in a poem titled "Poem for Don Cherry," and the third section is titled "Outer Egypt," an allusion to Pharoah Sanders' album *Tauhid*. The title of the series derives from Cherry's 1969 sessions in which he explored the musical influences he had absorbed during his years traveling in India, Turkey, South Africa, and Morocco. As Ekkehard Jost demonstrates, Cherry's playing during these sessions is most remarkable for his revolutionary relationship to theme and improvisation. While in the free jazz of musicians such as Ornette Coleman (whose group Cherry had left not long before the "mu" sessions) and Cecil Taylor, there is still generally an identifiable distinction between the thematic material and the improvisation upon that material, Cherry pushes these conventions to such an extent that in his music, "both 'theme' and 'improvisation' require a new definition."[53] Jost enumerates seven largely culturally situated themes that preoccupy Cherry and compellingly describes two modes of Cherry's improvisation, one as a matter of selecting from this catalog of ready-made themes and the other as a development of patterns within themselves while the model is still "in the works," the resulting patterns sharing broad contours with the original but being far from identical with it.[54] These practices of improvisation make Cherry's music both a kind of bedouin patchwork of styles, instrumentation, modes, and references and lend it a sense of organicism or evolution. Nevertheless, as Jost argues, "there is a factor that links all of Cherry's music together: it is not a stylistic concept of homogeneity of means, but a consistent inconsistency. The essence of Cherry's music lies in its contradictions. It is at once humorous and melancholy, full of pathos and full of fun, energy-laden and meditative, songlike and chaotic, complicated and simple, with complexity often giving an impression of simplicity, too."[55]

Jost's analysis of Cherry also provides a framework for understanding Mackey's poetics of the unexpected and the heterodox. The link between Cherry's practice and Mackey's response illustrates the ongoing role that music plays in Mackey's conception of the Orphic voice of the poet. One of the most compelling features of Cherry's "mu" recordings is the way in which he uses his voice as an instrument, particularly on the track "Teo-teo can," a title that is also a line in Mackey's "Poem for Don Cherry," coming midway through "'mu' second part." The phrase, both as a title on Cherry's recordings and as a line in Mackey's work, is onomatopoeic, replicating the glottal, birdlike sounds that characterize Cherry's voice on the recording: "Teo-teo can" as instance and indicator of *duende* in the Orphic voice, then. Against the background of Blackwell's jangling bells, Cherry begins by singing a brief phrase that vibrates between notes and phonemes. He repeats the phrase in a higher register, then alternates between these two registers, introducing a multiplicity of voices within his own. He then turns to his flute, playing a theme reminiscent of but not identical to these sung phrases, to recall Jost. Alternating between the wind instruments of voice and flute, Cherry turns the phrase increasingly melodic, though straining, in the flute. This approach to melody culminates in a shift in instrumentation and idiom for the last two minutes of the piece. As Cherry moves to the piano and Blackwell from the bells to tom-toms, the piece takes on a completely different tonal and rhythmic identity, with the phrase seemingly bifurcated into the regularized beats of Blackwell's tom-toms and the surprisingly melodic lines of Cherry's piano. In fact, the entire piece can be heard as a bit of historical musicology in miniature, actuating in its movements the incorporation of the extra-semantic voice into instrumental music.

Mackey's thematic concerns in "Poem for Don Cherry" revolve around just this link between the voice of the Orphic poet and song. Italicized on its own line and coming after the lines "Noises / came out of it / Calls," the immediate function of "teo-teo-can" in the poem is again onomatopoeic, much as it was in Cherry, voicing the "noises" suggested in the first section of the poem. The remainder of the poem takes the phrase as its subject, thematizing and tracking the changes in Cherry's performance. Thus, as Cherry's playing moves from his voice to the flute and then finally the trumpet, the poem reads,

> The coarse
> cloth of Moorish cante
>
> The fluted
> bone of our lady's

> blown upon thigh
>
> The
>
> enormous bell of a
>   trumpet's inturned
>   eye, an endangered
>
>   isle, some
>
>   insistent Mu,
>   become the
>   root of whatever
>
>   song[56]

The poem moves through reflections on Cherry's playing, highlighting the connection between Cherry's performance and the mythological concerns common for Mackey. Recalling the cultural responsibility of the Orphic poet, Mackey's poem thus makes the traditions from which Cherry draws more evident and also emphasizes the thematic concern of genesis. Thus, Cherry's vocalizing is given a location, a reference by becoming "the coarse cloth of Moorish cante," his flute playing actuates the myth of the flute as the thigh bone of the goddess, and the tiny bell of his pocket trumpet expands inward to give voice to the lost island of Mu. As an act of language, it seems fitting that the poem should end these musings by bringing to mind the etymological significance of "mu" as a root, the base of muse and music (and myth, *muthos*), the very possibility of lyric. The Orphic logic in the chain of associations across the poem is consistent with the open, exploratory nature we identified in Mackey's fiction; here, unifying each of these images, of course, is their productive hollowness, each instrument signifying not because of its precision but because of its particular "grain."

While the thematic elements of this passage clearly invoke Cherry's playing, Mackey's prosody does not seek to mimic the music—something that would, no doubt, be possible given this passage's proximity to speech. Instead, the velocity and syncopation that characterize these lines stem from attention to the properties of the language: the New American use of the line; the use of enjambment and caesura; and, above all, the sound pattern achieved through the intricate permutations of "ü" and "ī" vowels. Thus, though the poem is inspired by Cherry's work, here, at the very point where its thematic relationship to Cherry's music is most evident, the poem insists on its own capacities as an aesthetic use of the sonic properties of language.

Mackey's contemplation on Cherry's performance also recalls his frequent concern with the recollective preoccupations and retroactive action so important to Orphic poetics. Remembering and making present that which is irretrievably lost, making real a time of unity that never existed, Mackey's engagement with Cherry's music both enacts the voice of the muses of the "endangered isle" and, in so doing, delineates a temporal seam. "'mu' first part" begins with temporal concerns, the first two lines reading, "The day before the / year begins woke to a."[57] While this may simply indicate anticipation of the New Year, it more radically suggests a moment on the cusp of history, the time before the birth of song that we get at the end of the poem. The earthly sensuality of this impending change, this coming time, is suggested by the "scratchy legs" of the speaker's partner and even more strongly when, in the next two stanzas, one of the characters (it's not clear which) is described as "Lotusheaded" in the position of prayer next to the bed and then as waiting on the top of a hill either "for rain or [to] watch the sun set." "'mu' first part" ends by describing this vantage point as an opportunity not only to survey the possible coming rain or the sunset but also to enjoy temporal reflection. In lines that are markedly shorter and more widely spread across the page than earlier in the poem, the senses of spatial and temporal movement are brought even more closely together, as the characters pause to "see / how far the way we'd / come / went back." Apparently looking back on the progress up the mountain, perhaps the days' journey from that morning's bedside, the characters also partake in a reflection upon their source. Standing at the brink of the new year, at the moment before time begins again, and looking back through their history, the characters reside at the moment of song's birth.

"'mu' second part," enacts this birth of song as an Orphic rite or ritual. The first half of the poem, before the line "*teo-teo-can*," draws together images of physicality and rebirth and articulates them in prosody that itself emphasizes temporality. Thus, the image of the female character's hairy legs returns from the first section, alongside that of "her bald feet" and "all the mud, alive / with eggs, with likenesses." As the fertile riverbed teams with the near-identical, still embryonic life, it gives rise to the "Noises" that culminate in "*teo-teo-can*." While these images in themselves would suggest a scene of birth and spirituality, Mackey's prosody here emphasizes the process of desire that resonates through them. Here, as is so often the case in Mackey's poetry, the overriding effect of the prosody is that of deferral. Phrases, clauses, and images shift before giving a sense of having been completed. As the poem resists the closure offered by conventional grammar or syntax, it insists on the time of its own telling and thus constitutes itself as an act of desire. Thus, here, the birth of song, the very emergence of that "*teo-teo-can*" that preoccupies the second half of the poem, comes perhaps from the mouth of the female character and perhaps from the riverbank, giving voice to the yet-to-be-born hatchlings:

> The mouth she wore
> who although she wore jeans I
> could see she grew hair
> on her legs,

her bald feet

And at the Stream,
who in her cupped hands held it,
thirst,

or some worship,
whichever

All the mud, alive
with eggs, with likenesses

Noises

came out of it

Calls[58]

The series of deferrals that arrive throughout this section are first announced by the distinction between her and "the mouth she wore," her assuming a voice as a mask, an association that immediately aligns this mask with her apparel. In the second strophe, the process of expectation and deferral continues as we first see her at the stream and then find that she holds not water in her cupped hands but "thirst." As her hands hold the absence of that which they desire, they are also in the position of prayer, "some worship." The next strophe again defers a sense of completion, this time by introducing the images of the eggs in the riverbank so that by the time we reach the last three lines, it is ultimately impossible to say from where the "Noises" that are transformed into "Calls" originate. The poem does not describe the moment of the birth of song so much as it puts us in the position of the Orphic speaker as they experience the act of desiring this birth. In terms of thematic development, this passage coheres not by way of linearity or parataxis but, rather, by a persistent turning inward on itself. The imagery travels from the mouth she wore to the jeans she wore to the hairy legs beneath those jeans to the bald feet at the base of the jeans, then to the hands holding not water but thirst. As the cupped hands resonate for their hollowness, the imagery draws together religion and reproduction, traveling from the human through the reptilian to the prehistoric, alluvial riverbank, back in time such that the Orphic "Calls," the birth of music, now sound like primordial birdsong.

In "Poem for Don Cherry," the thematic concern with voice, temporality, and the origins of song exists alongside and is troubled by a quintessentially Orphic prosody engaged with revisitation and return. The thematic recursiveness in the poem, the way that its thematic turning inward upon itself demands a kind of recursive, even retroactive reading, is amplified in the acoustic relationships between "'mu' first part," "'mu' second part," and "teo-teo-can." The opening lines of "'mu' first part" are defined by enjambed iambs:

> The day before the
>   year begins woke to a[59]

The line break interrupts the iambic pattern that is maintained in the sentence until "woke," so that the second line scans as two amphimacers, or cretics.[60] The hitch in the pace introduced by this line break is picked up in the second line with the two consecutive accented syllables in "begins woke." This contact point between the two amphimacers thus becomes a kind of caesura, all the more rhythmically effective because of the alliterative relationship between "begins" and "before,"[61] coupled with the near vowel–rhyme between "before" and "woke." Thus emphasizing the waking of these two lines, the poem concludes with two accentually identical lines, "glimpse of her / scratchy legs."[62] As the amphimacer pattern that defines the six syllables of the second line is here spread across two lines, the opening strophe of the poem concludes with a sense of formal completion. The next strophe, consisting of only two lines, picks up on this pattern, as each line consists of six syllables, with the first line following a perfect trochaic pattern and the second two troches followed by an iamb (thus echoing the chiastic patterning we saw in the second line of the first strophe). As these sound patterns build on one another and shift, even in this short passage from the opening of an ongoing serial poem, they enact a level of acoustic signification that is equally as effective (and affective) as the thematic developments in the poem. In these first gestures, the sounds of the words themselves present an evolving pattern not of metrical fixity but of open-ended, propositional relations.

The opening lines of "'mu' second part" are acoustically related to those of the first poem in a way that recalls Jost's description of the loose and evolving relationship between thematic material in Cherry's playing. Just as Cherry's themes evolve within themselves, shifting their characteristics from iteration to iteration, so does Mackey's use of sound in the first lines of "'mu' second part" invoke the sonic imprint of the opening of "'mu' first part." As with the first part, "'mu' second part" begins with insistent iambs: "The mouth she wore."[63] However, while the line from the first poem goes on to be enjambed, the first line of the second poem breaks after the second iamb and continues, "who although she wore jeans I."[64] In this instance, the "who" serves as a kind of rhythmic excess, syncopating what would otherwise be the continued iambs of "although she wore." In fact, were it not for "who," the second line of the second poem would also have the same syllable count as that of the first poem, and its accentual pattern would recall that of the first, though not repeat it. Here, in place of the first section's cretic, we would have two iambs followed by a spondee. Interestingly enough, the inclusion of "who" makes a cretic of the would-be iamb "although." Further resonating with the first lines of part one, the second line's internal rhyme with the first line occurs at one of the terms of the consecutive accented syllables, though here at the first term, "wore," instead of at the second, as it was in the first poem. Finally, as with the first poem, the first strophe of "'mu' second part" concludes with two lines of three syllables each. Emphasizing the evolution of the acoustic relation, the first line is a cretic, again as in the first poem, while the second is its inverse, an amphibrach, "her bald feet."[65] In these two opening strophes, then, we have an acoustic relation that is defined by a sense of evolving similarity. While the opening lines of "'mu' second part" clearly are not prosodically identical with those of the first part, they do recall its pattern even as they develop a pattern of their own. To borrow a phrase from Mackey's "Alphabet of Ahtt," this is a prosodics of "palimpsestic stagger."[66] As the poem continues, as it begins again at the opening of the second part, it revisits the acoustic patterns of the first part and writes over them, neither erasing nor obliterating them but, instead, writing them anew. As such, this palimpsestic prosody itself recalls Mackey's aligning of the Orphic and the orphaned, actuating in the text's acoustic materiality that which is also a thematic preoccupation.

In this first installment of the "mu" series, then, Mackey demonstrates an Orphic poetics in which musicality takes on the nature of the palimpsest, encompassing both the thematic and acoustic registers of the concern with an impossibly lost originariness, compensated for by return and revisitation. In the installments of the "mu" series included in Mackey's next collection, *School of Udhra*, the particular musicality of the series becomes more structurally evident as he introduces two poetic devices: under-the-line poems and anagrams. That is, *School of Udhra*, which consists of installments of his "Song of the Andoumboulou" as well as the "mu" poems, contains untitled poems written beneath a long horizontal bar.[67] As Mackey tells Peter O'Leary in an interview, the under-the-line poems proliferate the possibilities of the text, as they were meant to "suggest that even within the book there is another book, there's this 'under-the-line' book. And by citing them specifically that way in the table of contents, it's like saying they are works unto themselves in some ways. I was trying to suggest the possibility of a multiple reading. . . . It was another way in which I was working to unsettle and multiply the possible relations of the parts."[68] Brent Hayes Edwards has perceptively commented on these under-the-line poems as enacting a "poetics of reprise."[69] Employing the musical idea of the reprise, the "jump from the end of a song back into its theme,"[70] Edwards argues that Mackey's under-the-line poems are best understood as "a singularity repeated, a definitive closure re-opening to close again."[71] As such, the under-the-line poems understood as reprise tear at the boundaries of the work, multiply its formal possibilities, and structure its serial continuation. That is, though the under-the-line poems may bear troubled relations to the surrounding poems, they do not "represent redundancy, but a way of taking the groove beyond itself, opening the way for other voices or other levels in the music."[72]

The reprise is a mechanism for extending the performance possibilities in jazz. While the reprise is partly stage technique, it is also the very metaphysical mechanism of the music. Thus, just as the reprise allows for the multiplication of voice, instrumentation, and performance, it opens the work to additional levels of signification. Recalling the piece, recasting its theme, the reprise is the sound of multiplicity within the voice as it reaches toward a perpetual beyond. Edwards's "poetics of reprise" captures well the idea of a structuring musicality in Mackey's work, and I would cast it further by aligning it more explicitly with the visionary free jazz of Don Cherry and Cecil Taylor, to whom the poem "Alphabet of Ahtt" is dedicated. In *Free Jazz*, Jost's treatment of Taylor's music and aesthetics usefully demarcates two veins in free jazz, both defined by their relation to the ideas of "swing and energy." Citing saxophonist Archie Shepp, Jost describes the difference between "post-Ornette players" and "energy-sound players. That is, while musicians we might group alongside Ornette Coleman 'integrated [the old swing] into a new context,' Cecil Taylor . . . does not refashion swing by placing it in a new setting, but replaces it entirely by a new quality, energy."[73] If Cherry's "mu" sessions reconfigured notions of theme and improvisation, Taylor's music, as Jost suggests, is perhaps most revolutionary in its relationship to rhythm. As Jost argues with respect to Taylor's seminal recording, *Unit Structures*, Taylor's music "balanc[es] in equal measure emotion and intellect, energy and form."[74] For example, in each piece on *Unit Structures*, "there are three contrasting blocks: Anacrusis, Plain, and Area."[75] These three sections are intended as compositional frames, each serving a particular purpose. However, as Jost argues, "the formal disposition of Anacrusis, Plain and Area does not create boundaries, but directions, not predictable structures, but progressive developments."[76] Throughout *Unit Structures*, then, as elsewhere in his music, Taylor eschews clear metrical identity, achieving its rhythmic qualities both within and across these blocks by the rise and fall of "energy," which Jost identifies as "the relative density of impulse series," the frequency, not the regularity, of accents in time.

A similar notion of temporality as achieved by way of fluctuating energies is at work in the Orphic logic of Mackey's under-the-line poems, as well as his use of the anagram "ahtt." The appeal of the musical mode identified by Jost for Mackey's Orphic disposition is clear: insofar as Orpheus embodies and enacts an epistemological mode defined by its open and exploratory nature, musical practices that build "progressive developments" centered on momentary nodes of "energy," instead of conventions of teleology, provide strategies for keeping the work both coherent and open-ended. Insofar as Mackey's use of the under-the-line-poems and the reprise both speak to a particular interest in possibility and permutation, they also function as a particularly poignant way of bringing out the acoustic qualities of the alphabetic, operating as nodes of intensity that reach across the under-the-line poems and their poetic surroundings. This anagrammatic ligature makes its most conspicuous appearance in the title of the poem for Cecil Taylor, "Alphabet of Ahtt," and it recurs throughout the four under-the-line poems that follow. Like many of the installments of the "mu" series collected in *School of Udhra*, "Alphabet of Ahtt" is not numbered as one of the series in its subtitle, though its position in the order of poems in the book indicates that it is the tenth part of the series. Much like the first and second parts of "mu," "Alphabet of Ahtt" begins with thematic information that is intricately interwoven with a conspicuous recourse to the acoustic qualities of language. The first lines of the poem not only introduce the thematic interest in anagrams but do so in a self-referentially pedagogical way. That is, as Jost says of Taylor's Anacrusis blocks, these lines "lay down a general 'programme' rather than . . . material for improvisatory elaboration."[77] In the poem, this program is presented both by way of its thematic information, and, just as powerfully, by the sound of the words. The poem begins:

> Anagrammic scramble. Scourge
>   of sound. Under its brunt
> plugged ears unload . . .
>   Tight squeeze
> toward a sweatless heaven.
>   Anagrammatic tath. Anagrammatic
>   that . . .[78]

Thematically, the anagrammatic play in these lines extends from the self-reflexive quality of the opening lines to the subsequent permutations of the anagram, including "tath," which the *OED* tells us ranges from the act of manuring a field, usually said of a cow, to an eighteenth-century Irish measure of land, to a now obscure form of the word "take." As such, the opening lines work to weave their way from a musical performance to the island imagery of the following under-the-line poems.

However suggestive the imagery of the poem's opening is, "Alphabet of Ahtt" achieves its initial poignancy predominantly by way of sound patterns. Unlike "Poem for Don Cherry," which achieved its acoustic effects primarily through attention to accentual patterns, "Alphabet of Ahtt" exploits phonemes. The first three lines of the poem present an evolving phonemic chain, with each word bearing acoustic resemblance to that which precedes and follows it, with one significant exception. The poem announces its phonemic concern in its opening word, the neologistic "anagrammic." Whereas the grammatically conventional "anagrammatic," which Mackey uses later in the poem, would have presented a metrical pattern consisting of a dactyl followed by two trochees, "anagrammic" presents two consecutive trochees, a metrical regularity that characterizes the opening word pair, "anagrammic scramble." Alongside this conspicuous metrical regularity, we also hear a progression of phonemes. The vowel rhyme between "anagrammic" and "scramble" turns to the alliteration of "scramble" and "scourge." The linkages continue in the next line with the alliteration between "scourge" and "sound," followed by sight rhymes and echoes between "sound," "under," "brunt," "plugged," and "unload." The only word that does not fall into this chain of sounds (even the preposition "of" echoes the recurring vowels), is "ears," thus leaping to the acoustic fore. The sound of these opening lines surely tells the reader to listen these poems, to "unload" our own "plugged ears."

Listening to the "mu" series, however, is not simply a matter of locating sound patterns within particular poems. It is also a matter of listening for nodes of energy across the poems, of considering the acoustic relationships in a broader, looser, more open-ended sense. For instance, in "Alphabet of Ahtt" and the four under-the-line poems that follow, all of which contain permutations of the anagram, reading becomes resounding based on the iterations of the anagram. Indicative of the retroactive nature of lyric under the aegis of Orpheus, it is in these resoundings that the anagram acquires significance. For the anagram does not begin with "Alphabet of Ahtt," though that is its most conspicuous textual instance. In fact, the anagram is first introduced in "Amma Seru's Hammer's Heated Fall," the installment of the "mu" series that immediately precedes "Alphabet of Ahtt."[79] Dedicated to the legendary Detroit jazz disc jockey, Ed Love, the poem's title itself is worth pausing over. It invokes the name of "Amma," as Christopher Funkhouser notes, "the first personalized being" in the Dogon mythology that is the preoccupation of Mackey's "Song of the Andoumboulou" series, and resonates with the phonemic play on "anagrammic" in "Alphabet of Ahtt." As such, "Amma Seru's Hammer's Heated Fall" not only cuts across Mackey's two serial poems, thus problematizing a sense of boundary between the two, but also demonstrates the significance of retroactivity. We cannot say that "Amma Seru's Hammer's Heated Fall" recalls "Alphabet of Ahtt," because it precedes it in the series. Rather, the title of the poem attains its acoustic significance in an after-the-fact fashion, just as does the anagram. In the poem for Ed Love, Mackey's speaker twice invokes Etheridge Knight's "Dark Prophecy: I Sing of Shine," a poem in which Knight recounts the triumphant legend of Shine, a Black boiler-room worker on the *Titanic* who escaped death by swimming home to Harlem. Mackey's poem explicitly references Knight's poem, with the speaker twice saying "I sing of / shine," each time intoning "taht" as an extra-semantic phrase that gives voice to "tauntsong's eternity."[80] That is, this phrase, which exists in excess of semantic demands, perpetuates the timeless tall tale of heroic Black escape and survival as contrasted with white arrogance, stupidity, and drowning. Thus, when we encounter "'Nathtess's melismatic / ttah,'"[81] in "Alphabet of Ahtt," we not only read a description of a performer's utterance (ta-dah) but also witness the anagrammatic repetition of the phrase activate a node of "energy" that gains its import through an after-the-fact acoustic chain of signification.

The anagrams in the four under-the-line poems that follow "Alphabet of Ahtt" thus powerfully recall Jost's analysis of Taylor's use of "energy." Each of these four poems contains a permutation of the anagram, and in each poem the anagram occupies a different grammatical place. Thus, for instance, in the first poem, the anagram has become "Ttha," a location to which "the tribes of Outlandish" have gathered, apparently as a means of escape.[82] Whereas the previous iteration of the anagram, "ttah," exploited the celebratory sound of consecutive plosives, here, "Ttha" seems to question the very prospect of pronunciation by how it slides off of the fricative. Serving as a miniature machine of acoustic retroaction, the opening lines of this poem read: "To've been there as they / began to gather. All the tribes / of Outlandish crowding the outskirts / of Ttah."[83] Ending on the extra-semantic anagram, we hear its sound above all else and retroactively re-mark the predominance of consonants that bear family-resemblance. At the same time, the anagram has shifted from being a non-semantic vocalization to a proper noun. As the poem continues, the preponderance of t's and th's becomes thema-tized in the connection between breathing and being. Beginning with the exhala-tion of "Ttah," the poem goes on to contemplate, "an intake / of breath by which birth might be proposed / of something said to've been known / as meaning made with a mouth filled / with air. The soul sucked in by something / said."[84] As the exhalation of the anagram is followed by inhalation, this poem enacts a bodily field of energy in which place is brought forth by the acts of breathing and of reading.

The anagram continues to go through grammatical and phonemic permu-tations throughout the three under-the-line poems that follow. In the second poem, it regains its original graphic identity and assumes a cumulative gram-matical one, as "ahtt" now indicates both voice and place. Or, more precisely, as "ahtt" demarcates both voicelessness and placelessness. As the poem concludes, "Ache of its they the inundated earth / we lament, as ours rises up, upended, / islanded, / Ahtt unsounded / sunk."[85] In the following poem, the accumulation of signification continues as the anagram becomes "ahttlessness," indicating the frustrated desire for equilibrium that the poem addresses. The poem concludes by addressing this "inverse hoist" and the inevitable inequities associated with it not simply as a matter of social justice but also as an ontological state in which voice, place, and knowledge itself can only ever be "held on to / intangibly, / known as it / splits apart."[86] The acoustic qualities of the anagram again become central in the final under-the-line poem. As the anagram returns to its noun-form, "Ahtt," its initial vowel resonates throughout the poem's seven lines in such key words as "awoke," "aroused," "arrival," and, hauntingly, the final word, "away."

Mackey uses the anagram as an Orphic tool whose nodes of aural and the-matic intensity provide shifting points of connectivity across the "mu" poems and the under-the-line poems. Thus, just as these devices provide instances of a "changing same," they also embody the sense of temporality that is at work in Mackey's Orphic poetics. At once retroactive, premonitory, and imminent, this is the temporality of musical meaning under the banner of melody, *melos*, and in the name of Orpheus. The proceduralism of Mackey's Orphic poetics employs *melos* as malleable and evolving, drawing our attention to the fleeting, shifting moments of acoustic resonance and capable of equating different amounts of time as musical phrases. Perpetually unfolding in time, like Cherry's endless melodies, Mackey's poetics of radical musicality thus consistently foregrounds the action of the poem itself. As such, the epistemology of the poem is located not in its ability to recapture that which is lost but, rather, in its articulation of the experience of desire by consistently proposing and sounding those lost possibilities of knowledge about place, about belonging, and about identity.

In 2002, Mackey published *Splay Anthem*, the book for which he would win the National Book Award and one that contains a form of confession: the serial poem, "*-mu,*" was, in fact, not so much separate from that of "Song of the Andoumboulou" but a parallel project that was by turns intertwined, richly resonant, and contrapuntal to it. In the preface, Mackey says of the two serial works: "Each is the other, each is both, announcedly so in this book by way of number, in earlier books not so announcedly so. By turns visibly and invisibly present, each is the other's twin or contagion, each entwines the other's crabbed advance. They have done so, unannouncedly, from the beginning, shadowed each other from the outset, having a number of things in common, most obviously music."[87] Mackey's sense of the poet's occupation as defined largely by recurring preoccupation recalls the importance of the turn, of returning, and of repetition to Orphic poetic practice. What's more, if Mackey's work often gives the sense that music exceeds speech as an aesthetic ideal and is thus the repository of the unsayable, one of the most powerful aspects of *Splay Anthem* is how it ruminates on music itself as circumscribed. Mackey's intertwining of the two serial works is consistent with his quest for compositional principles that will allow the work to adhere without closure and is an upping of the ante for his Orphic poetics in its acknowledgment of an underlying unity of purpose.

In the preface to *Splay Anthem*, Mackey's Orphic poetics are on full display as he also returns to "Sound and Sentiment, Sound and Symbol," revisiting the key elements of this argument (including the story of the muni bird) and commenting on the act of authorial return or preoccupation. As he observes, "one echoes oneself. . . . One finds oneself circling, the susceptibility of previous moments in the work to revisitation and variation conducing to a theme of articulation's non-ultimacy, a theme too of mortality and new life. Earlier moments can be said to do and live on as echo and rearticulation, riff and recontextualization, alteration and reception. The song of the Andoumboulou is one of burial and rebirth, *mu* momentary utterance extended into ongoing myth, an impulse toward a signature, self-elaboration, finding and losing itself."[88] The interest in contingent and continual development in this passage is both essential to Mackey's conception of music and the basis on which music and dream are so closely aligned in the Orphic poet's quest for new orders of knowledge: each "a way of enduring reality" and "a way of challenging reality . . . an ongoing process of testing or contesting reality, subjecting it to change or a demand for change."[89] For the Orphic poet, music and the musicality of poetic language function like this dream state, enduring, challenging, and contesting the reality we are given. Even so, while the epistemological bent of Mackey's interest in music has been present throughout his career, it becomes most prominent, most urgent, and most vexed in *Splay Anthem*. This shift is evident even in the preface, the first written for one of his poetry collections and one that uncharacteristically and bluntly considers its contemporaneous political climate, noting that the migration of peoples, which is a thematic touchstone in the *Andoumboulou* poems, is, in the real world, most often the result of political unrest and military conflict and bemoaning the "imperial, flailing republic of Nub the United States has become," under the presidency of George W. Bush.[90]

The senses of revisitation, return, and perpetual preoccupation that Mackey contemplates in the preface to *Splay Anthem* are indexes of his Orphic poetics. Just as Orpheus's practice depends upon the trauma of Eurydice's death and revisits it each time he sings, so, too, does the Orphic poet return, even unwittingly, to those foundational crises, registering them in endless variations on images, themes, ideas, and prosody that characterize the poetry's own unique Orphic vision. In *Splay Anthem*, this vision most powerfully manifests itself in the book's drawing together of the two ongoing serial poems. The book is full of instances of cross-pollination between the two poems: for instance, the first poem (in the section aptly titled "Braid") is titled "Andoumboulouous Brush" and subtitled "'mu' fifteenth part," and themes, images, phrases, and titles are interwoven throughout the book. What's more, three poems continue the process of "taking up and taking further" the ideas found in the essay "Sound and Sentiment, Sound and Symbol": "Sound and Semblance," "Sound and Sentience," and "Sound and Cerement." The titles of the three poems not only announce their relationships to the earlier essay but also imply a progression from emerging awareness to knowledge and on to death and rebirth. Thus, in the first of the poems, "Sound and Semblance," Mackey revisits the story of the muni bird, here framed as an acoustic coronation, as the speaker and his companions transform into "red-beaked / birds / known as muni what we were, heads crowned / in / sound only in / sound";[91] and, in the ghostly, otherworldly dreamscape of "Sound and Sentience," in which "earth [is] a / dream / of drums come / true,"[92] sound becomes a mode of inquiry and apprehension characterized by "Endless / reconnoiter, endless vex, revisitation";[93] and in "Sound and Cerement," it is "beginning to be the end it seemed . . . / Ending begun to be come to again,"[94] as the speaker finds himself "at the beginning / again, / wanting to undo and redo what was / done. I was only what was left."[95] As the poems elaborate a world founded on music, they reiterate the temporal circularity with which they began in the first "mu" poem, establishing a temporal seam that collapses beginnings and endings, lifting the poem above the current of chronology, and leaving the subject as a kind of residue amid this practice.

The developing ideas across "Sound and Semblance," "Sound and Sentience," and "Sound and Cerement" further demonstrate the notion of "ythm," the neologism first used in the poem "Alphabet of Ahtt" to link rhythm and myth. When Mackey returns to the idea of "ythm" in the preface to *Splay Anthem*, there is a slight but compelling addition to its string of attributes. What had been "anagrammatic / ythm, anagrammatic myth," is now, "clipped rhythm, anagrammatic myth."[96] This small, subtle change attenuates poetry even as it is invoked, a double motion that is found throughout *Splay Anthem* in a set of rhetorical gestures and phrasings that qualify music or set it to the side even as they turn toward it. For instance, in "Song of Andoumboulou" 42, the speaker participates in a chain of remembrances, after which "the dead and the living dead . . . bid [themselves] / goodbye," only to beg off leaving before the assertion: "better / said or sung than done it seemed [they] / reasoned, leaflike the trembling / skin [they] strode inside."[97] As the speaker and his apparitional companions move about the book in which they find themselves (or, perhaps, within the material of the cerement), action within language (saying or singing) takes precedence in a move that insists on the song as a philosophically and linguistically performative act. And yet, in the section of the same poem written beneath the horizontal line dividing the page, we read, "Sang with a catch in our throats, / cough caught in our throats . . . / Sang to / have been done with singing, / song / not enough."[98] In some ways, these lines again recall the notion of *duende*, but the qualification of music as the lines continue seems more radical, more dramatic, potentially even more traumatic, given Mackey's frequent association of song with the moment and process of creation. Singing to be done with singing, the speaker and his companions here do not so much give voice to their own struggles as seek a kind of self-annihilating end to those struggles that would be registered in the end of song, in the silence that remains after the exhaustion of the voice.

In fact, this sense of approaching the exhaustion of song is a recurrent motif in the book. Thus, in the dreamlike landscape of "Andoumboulouous Brush," we read: "Sang through / the / cracks a croaking / song / to end all song,"[99] and then, "Spoke with a muzzle on its / mouth, / called it music, / partings more than / words could number, / made myth, / 'mu's / equivalent, lisp . . . / imminent departure / made more poignant"[100] and "audible witness / all but out of ear's / reach,"[101] these last lines recalling the title of Mackey's first collection,

Eroding Witness. The case seems to become even graver in "Song of the Andoumboulou" 46, as "All songs had long been sung," the sense of exhaustion reiterated a few lines later: "All the songs / had long been sung, numb choir, / sandpaper / coating our / throats."[102] In "Song of the Andoumboulou" 48, music is ambient and unrooted: "what there / was wasn't music, but music / was there. Where it came from was nowhere, we heard it / nonetheless, not hearing / it / before put us there";[103] and again, "not moved if not by reread / meaning, moved, music now / we / saw, beside the point."[104] This curious and persistent setting aside and troubling of music in these lines and others like them are reinforced by a predominance of conditional phrases, variations on the description of the "nonsonant ring shout" in "Song of the Andoumboulou" 50: "a healing / song / we sang had there been a song we / sang."[105] This formula of naming music, song, or sound as that which would be but is not present recurs throughout the book and performs key imaginative and even epistemological work—naming and making knowable that which is not there.

These apophatic gestures radicalize Mackey's Orphic project insofar as they further project music and musicality into spheres further removed from the material world. Describing song and music as variously muzzled and exhausted and setting it aside as what the actors in the poems *would be* doing, these passages foreground the ineffability of music and ascribe an indexical function to it. In doing so, Mackey further radicalizes music's role as that phantom limb that would point to or suggest what is not present in the given world. When music itself is so often what is not there, the prospect of attaining a "musical state" becomes that much more unlikely and therefore that much more important. It is just this sensibility that underwrites the poems in which music is embraded, such as "Go Left Out of Shantiville," "mu" 22: "Music / the breath we took. . . . It was only / there we wanted to be, the everywhere we'd always wanted, ours, / albeit / only an instant, forever, never to be / heard / from again."[106] This utopian depiction of music—as the air we breathe, as the place we live, and as what we do—is made possible not in spite of but precisely because of music's ephemeral and ineffable nature. For Mackey, music and the musicality of poetic language embody an epistemological order not because they yield reliable or predictable answers but because they stubbornly persist in the optative mood. As he concludes the preface to *Splay Anthem:* "Kaluli poetics posits poetry and music as quintessentially elegiac but also restorative, not only lamenting violated connection but aiming to reestablish connection, as if the entropy that gives rise to them is never to be given the last word. As with the Dogon trumpet blast or the post-burial parade in New Orleans music, something undaunted wants to move no matter how inauspicious the prospects, advance no matter how pained or ungainly."[107] Throughout his criticism, his prose, and his poetry, Mackey, more than any other living writer, continuously makes such limping, lucid advances along the Orphic bend.

Conclusion

The poets considered in *Orphic Bend* are part of a much wider and deeper tradition of poets who turn to the myth of Orpheus and its attendant framing of the relationship between poetry and music. As we have seen, these projects situate twentieth- and twenty-first-century writers on a through line of artistic practice that extends at least from the Renaissance birth of opera up through the present day. More narrowly, these poets are major participants in the lineage of the New American Poetry, working in the tradition articulated by Ezra Pound, William Carlos Williams, and Louis Zukofsky, and the importance of music to their poetry draws our attention to the broader role of music in modern and contemporary American writing. What's more, these writers are active during a period that has seen dramatic changes in acoustic culture, including the proliferation of sonic media, technology, and environments that parallel and underwrite era-defining phenomena such as the emergence of jazz-inflected writing, sound poetry, and popular music, even as these events return us to the originary text-music problematic. In a very real way, the past century has been defined by the fact that music is simply more accessible and more pervasive than ever before, rendering the modes of musical imagination and musical meaning making as seen in Bernstein, Creeley, Taggart, Morris, and Mackey unprecedented in their relevance.

Among the most important voices in this tradition of Orphic experimentation in American poetry is that of Robert Duncan. A major successor to Pound, close contemporary of Creeley, and primary influence on Taggart and Mackey, Duncan frequently invoked the myth of Orpheus as a figure for the modern poet. As Michael Palmer notes in his introduction to the posthumous edition of *Groundwork*, which brings together the two volumes *Before the War* and *In the Dark*, "Duncan was prominent among a generation of poets who sought to recover poetry's exploratory capacity from the strictures of orthodox critical propriety. Perhaps no one among his peers committed himself more profoundly to the magical, Orphic dimension of the poetic voice, and to the dynamic tension between the flowing currents of a restlessly associative mind and the demands of construction."[1] In Duncan's open-field poetics, the Orphic vision of the poet allows him to perceive and become immersed in hidden, mysterious, often mystical truths, and the task of the poet is to construct a field of ever-expanding interrelation between these exceptional perceptions. For Duncan, Orpheus's ability to thus sing his way into and out of the depths of Hell speaks to the profundity of his power, and, as Peter O'Leary has noted, means that in Duncan's cosmology, "Orpheus has pride of place, followed by Christ. . . . Orpheus is the reflected image of the man torn apart, and man himself is the ape to spiritual man."[2] As O'Leary summarizes, for Duncan, "Orpheus is post-Eurydice, already dismembered,"[3] and it is in this state of singing the double tragedy of Eurydice's and his own deaths, exploring and forging an ever-expanding unity, that the voice of the Orphic poet operates.

In his collection *Bending the Bow* (1967), Duncan demonstrates the work of the Orphic poet in the context of endemic political dishonesty, horrific war, and skepticism.[4] For Duncan, while these may be failings typical of humanity, the task of the Orphic poet is not to reject or compensate for them but, rather, to integrate them into a larger and more-encompassing system. As he argues in the introduction to *Bending the Bow*, "The old doctrine of correspondences is enlarged and furthered in a new process of responses, parts belonging to the architecture not only by the fittings—the concords and contrasts in chronological sequence, as in a jigsaw puzzle—by what comes one after another as we read, but by the resonances in the time of the whole in the reader's mind, each part as it is conceived as a member of every other part, having, as in a mobile, an interchange of roles, by the creation of forms within forms as we remember."[5] Duncan's practice, here, extends from the large-scale poetics of Pound, H.D., Zukofsky, Williams, and Olson, continuing the development of the American modern and postmodern long poem, and radicalizes the premise of his predecessors as he articulates his vision for open-field poetics and extends the traditional Orphic task of the poet. There are analogies, too, in the mobiles of Alexander Calder and the tone-rows of modernist music,[6] each medium eschewing conventions of static subordination and linearity in favor of the development of forms of vast and varied interrelation. Interestingly, Duncan's framing of his poetics, here, also frames the experience of the form of the poem in decidedly musical terms—we apprehend and understand the form of the poem as we do a piece of music, in recollection after having heard it. Only once the piece is over do we have all of the requisite parts, and so the experience of the poem, and the song, involves a kind of temporal stutter: while the artwork unfolds in time, it is complete only once it is out of time.

In the title poem of *Bending the Bow*, Duncan is explicit about the Orphic disposition of the poet. The poem begins by juxtaposing the different surfaces and materials of the objects at the poet's table, "the whole / composition of surfaces leads into the other / current disturbing / what I would take hold of."[7] The visual reverie of the moment is the condition of the poet's receptivity, resisting the temptation to stop at individual objects or details and, instead, remaining on the slippery surface of perception. The poem becomes self-referential, as Duncan notes, "I'd been // in the course of a letter—I am still / in the course of a letter—to a friend, / who comes close in to my thought so that / the day is hers,"[8] his friend taking up residence in his imagination, an epistolary action embedded and doubled within the writing of the poem. For Duncan, she is as present in her role as the letter's audience as she would be were she physically in the room. As the poem's self-reflectivity integrates the imagined recipient of his letter into the act of writing the poem, the anticipated reader soon takes on the qualities of Eurydice. The speaker addresses her, "You stand behind the where-I-am. / The deep tones and shadows I will call a woman," and continues, "I would play Orpheus for you again, / recall the arrow or song / to the trembling daylight / from which it sprang."[9] Duncan's analogical thinking aligns the arrow and the song. The bow, of course, is a reconfiguration of Orpheus's lyre into a resonant weapon, such that the song follows the flight of the arrow, shot by the singer-poet-archer into the daylight as if returning from the dark depths of the underworld.

Duncan's recourse to the myth of Orpheus frames his treatment of music, which he often invokes as exemplary of the "correspondences" to which the Orphic poet is attuned, recalling classical notions of the music of the spheres. In his poem "The Law of Love Is Major Mover," for instance, Duncan thus invokes music as an exemplary mode of interconnectivity and as a tool for recovering a lost pastoral ideal. As he argues, "there is no touch that is not each / to each reciprocal. // The scale of five, eight, or twelve tones / performs a judgment / previous to music. The music restores / health to the land."[10] In this passage, Duncan links the reciprocity of touch with the relationships between musical scales ranging from the perfect fifths of Pythagorean tuning through the octave-based tunings of classical music and on to the twelve-tone compositional practices of the European avant-garde. As such, the argument of the poem is that any musical model, regardless of historical circumstance or usage, reveals a restorative truth. What's more, the nature of that truth, for Duncan, is one of "judgment," an act of reason, a discernment of facts, the passage of a sentence, a juridical resolution that has been pronounced.

This figural role of music and its Orphic connection to poetic practice is central to several installments of Duncan's serial poem "Passages." Thus, in "Moving the Moving Image: Passages 17," Duncan explicitly aligns Orpheus with Jesus Christ by equating the Crucifixion with the dismemberment of Orpheus and links this composite figure with music as a divine power. As Duncan envisions, "The Orphic Xristos descends in the magic rite— / the driving of the nails into his hands and feet, / the briar crown, and, before: the sweating, stumbling / destitute carrying of the instruments of his death / to the place of His death."[11] With Christ as a surrogate for Orpheus, the poem proclaims the persistence of his truth in music: "As for Music—to know this is to know the order of all things / set together in a key of diversities // is a sweet harmony."[12] Later, in "The Concert: Passages 31," Duncan returns to the primal power of music and again ascribes to it an Orphic quality: "first there is the power, and in the power / is the tone or tune, / so that all of creation moves with / a music."[13] As Duncan identifies this moving musical form that accommodates and incorporates even the dissonances of life, he tells us, "the musician / has wound up his pegs / and tuned his strings. He bends his head / to hear the sound he makes / that leads his heart upward, // ascending to where the beat breaks into an all-but-unbearable whirling crown / of feet dancing, and now he sings or it is / the light singing, the voice / shaking, in the throes of the coming melody, / resonances of meaning exceeding what we / understand, words freed from their origins."[14] For Duncan, even as music embodies and projects a celestial order, it ultimately becomes an order to which we may have only fleeting and imperfect access, a framing of music as an unearthly, suprahuman order of knowledge that, as we have seen, clearly underscores the work of Duncan's major successor, Nathaniel Mackey. As the poem concludes, Duncan returns to the directives of Charles Olson's projective verse, "MOVE, / INSTANTER, ON ANOTHER," and the poem virtually unravels in visionary ecstasy, with "majesty thwarted."[15]

Duncan's invocations of the Orpheus myth, and the attendant relationship between poetry and music, should be understood as part of a conversation among his peers, including his Black Mountain fellows, Creeley and Olson, as well as his compatriots of the San Francisco Renaissance. Among the Bay Area poets, Jack Spicer, Duncan's sometime collaborator and sometime nemesis, developed what certainly stands out as one of the most thoroughgoing and imaginative uses of the myth of Orpheus. Spicer repeatedly returns to the myth in both his poetry and prose, including in the first of his landmark "Vancouver Lectures," titled "Dictation and 'A Textbook of Poetry,'" presented at the Vancouver Poetry Conference in 1965, on the one hundredth anniversary of W. B. Yeats's birth. In this lecture, Spicer explicitly invokes Orpheus as a figure for the poet involved in "the poetry of dictation," drawing a parallel with the practices of William Blake and Yeats. Although he seems to disbelieve the veracity of Yeats's specific claims about his wife, Georgie's, visions, Spicer nevertheless seriously entertains the core of the proposition that the Yeats's experience demonstrates the presence of an "Outside" that speaks through the medium of the poet: "In other words, instead of the poet being a beautiful machine which manufactured the current for itself, did everything for itself—almost a perpetual motion machine of emotion until the poet's heart broke or it was burned on the beach like Shelley's—instead there was something from the Outside coming in."[16] As the lecture continues, Spicer develops the analogy by turning to the title character in Jean Cocteau's film *Orphée* (1950), which wildly reenvisions the mythical poet as a character who receives poetry as messages via a car radio.[17] Spicer proposes that "essentially you are something which is being transmitted into, and the more that you clear your mind away from yourself, and the more also that you do some censoring—because there will be all sorts of things coming from your mind, from the depths of your mind, from things that you want, which will foul up the poem."[18] Spicer adopts Cocteau's depiction of Orpheus as he substitutes receptivity for creativity and brackets the will of the poet. As Peter Gizzi has usefully summarized, Cocteau's film provided Spicer with "a seductive combination of ancient mythology, popular psychology, avant-garde aesthetics, and poetry. . . . [The poet] is not a Romantic genius but a scribe, taking down what this machine of sound transmits."[19] As Spicer rejects the Romantic ideals of genius and creativity, he turns to and reconfigures the myth of Orpheus as a metaphor not for artistic control, mastery, or even vision but, instead, for one of radical receptivity and transmission.

The extent to which Spicer radicalizes the myth of Orpheus is evident in the extremes to which he pushes the analogy, casting the work of the poet as being spoken through by the voices of the dead and communing with the unearthly and inhuman in a tirelessly forward-looking process. Beginning with his pivotal collection *After Lorca* (1957), Spicer committed himself to an exploratory serial mode in his poetry, rejecting his previous work as so many "one-night stands," a conviction serious enough that his *Collected Poems* from 1996 begin with *After Lorca*. As Gizzi notes, Spicer's relationship to Lorca fuels his Orphic poetics: "[Lorca's] position offers unique connections to the underworld for an Orphic poet, and he provides both the perfect vehicle for unrequited love and the perfect emblem of literary inheritance and tradition."[20] Lorca provides an Orphic voice from the dead whose words can be received and transmitted by the subsequent Orphic poet, Spicer, thereby establishing an ongoing chain of Orphic communication. Spicer goes on to equate this ventriloquizing of the voices of the dead with his other primary model for the "poetry of dictation": the poet as a receiver of messages from Martians. Partly drawing upon the prevalence of Martian invasion narratives in mid-1950s popular culture, Spicer's ludic invocation of Martians further divorces the will of the poet from the act of creation. For Spicer, the contents of a poet's mind—the language he speaks, the things he knows, the experiences he remembers, and so on—are merely "the furniture in the room," to be moved around and organized through the voice of the Martian. What's more, the myth of Orpheus provides the commandment for unidirectionality that Spicer ascribes to his post-*After Lorca* serial poetry—just as the mythical poet is directed not to look back, so, too, should the serial poet consistently project him- or herself forward, eschewing the order-making, sense-making, self-imposing gesture of considered recollection.

In his poetry, too, Spicer frequently turns to the myth of Orpheus. Amid the "one-night stands" of his early poems is an Orphic trilogy, predating Spicer's commitment to seriality, Cocteau's Orpheus, and Martians as metaphors for the poetry of dictation. The three poems, "Orpheus in Hell," "Orpheus after Eurydice," and "Orpheus's Song to Apollo," are brief contemplations on key elements of the myth. The first two poems follow the chronology of Orpheus's journey, with the first providing a typically Spiceresque view of the underworld, in which he wonders "if all of hell were without music," and his song is drowned out as "pain / was screaming on the jukebox."[21] These screams are cut through by "a voice" calling his name, after which Orpheus returns to the gateway; the poem concludes, "Later, he would remember all of those dead voices / And call them Eurydice."[22] While the voice that calls to Orpheus seems to belong to Eurydice, the fact that Spicer generalizes it as "a voice" and then includes it alongside all of the voices of the dead both dematerializes and pluralizes Eurydice. She is no longer his lost beloved but, rather, a conceptual placeholder for the many voices that will speak through the Orphic poet (including, later, the voice of Lorca). The subsequent poem turns to Orpheus's condition after Eurydice's second death, full of grief and intoxication as he both envisions his lover as "a god" and laments the irrecoverability of that love. The speaker twice intones, "Mella, mella peto / In medio flumine," as Maria Damon has noted, "an Ovidian proverb meaning a vain and futile attempt—to seek honey in the river."[23] The last of the Orpheus poems is a reproach to Apollo for having "yoked [his] horse / To the wrong sun" and a riff on the associations and associative habits of Greek mythology, with Apollo having "picked the wrong flower" in his beloved Hyacinth instead of the rose. Addressing "Fool Apollo," the speaker concludes, "I like your aspiration / But the sky's too deep / For fornication,"[24] Orpheus's grief having apparently transmuted into a renunciation of the material world.

While this trio of Orpheus poems presents rather direct and playful contemplations of the myth, Spicer approaches the myth very differently when he returns to it in his collection *The Heads of the Town Up to the Aether* (1960). Now fully committed to serial poetry and the poetry of dictation, Spicer notes in "Dictation and 'A Textbook of Poetry'" that the first section of the book,

"Homage to Creeley," "is based almost entirely on Cocteau's *Orphée*."[25] Dedicated to Duncan's Orphic contemporary, "Homage to Creeley" utilizes a horizontal division of the page not unlike, and possibly prefiguring, what we saw in Mackey's use of a horizontal bar to divide his poems into upper and lower parts. Whereas Mackey's use of this horizontal dividing line presents something akin to a musical reprise, Spicer clearly divides the page into "Homage to Creeley" above the line and "Explanatory Notes" below. While this seems to present an orderly relationship in the form, as Robin Blaser has noted, "'Homage to Creeley' becomes a hell of meanings," a juxtaposition of images, ideas, and snippets of found and invented language so radical that "everything slips or slides into nonsense and is haunted by meaning and laughter."[26] Blaser goes on, "In Jack's work [the surrealism of the poet is] the mode of an operational language distinct from a language which stops the world. And it is attached to an Orphic methodology of great complexity, which the book keys by way of dedications to the figures of Cocteau's *Orpheus*."[27] Ellingham and Killian similarly note the rich verbal field of the collection: "The whole of 'Homage to Creeley' is studded with allusions and quotes from Spicer's favorite writers: these were the 'furniture in the room' which the Martians came in and arranged. Nursery rhymes, spells and incantations, folk and pop music, medieval riddles, bardic incantations, drinking songs, stage directions, radio jingles: these were the materials of the weird science fiction landscape Spicer's poetry now pushed him into headlong, dreaming."[28] In the explanatory notes, running beneath this manic linguistic menagerie, Spicer frequently points the reader to the role of Orpheus in the poetry, although the explanatory power of these notes is often tenuous, at best. For instance, the poem "The Territory Is Not a Map" is populated by lobsters, sugared groins and sugared hair, and half-squinting and oily eyes, while we learn from the "explanatory note" that "Orpheus and Eurydice are in their last nuptial embrace during this poem."[29] Similarly, the poem "When You Go Away You Don't Come Home" concludes with the final two lines, "And what are is bigger than the moon, I guess, / Bigger than that boy's pants," which the note proclaims is "an obvious reference to Eurydice. What doesn't cast shadows is obvious to everyone."[30] The reference to Eurydice is, of course, anything but obvious, as is the relationship between the poetry and the "explanatory notes" throughout "Homage to Creeley," with the notes routinely invoking Cocteau's retelling of the Orpheus myth as explanation for poems that have no apparent bearing whatsoever on the myth.

If moments such as these embrace hypotaxis to the level of the absurd, other moments in "Homage to Creeley" do follow the logic of proposition and explanation, such as in the poem, "Elegy." The poem reads,

Whispers—

Eurydice's head is missing

Whispers—

Get out of hell—

Whispers—

You big poet

We soldiers from hell's country

Here

Safe as you are

You write poetry

For dead persons[31]

The poem's "whispers," image of a decapitated Eurydice, and admonition that the poet should "get out of hell" give it a haunting, foreboding quality such that the note is plausible when it confidently describes the poem as "definitely a warning to Orpheus which he does not understand—being an asshole. This is too bad because there would have been just as much poetry if he had understood it."[32] Later, Spicer conceptualizes the relationship between Orpheus and Eurydice after her death in terms consistent with that of Blanchot and Bruns, whose framing of her death as a tragic precondition for the birth of lyric we saw in relation to Creeley's Orphic poetics. The note to the first and untitled poem of section 2 tells us that "Eurydice is miles away" and concludes, "She is almost a function of them," a reference to the interaction between the characters of Orpheus, Cegeste, and the Princess in Cocteau's film. By oscillating between these modes of explanation that is at times fanciful, at times misleading, and at times illuminating, Spicer demonstrates that his Orpheus is a poet in the throes of his defining tragedy; his task is not to provide shape to the world around him but, rather, to report back to us on the disorder and disharmony of the land of the dead.[33]

While Spicer's invocations of Orpheus focus primarily on reconceiving the conceptual power of the myth as it configures the work of the poet, they should also be understood in relation to his use of music. Spicer concludes his "California Lecture: Poetry and Politics" by noting the role of music both in his work and as a broader artistic practice in relation to community building. Throughout his collected lectures, Spicer attends to both the conceptual claim that poets (like musicians) build imagined cities through their work, including through their imaginations of their readership and their incorporation of the voices of their predecessors, and the practical concern of community building through publishing practices. He concludes the "California Lecture" by explicitly linking poetry and music in this process: "I have used songs in my poems all along. In *Language*, there are about five places where you have to sing the thing in order to get it, and anyone who doesn't know the fact that it's a song—since it's a popular song like 'The Frog Went A-Courtin'—well, doesn't belong there. . . . But certainly it appeals to me. Really, if there's any way of getting the poet, the individual, and society together, it would be the song. But I haven't yet been able to do it."[34] Spicer's hope for popular song as a way to reunite the poet with society, a split that he elsewhere sees as almost complete, suggests that the traditional invocation of Orpheus as a figure for unification courses beneath the fragmentation of Spicer's texts, the fragmented relationship between the poet and society, and the fragmentation of society itself. As Gizzi notes, "The significance for Spicer of [the] act of community building through song leads him to an imaginary association with Charlie Parker—the 'bird' of Spicer's 'Song for Bird and Myself'—whom Spicer again invokes in *Language* as dancing 'now in some brief kingdom (Oz)' that is created through its unique pairing of the phonemes /ä/ and /z/, 'two phonemes / That were never paired before in the language' (*L*, 237). While the 'brief kingdom' could be an afterlife for the posthumous Parker, the kingdom's 'briefness' and the reference to Oz suggest that it is an imaginary world created and entered only in the act of song."[35] Spicer's identification with Parker as a kindred spirit, a figure for the Orphic poet, and a model for the hope of community building in and through artistic practice powerfully presages the role of John Coltrane in the poetics of John Taggart, as discussed in chapter 3; both Spicer and Taggart turn to these icons of the innovative jazz that emerged in the postwar period as their benchmarks.

    In 1956, the year following Parker's death, Spicer wrote, "Song for Bird and Myself" and its bleakly titled counterpart, "A Poem without a Single Bird in It." In the first poem, Spicer identifies with the "neoclassical" Parker as an artist who torques the materials of his medium. Thus, much like Spicer's poetic practice puts language under various forms of duress, Parker pushes against the material of music itself, "Distrusting the reality / Of every note. / Half-real / We blow the sentence pure and real / Like chewing angels."[36] For Spicer, his poetic practice, like Parker's, cleanses the medium of convention, finding or giving voice to a pure truth that is otherwise unknowable. In the final stanza of the poem, Spicer's identification with Parker carries through to the musician's death and returns to the notion of "Outside" that is so important to Spicer. He writes, "So bird and I sing / Outside your window / So bird and I die / Outside your window," the syntactical parallelism of the poem aligning song with death.[37] At first glance, the poem seems to simply offer a scene of the song of the poet, like that of the musician, carrying through an open window; Spicer's use of the word "Outside," though, suggests a more radical possibility. Although Spicer won't formalize his sense of "Outside" for a decade, this poem seems to anticipate his sense that the poet (and the musician) are spoken through by forces outside of themselves. Here, in lines written after Parker's death, the poem suggests that these songs, this poem, are windows through which the Outside that is death passes. In "A Poem without a Single Bird in It," Spicer returns to this linking of death as the root of lyric, twice encouraging his muse to "Commit suicide. Go mad," concluding that, in the end, "There will be nothing left / After you die or go mad, / But the calmness of poetry."[38] In the "Bird" poems, even before the "practice of outside" has taken hold, Spicer invokes Parker as an Orphic kinsman, an artist-as-vehicle through which an outside sings and will continue to sing long after the death of the poet and the musician.

Spicer's invocations of Charlie Parker in these poems of the 1950s antici-pate one of his more wryly humorous collections, *A Book of Magazine Verse*, his last book, published in 1965. As Spicer notes in his third Vancouver lecture, the book consists of "poems written for magazines that would not print them," in-cluding as its last section, "Ten Poems for *Downbeat*," the standard-bearer of jazz publications.[39] Written in the spring and summer of 1965, the poems date from the year-end issue in which the magazine's readers' poll proclaimed "The Year of John Coltrane" on the front cover. However, Spicer does not invoke Coltrane in these poems, nor does he reach back to Parker; instead, the poems include several quotations from the lyrics to the popular song "Sweet Betsy from Pike," a song whose lyrics were included in Carl Sandburg's 1927 *American Songbag* and, more suggestively, recorded by Johnny Cash on the album *Johnny Cash Sings the Ballads of the True West* in September 1965. The presence of these lyrics partly sig-nals Spicer's commitment to California, as does his invocation of the Donner Party's infamous crossing of the Sierra Nevada, the image of the "heathen Chinee [*sic*] / Building a railway," and his confident assertion that "We are a coast people / There is nothing but ocean out beyond us. We grasp / The first thing com-ing."[40] For Spicer, the traditional American folk song is fundamentally linked to the westward, Orphically apt forward-looking disposition he identifies as funda-mentally Californian.

Elsewhere in *Ten Poems for Downbeat*, Spicer similarly invokes popular music and links it to his sense of geography. For instance, the fourth "Poem for *Down-beat*" also includes a lyric from a similar folk ballad, "Wreck of the Ole 97," which tells the story of a 1903 train wreck in Virginia, although the poem does not include the details of the line's context. In fact, the poem presents it as a prose quotation: "It's a mighty rough road from Lynchburg to Danville, declen-sion on a three mile grade."[41] The poem continues with the stern observation, "You either pick up the music or you don't," and then shifts to the geography of "British Columbia" and "Western Imperialism."[42] In this brief gesture, Spicer lifts a line from the tradition of American folk music, assumes the knowledgeability of the reader, and then transplants the line to the Pacific Northwest; and he does all of this in the context of poems sardonically destined for non-publication in a

jazz magazine. As such, the poem, and the whole of *Ten Poems for Downbeat*, cri-
tiques the compartmentalization of aesthetic experience and knowledge, a cri-
tique that would encourage us, for instance, to consider the relationship between
the emerging visionary jazz of the mid-1960s and vernacular and popular tradi-
tions of music. While market forces and listening habits tend to separate these
fields of musical expression, Spicer's juxtaposition of these works would encour-
age us to see the link, for example, between pieces of musical Americana such as
these lyrics and the performance practice of musicians such as Coltrane, Ornette
Coleman, Charles Mingus, and Archie Shepp, among many others.

Ultimately, Spicer's Orphic poetics are fueled by his conviction that the poet
must harrow the depths of hell to gain access to a truth that can then speak
through him, yielding the dead-but-singing body of Eurydice in and as the body
of the poem. Inasmuch as he turns to Parker, he seemingly does so partly be-
cause of his shared status as a suffering artist, perhaps even one whose drug ad-
diction resonates with Spicer's own alcoholism, and partly because of the com-
munity building he sees made available in and through Parker's playing. Insofar
as Parker's innovations in jazz are both steeped in the traditions of the form and
break radical new ground, they share the architecture of Spicer's sense of the
coexistence of the old and the new; what's more, insofar as the improvisatory na-
ture of bebop performance depends upon the fluid mobilization of a musician's
catalog of musical gestures, including those that arise in the moment of the per-
formance, it is also analogous to Spicer's argument that the poem is the result of
the poet's language and mental landscape being so much furniture arranged and
rearranged by the aliens in the making of the poem.

In contrast to Spicer's long-standing interest in the Orpheus myth and the
proximity of poetry and music is the notably singular turn to the myth by an-
other of Spicer's contemporaries, John Ashbery. In his 1977 poem "Syringa," Ash-
bery juxtaposes the myth of Orpheus with that of Syrinx, using these competing
and irreconcilable mythological frameworks as material for his common practice
of setting up irresolvable tensions in his poem, a practice he seems to define in
his earlier poem "Soonest Mended," "a kind of fence-sitting / raised to an esthetic
ideal."[43] "Syringa" begins its fence-sitting with an immediate displacement: while
the title invokes the myth of Syrinx, the first word of the poem names Orpheus,
and the most obvious project of the poem is a kind of cool, half-ironic contem-
plation of the myth of Orpheus. But, Syrinx comes back, about two-thirds of the
way through the poem, and the linkage between the two myths is the subject of
the poem's concluding lines. We should recall, then, that Syrinx is transformed
into reeds by the river nymphs in order to avoid being raped by Pan and that it
is from these reeds that Pan fashions his pipe. That is to say, the story of Syrinx
is the story of music as linked to the breath and the body, a transmutation of the
human voice through the vehicle of the musical instrument. The myth of Syrinx

thus presents a sharp contrast to that of Orpheus, whose instrument is the Apollonian lyre, a difference that, among other things, leaves his mouth free and able to sing.

The project of "Syringa" is largely to put these competing models of music into irresolvable and mutually sustaining tension with one another. Ultimately, "Syringa" suggests the interchangeability of these competing conceptions of music. As the poem concludes, "an arbitrary chorus / speaks" not of the subjects that have occurred in the poem but of, rather, "a totally different incident with a similar name / in whose tale are hidden syllables / of what happened so long before that / in some small town, one indifferent summer."[44] Ashbery's gestures of temporal and geographic inconsequentiality, here, serve to blur the distinctions between the incidents and to highlight their similarity within language— the "hidden syllables." That is to say, the poem suggests, in its conclusion, that the myths of Orpheus and Syrinx are importantly the same.

On one level, the nature of this similarity between the two myths operates much as Ashbery describes music as a kind of logic. In a statement published in the 1965 collection, *A Controversy of Poets*, Ashbery describes his appreciation of music: "What I like about music is its ability of being convincing, of carrying an argument through successfully to the finish, though the terms of this argument remain unknown quantities. What remains is the structure, the architecture of the argument, scene or story. I would like to do this in poetry."[45] Likewise, the poem has an ability to convincingly seem like an argument, in this case, for the persuasive logic of mythical narrative. As the poem tells us, while some may believe that the Bacchantes tore Orpheus limb from limb, "for his treatment of Eurydice," actually "probably the music had more to do with it, and / the way music passes, emblematic / Of life and how you cannot isolate a note of it / And say it is good or bad. You must / Wait till it's all over."[46] While Ashbery does not take up the composition-by-field processes that would define Duncan's and Spicer's poetics, his view of music, here, resonates with their drive toward an aesthetic of interrelationality. For Ashbery, it is precisely music's stubborn irreducibility that triggers the Bacchante's fatal rage, and it is also that quality of music that makes it paradigmatic of the structure of life—as with a life, no single element of a piece of music can be evaluated in isolation, and the final merits of the life or the music can only be accounted for once they are over, the song completed and the life lived.

In addition to this sense of music as structure, the poem makes another, more specific case for the similarities between the myths of Syrinx and Orpheus. While music is the medium under question in both of them, they are also linked by their use of sexual violence at key points: just as Syrinx escapes the predations of Pan, Eurydice dies from the bite of a viper suffered while she was fleeing from the similar advances of Aristaeus, suggesting that the threat of sexual violence is the precondition for the birth of music. The narrative of Ashbery's poem clearly derives from the myth's tragedy, although it strategically, even conspicuously evades any depiction of it. The poem begins, in Ashbery's characteristic offhand tone, "Orpheus liked the glad personal quality / Of the things beneath the sky. Of course, Eurydice was a part / Of this. Then one day, everything changed."[47] The poem recounts neither the death of Eurydice nor Orpheus's descent to the underworld but, instead, leaps ahead to the third phase of the myth, after Eurydice has been lost and Orpheus left only to lament. Even as the poem elides the cause of Eurydice's death, she is, in fact, not dead but "a part of this," an irreducible part of the myth as it exists in the cultural repository.

While myths of music are clearly at the heart of this poem's drama, then, the status of music is hardly idealized as the poem deeply problematizes the models presented by both Syrinx and Orpheus. If the bodily music of Syrinx is invoked and then withdrawn, she returns in a rather diminished mode, "the tossing reeds of that slow, / Powerful stream, the trailing grasses / Playfully tugged at, but to participate in the action / No more than this."[48] Instead of idealizing or even elaborating upon Syrinx's role in the myth, Ashbery's invocation of her reduces her role in the story to a minimalist state, as if the waving reeds from which she is made now merely register the passage of the stream, just as her music does no more than merely register the passage of time. As the poem continues, so, too, does this constriction of the role or possibility of music:

> The singer
>
> Thinks constructively, builds up his chant in progressive stages
>
> Like a skyscraper, but at the last minute turns away.
>
> The song is engulfed in an instant in blackness
>
> Which in turn must flood the whole continent
>
> With blackness, for it cannot see. The singer
>
> must then pass out of sight, not even relieved
>
> Of the evil burthen of the words.[49]

At first, these lines seem to suggest that the poet can sing constructively, much as he thinks, and build a reality skyward (or out of the depths of Hades). In doing so, he would adopt and adapt the ideal of music as registering the eternal truths of the music of the spheres, toward which the art of music might help us to aspire. However, such a vision is ultimately impossible for Ashbery. Music, here, is neither Orpheus's Apollonian lyre, nor his well-ordered, all-pervasive, and omni-persuasive song, nor the bodily expressivity of panpipes. That is to say, neither myth holds. Rather, music, like the structural similarities in the myths, is syntactical, an endless procedure of ordering that gives at least the impression of adding up to an as-yet-undecided sense.

It is worth noting that the three poets I just discussed—Duncan, Spicer, and Ashbery—all not only turn to the myth of Orpheus but also were gay poets of the generation that solidified in contrast to the cultural conservatism of the 1950s (they were born within eight years of one another, Duncan in 1919, Spicer in 1925, and Ashbery in 1927). I would not want to make any programmatic claims about the relationship between these facts, particularly insofar as the relationship between poetic practice and the poet's sexuality operates very differently for each of them.[50] Nevertheless, part of Orpheus's myth is that after the loss of Eurydice, he foregoes the love of women and substitutes for it homosexual love, the consequence of which is his refusal of the advances of the Bacchantes (Ashbery's "Ciconian women"), who then tear him limb from limb. Both Duncan and Spicer published work directly related to the status of homosexuality in postwar America: Duncan's essay "The Homosexual in Society," from 1944, and Spicer's dada-esque "The Unvert Manifesto," from 1956. Duncan's essay is a powerful statement of belief in fundamental human equality and the costs of a closeted life, and his argument for political and social equality is consistent with and an extension of the inclusiveness that characterizes his open-field poetics and his broader Orphic vision. Throughout the essay, Duncan explores the effects of homophobia on gay writers, focusing on the ways in which closeted writers develop coded narratives, as well as his own complicated relationship to the idea of community. He argues, "What I think can be asserted as a starting point is that only one devotion can be held by a human being seeking a creative life and expression, and that is a devotion to human freedom, toward the liberation of human love, human conflicts, human aspirations. To do this one must disown *all* the special groups (nations, churches, sexes, races) that would claim allegiance. To hold this devotion every written word, every spoken word, every action, every purpose must be examined and considered."[51] For Duncan, this absolute devotion to individual freedom originally made him suspicious of the idea of community as such, a suspicion that subsides later in his career after he found personal relationships based upon shared experiences, goals, and desires and the affection of a durable personal relationship with the artist Jess.

While Duncan's essay is a serious contemplation of the effects of homophobic culture in America, Spicer, for his part, turns to the absurd in describing the "unvert." He deploys the term in inconsistent and contradictory ways, at one point, for instance, proclaiming that "an unvert must not be homosexual, heterosexual, bisexual, or autosexual. He must be metasexual."[52] For Spicer, the "unvert" is a category of person, and a descriptor of behavior, that exceeds all possible social norms and conventions, even those that might adhere around recognized minority groups. It is, we might say, another practice of "Outside," here, less as a matter of receiving messages from elsewhere as of rejecting any given category of social, sexual behavior. In the midst of the "Unvert Manifesto," Spicer turns again to his favorite Cocteau film and narrates a rather pathetic and inconsequential Orpheus, one whose art is largely unheard: "Only a few people turned around to look at Orpheus," who was "singing and making horrible noises on his guitar or whatever it was."[53] Ultimately, we learn that "Orpheus . . . was on a spaceship and Eurydice couldn't see him anymore," a framing that shifts the narrative such that Eurydice's residence in the underworld becomes the baseline and Orpheus's typical return to the world of the living is actually an extraterrestrial visit to Spicer's beloved Martians. At the conclusion of the "manifesto," in a scenario in which Spicer deploys the characters from the 1960s television show *Perry Mason*, Orpheus's fate at the hands of the maenads returns in the whispered remark that private investigator Paul Drake makes to the eponymous defense attorney, "You can tear him to shreds on cross-examination."[54]

The surprising durability of the myth of Orpheus suggests that it continues to speak to a cultural or aesthetic need. As the examples of Duncan, Spicer, and Ashbery demonstrate, the persistence of Orpheus as a figure for the lyric poet works to retain the proximity of poetry and music, even as both the nature of music and the nature of its relationship to poetry are thereby often put under pressure. More than merely an abstraction, this interdisciplinary, cross-media relationship is often of material, practical importance to poets operating in the Orphic bend. It is no surprise, then, that many of the poets treated in this study have turned to collaboration with musicians. As we see with Bernstein's opera and Morris's sound poetry, the text-music nexus illuminates and animates the projects of these poets in important ways: for Bernstein's part, it is the mechanism by which his opera jousts with the legacy of Pound, while, for Morris, it is the vehicle of her vision of performativity. Collaboration is also important in the oeuvres of Creeley and Mackey, both of whom have recorded their work with musical accompaniment.

While Creeley collaborates with musicians who have very different musical aesthetics, the collaborations all center on his defining meter, or "measure." In 1979, the jazz bassist Steve Swallow recorded the album, *Home*, consisting of ten tracks that feature the vocalist Sheila Jordan singing portions of Creeley's poems, primarily from his collections of the early 1970s. Each track takes its title from a Creeley poem or, as in the case of "She was Young . . ." and "Nowhere One . . .," from lines embedded within longer poems. Each of the ten songs includes either only a brief poem or a brief passage from the longer poems, without repetition. Swallow's ambient, softly straight-ahead idiom, echoed in Jordan's breathy singing of the lines, transmutes Creeley's poetry into song lyrics that, for the most part, retain Creeley's characteristic prosody. This attention to the music of

Creeley's language is more pronounced when Swallow returns to Creeley's work on his album, *So There*, which includes material from recording sessions in 2001 and 2005, and was released in 2006, the year after Creeley's death (the album is dedicated "to Bob" in the liner notes). Unlike on the previous recording, *So There* features Creeley reading poems to the accompaniment of Swallow, along with the pianist Steve Kuhn and the Cikada Quartet, featuring Henrik Hannisdal and Odd Hannisdal on violin, Mark Konstantynowicz on viola, and Morten Hannisdal on cello. *So There* draws upon poetry from across Creeley's career, including his most famous poem, "I Know a Man," which was originally published in his landmark 1960 collection, *For Love*, up to and including poems from his 2001 collection, *Just in Time*. The album does not follow the chronology of the dates of composition or publication for the poems but, rather, traverses Creeley's career and sets the poems in Swallow's lyrical musical idiom, with lush strings, sparkling piano, and a steady swinging bass line (a notable exception being the dissonant strings that open "Ambition"). The album's most striking pieces feature syllabic text setting that draws upon and accentuates Creeley's voice. Most markedly on tracks such as "Ambition" and "I Know a Man," Creeley's signature rhythm is stylized or accentuated and the rhythm derived directly from his words such that the music provides an undeniable emotional arc to the poems.

The subtle attention to Creeley's prosody that informs Swallow's recordings with him is dramatically foregrounded in Creeley's collaboration with the soprano saxophonist Steve Lacy. Lacy's idiom is entirely different from Swallow's, with its characteristic angularity, dissonance, and combined avant-gardism and lyricism, and his two recordings, *Futurities I* and *Futurities II*, recorded in 1985 and 1989, respectively, are the most significant examples of Creeley's collaboration with musicians. The albums feature Steve Potts on alto and soprano saxophone, George Lewis on trombone, Gyde Knebusch on harp, Barry Wedgle on guitar, Jef Gardner on piano, J. J. Avenel on bass, Oliver Johnson on drums and percussion, with vocals by Irene Aebi. The two albums set poems from across Creeley's career, up to and including his collection *Mirrors* (1983). The recordings are the result of the poet, critic, and translator Pierre Joris having put Creeley and Lacy in touch with one another in 1983, at which time they recorded an improvised reading of the poems with accompaniment by Lacy. As Joris recounts,[55] much to his surprise, Lacy continued to work with the materials from that point, setting the poems to music in fully developed compositions and then as the text for a music-text-dance piece that was debuted at the 1984 Festival in Lille. After the Lille performance, Lacy returned to the pieces and developed the versions that are featured on the recordings. Throughout the process, Lacy demonstrated what Joris describes as "rare care" for the language of Creeley's poetry, insisting that it remain intelligible to all of the performers as well as the audience. As Peter Kostakis describes in the liner notes to the second recording, each piece consists of five parts: an introduction; a sung poem, repeated twice; a tag (a "last phrase," repeated twice); a return to introduction; and an improvisation, using one instrument or a combination of instruments.[56] In this structure, Lacy's treatment of Creeley's text is a process of syllabic text setting, often matching Creeley's voice to two instruments simultaneously. As Kostakis notes, this fidelity to Creeley's prosody is central to Lacy's project: "Creeley's serpentine line and surprise syntax hook into the astute quirks of intervallic melody, purposeful repetition, and stretching harmony that are Lacy trademarks. Listen more closely and you appreciate *Futurities*' accord with the poet's view of form as 'the extension of content.' The soprano saxophonist did more than fit notes to syllables when he composed and arranged: he located—in scoring *and* performing—the just right emotional correlatives to the lyrics. . . . This feat is important for a work of art because, as Creeley quotes Pound, 'only emotion endures.'"[57] Indeed, even as the pieces are sung by a voice other than Creeley's (Aebi's), they perform precisely the kind of work that Creeley and, behind him, Pound ascribe to rhythm at its most profound—an instantiation of the poet's self that can be reanimated by reading/performing his words.

A compelling example of the literalization of Creeley's belief in the importance and durability of song is the first track on *Futurities II*, "Sad Advice,"[58] a poem originally published in *Mirrors*. The poem reads in its entirety:

> If it isn't fun, don't do it.
>
> You'll have to do enough that isn't.
>
> Such is life, like they say,
>
> No one gets away without paying
>
> and since you don't get to keep it
>
> anyhow, who needs it.[59]

Interestingly, Swallow also set this poem. On the album *So There*,[60] recorded some twenty years after Lacy's performance, Swallow's recording focuses on the melancholy undertone of the poem, and Creeley's reading on the track adheres closely to his lineation, with three distinct couplets operating as units of both prosody and argument. After Creeley's reading of the poem, which concludes approximately one minute into the piece, the remaining two minutes continue in the opening mood with thin, quiet layers of piano, guitar, and violin. Lacy's rendition of the poem couldn't be more different. It begins with the soprano and tenor saxophones repeating a brief phrase in unison, after which Aebi's vocals enter, demonstrating that the opening musical phrase is actually derived from the rhythm of Creeley's line. That is to say, Lacy's process here recalls nothing so much as how Ezra Pound described his setting of the poetry of François Villon, as discussed in chapter 1—an attempt to derive musical material from the patterns of language. What's more, with the entrance of the high-hat, the faster tempo, the swinging beat, and the interplay between soloing instruments, the tone of Lacy's "Sad Advice" is wryer and wittier than it is melancholy. Like the songs throughout the *Futurities* recordings, "Sad Advice" is a powerful instance of Creeley's measure, his Orphic voice literally resonating, sounding through the performer's instrument, be it saxophone, trombone, percussion, or voice itself.

Like Creeley, Mackey's collaborations with musicians are important exempla of his Orphic poetics, particularly of the way Mackey's poetry engages musicality as a mode of understanding. Working in conjunction with musicians literalizes the ensemble imagination that is at work throughout his poetry and prose, the vocal performance of the text animates Mackey's use of puns, homophones, and other productive linguistic slippages, and the interaction between the text and music both enriches the musicality already present in the language and creates new musicalities. Mackey's first recording of these collaborations is his album, *Strick: Song of the Andoumboulou 16–25* (1995), featuring Royal Hartigan and Hafez Modirzadeh. *Strick* received substantial treatment in the 2000 special issue of the journal *Callaloo* dedicated to Mackey's work, in which both Jeffrey Gray and Richard Quinn explore how Mackey's read text interacts with the music of Hartigan and Modirzadeh to test the boundaries between poetry and music. As Gray summarizes, "*Strick* is . . . the narrative of a journey across desert spaces, a journey in which layers of voices, histories, and melodies replace chronology as a way of organizing time."[61] Even as *Strick* embraces a musical mode of coherence, as Gray notes, it is also powerfully shaped by musical genre, with Hartigan and Modirzadeh drawing on veins of jazz and world music, including "musics of Iran, India, China, the Philippines, and West Africa," which resonate powerfully with both Mackey's poetics and the quest narrative at the heart of the "mu" series. Similarly attending to the ways the work resists conventional categorization, Quinn describes Mackey's "aural oscillation," "a movement in sound which critiques word, thought, concept or category as rigid products."[62]

The characteristics of *Strick* that Gray and Quinn discuss also pertain to his later collaborations with musicians. Notable instances include a performance with the Creaking Breeze Ensemble in 2019 (consisting of Billy Steiger, Evie Ward, Paul Abbott, Seymour Wright, and Ute Kanngiesser), unfortunately not available for study, and a September 22, 2019, performance with the saxophonist Marty Ehrlich, available on PennSound. Perhaps most compelling of Mackey's recent recordings is an April 15, 2015, performance at Duke University with bassist Vattel Cherry. The performance with Cherry features recent installments in the now intertwined serial poems, "mu" and "Song of the Andoumboulou," the relationship between which was discussed in chapter 5. The acoustic world of

Cherry's performance is made up of his double bass, bells hung from the scroll of the bass and worn on his left ankle, and a xylophone. The performance begins with Mackey reading "Sound and Semblance: 'mu' twenty-sixth part," from *Splay Anthem* (2002), while Cherry's rhythmic xylophone playing, punctuated by the jangle of the ankle bells, grows and diminishes in volume, giving the sense of traveling through space, much as Gray notes in *Strick*. Cherry shifts to the bass roughly two-thirds of the way through the first poem, as the poem's fictional travelers are joined by jazz royalty, "kings and queens, crowned ourselves / in sound. Duke was there, Pres, Lady, Count, Pharaoh came later. The / Soon-Come Congress we'd heard so much / about, soon come even sooner south."[63] After a pause, Mackey's reading resumes, noting that "there was a new mood suddenly, blue / but uptempo," and Cherry's playing follows suit. Cherry then plays a brief bass solo, after which Mackey reads his poem "Day After Day of the Dead," which is not, however, the next poem in the series but, instead, "'-mu' forty-eighth part," published a decade later in his collection *Nod House* (2011).

This leap across moments in Mackey's career is unremarked in the performance as Mackey and Cherry collaborate to create a temporal experience in performance that collocates chronologically disparate materials. Cherry's music bridges across the poems, making them contiguous with one another in spite of the years that have passed and the twenty-two intervening poems. The title of the second poem of the performance, "Day After Day of the Dead," is not read until it comes as a line halfway through the poem, following a break marked by a dot, a sectioning of the poem common in Mackey's work. The performance follows this form of the poem, as Cherry fills the textual space with an extended solo. The title also recalls the phrasing that began the first poem in the "mu" series, as discussed in chapter 5, which reads, "The day before the year / begins."[64] As Mackey echoes the poem that initiated the series, he both marks the passage of time, from the eve of the new year to late fall, and continues his characteristically oblique phrasing—not New Year's Eve and not the Day of the Dead. It is as if Mackey's Orphic poetics frame time itself as knowable via suggestion but not via direct apprehension. The consistency of Mackey's project is also evident in how the performance recalls many of the animating features Gray notes in *Strick*, including Mackey's play with the tension between the scribal and the aural, such as when the Orphic lines "happy to / see / shadow, know touch," sounds like "happy to / see / shadow, no touch," and when the music and the poem react to one another, such as when Cherry shifts to bowing the bass as the poem describes a "requiem so / sweet we forgot what it lamented."[65] This blurring of the boundaries between individual poems is reinforced by the fact that the pause between them is no longer than some pauses within the poems, as well as the ongoing quest narrative, familiar thematic touchstones, and consistency of Mackey's signature prosody. The combined effect of the performance is to present a richly interwoven field of scribal-aural, textual-musical experience in which res-onance, the perception of patterns as they evolve over time, is proposed as a mode of knowing. On the one hand, what seems to be a unified textual-musical aesthetic experience is actually a collage-like composition made up of discrete and discontinuous pieces of an ongoing serial composition; on the other hand, what matters in Mackey's Orphic epistemology is precisely not chronology but the resonances that cut across it.

This exploratory, provisional, propositional mode of knowing in Mackey's po-etics is deeply rooted in his interest in post-bop jazz and world music, and it is no accident that jazz, in particular, is such a common touchstone in the pages of *Orphic Bend*. Every poet in this study has referenced jazz as a benchmark for their practice, and, for most, these literary practices are inconceivable without jazz as an aesthetic model, prompt, and interlocutor. While the tradition of poetry shaped by its relationship to music extends to the ancient roots of lyric, since the emergence of jazz as a defining force in American literature, it is the trajectory of jazz-inflected writing that most powerfully carves the Orphic bend.

Notes

Introduction

1. For a discussion of the role of music in lyric poetry, including the myth of Orpheus, see Robert von Hallberg, *Lyric Powers* (Chicago: University of Chicago Press, 2008).

2. M. Owen Lee, *Virgil as Orpheus: A Study of the Georgics* (New York: State University of New York Press, 1996), 3.

3. For an overview of the development of the myth of Orpheus, see John Warden, ed., *Orpheus: the Metamorphosis of a Myth* (Toronto, CA: University of Toronto Press, 1982).

4. Ovid, *Metamorphoses*, trans. Rolfe Humphries (Bloomington: Indiana University Press, 1968), 234.

5. Virgil, *Virgil's Georgics*, trans. Janet Lembke (New Haven, CT: Yale University Press, 2005), 69.

6. This gesture brings the myth of Orpheus in line with other myths that similarly invoke sexual violence as lying at the root of music. Particularly powerful on this account is the story of Syrinx, also recounted in Ovid's *Metamorphoses*. A river nymph known for her chastity, Syrinx escapes Pan's advances by being turned into river reeds, only to then be cut down by him and fashioned into his first set of pipes. The contrast between Syrinx's bodily, breathy music and Orpheus's lyre also frames John Ashbery's poem, "Syringa."

7. Kaja Silverman, *Flesh of My Flesh* (Palo Alto, CA: Stanford University Press, 2009), 7.

8. Maurice Blanchot, *The Space of Literature*, trans. Ann Smock (Lincoln: University of Nebraska Press, 1989), 176.

9. Silverman, *Flesh of My Flesh*, 6.

10. Silverman, *Flesh of My Flesh*, 4.

11. Lacan, *The Four Fundamental Concepts of Psycho-Analysis*, ed. Jacques-Alain Miller, trans. Alan Sheridan (New York: W. W. Norton, 1978), 72.

12. Lacan, *Four Fundamental Concepts*, 74.

13. Lacan, *Four Fundamental Concepts*, 83.

14. For discussions of the role of music in literary modernism, see Daniel Albright,

Untwisting the Serpent: Modernism in Music, Literature, and Other Arts (Chicago: University of Chicago Press, 2000) and Bradley Bucknell, *Literary Modernism and Musical Aesthetics: Pater, Pound, Joyce, and Stein* (Cambridge: Cambridge University Press, 2002).

15. For an essential discussion of the role of music in Zukofsky's poetry and poetics, see Mark Scroggins, *Louis Zukofsky and the Poetry of Knowledge* (Tuscaloosa: University of Alabama Press, 1998), particularly the section titled "*'A'*: Musical Form and Musical Knowledge," which provides three illuminating chapters on the subject.

16. Mackey cites Zukofsky several times throughout both of his collections of critical prose, *Paracritical Hinge* and *Discrepant Engagement*. See Nathaniel Mackey, *Discrepant Engagement: Dissonance, Cross-Culturality, and Experimental Writing* (Tuscaloosa: University of Alabama Press, 2000), and Nathaniel Mackey, *Paracritical Hinge* (Iowa City: University of Iowa Press, 2018).

17. Louis Zukofsky, *A* (New York: New Directions, 2011), 138.

18. Louis Zukofsky, *Prepositions* (Berkeley: University of California Press, 1981), 16.

19. Ezra Pound, *ABC of Reading* (New York: New Directions, 1960), 37.

20. Zukofsky, *Prepositions*, 78.

21. Scroggins, *Louis Zukofsky and the Poetry of Knowledge*, 218–19.

22. This framing of the argument is meant to recall two landmark works on the role of music in modernist poetry and poetics: Elizabeth Sewell's *The Orphic Voice: Poetry and Natural History* (New York: Harper & Row, 1971), and Walter Strauss's *Descent and Return: The Orphic Theme in Modern Literature* (Cambridge, MA: Harvard University Press, 1971).

23. John Taggart's interest in the visual arts is underscored in his work on Louis Zukofsky, particularly as it is found in his essay collection, *Songs of Degrees* (Tuscaloosa: University of Alabama Press, 1994); it is also powerfully apparent in his minutely meditative book, *Remaining in Light: Ant Meditations on a Painting by Edward Hopper* (Albany: SUNY Press, 1993).

24. For a discussion of Baraka's relationship to free jazz, see William J. Harris's essay, "'How You Sound?': Amiri Baraka Writes Free Jazz," in *Uptown Conversation: The New Jazz Studies*, ed. Robert G. O'Meally, Brent Hayes Edwards, and Farah Jasmine Griffin (New York: Columbia University Press, 2004).

Chapter 1

1. See Peter Kivy, *Osmin's Rage: Philosophical Reflections on Opera* (Princeton, NJ: Princeton University Press, 1988), esp. chapter 2.

2. See Mladen Dolar's contribution to *Opera's Second Death* (Abingdon, UK: Routledge, 2002), coauthored with Slavoj Žižek, for a discussion of how opera figures its larger politico-cultural moment.

3. For a discussion of the tension between purists and those more favorably inclined toward artistic collaborations, see Albright's *Untwisting the Serpent*.

4. Žižek and Dolar, *Opera's Second Death*, 4. Also, see Kivy's *Osmin's Rage* for its argument that opera is neither a compromise between music and drama nor a subgenre of either but, instead, a genre in its own right, the genre of "drama-made-music."

5. Brian Ferneyhough, *Collected Writings* (Reading, UK: Harwood Academic, 1995), 248.

6. Pound, *ABC of Reading*, 104–5.

7. Synopsis for *Shadowtime: An Opera with Music by Brian Ferneyhough and Words by Charles Bernstein* (Compact Disc. NMC, 2006), 13.

8. Humanism is a famously amorphous term, and it is well beyond the scope of this chapter to decisively define its parameters. Instead, I would simply note the specific role of Neoplatonic syncretism in the formation of opera, to which Pound returns and against which Bernstein rebels.

9. Margaret Fisher, *Ezra Pound's Radio Operas: The BBC Experiments, 1931–1933: The BBC Experiments, 1931–1933* (Cambridge, MA: MIT Press, 2002), xii–xiii. During the same period, Pound also composed a number of instrumental pieces, often using instruments made for him by the early-music enthusiast and instrument maker, Arnold Dolmetsch. In 1931, he also began work on his opera, *Cavalcanti*, and in 1932, he began work on a third, of which only the scene "Collus o Helliconii," on the Roman poet Catullus, is extant.

10. As A. David Moody's biography of Pound demonstrates, *Le testament* not only extends from Pound's lifelong interest in the relationship between poetry and music, but is preceded by a period in which Pound's life is deeply involved with a whole range of musical matters. See A. David Moody, *Ezra Pound: Poet; A Portrait of the Man and His Work* (Oxford: Oxford University Press, 2007).

11. Pound, *ABC of Reading*, 104.

12. Patricia Vacari, "Sparagmos: Orpheus Among the Christians," in *Orpheus: The Metamorphosis of a Myth* (Toronto, CA: University of Toronto Press, 1985), 68.

13. See the introduction to Walter Strauss's *Descent and Return: The Orphic Theme in Modern Literature* (Cambridge, MA: Harvard University Press, 1971), for his problematization of the distinction between the Apollonian and the Dionysian in the myth of Orpheus.

14. Strauss, in *Descent and Return*, usefully suggests that Romantic poets can be categorized according to their affinities for either Orpheus or Prometheus: "Certain Romantic poets are classifiable as Promethean (Shelley, Byron, Hugo) and others as Orphic (Novalis, Wordsworth, possibly Keats). . . . The differences can be summarized in this fashion: Prometheus and Orpheus are readily contrastable as half-gods and as mythological culture-heroes. Prometheus defies Zeus in behalf of mankind and is martyred for his deed; as a fire-stealer, he is at the same time the eternal rebel (joining forces with Faust, Satan, and Cain) and the representative of a 'progressive' Romantic humanism. Orpheus does not rebel; he refuses to accept the world as it is; he does not lead the people, he charms them. Prometheanism aims for an outer transformation of society; it proposes to ameliorate man's lot by external action. Orphism proposes to transmute the inner man by a confrontation with himself and to alter society only indirectly, through the changes that man can effect within himself. All of modern literature tends to fall within the area delimited by these two points of reference, rebellion and refusal" (10–11). While I recognize that Strauss's framework would clearly situate Pound as an inheritor of the Promethean disposition, my argument is that his turn to opera and his broader understanding of music and musicality demonstrate a powerfully Orphic sensibility, albeit one that clearly is not lost in dreamy contemplation.

15. Charles Baudelaire, "Richard Wagner and *Tannhäuser* in Paris," in *Selected Writings on Art and Literature*, trans. P. E. Charvet (London: Penguin Classics, 1995), 325.

16. Baudelaire, "Richard Wagner and *Tannhäuser* in Paris," 354–55.

17. Baudelaire, "Richard Wagner and *Tannhäuser* in Paris," 357.

18. For Emerson's role in Bernstein's poetics, see Joel Bettridge, *Reading as Belief: Language Writing, Poetics, Faith* (New York, Palgrave MacMillan, 2009).

19. Charles Bernstein, *Recalculating* (Chicago: University of Chicago Press, 2013), 124.

20. For a discussion of Bernstein's relationship to his predecessors, see Charles Altieri, "Avant-Garde or Arriere-Garde in Recent American Poetry," *Poetics Today* 20, no. 4 (1999): 629–53.

21. Charles Bernstein, "State of the Art," in *A Poetics* (Cambridge, MA: Harvard University Press, 1992), 8.

22. Kivy, *Osmin's Rage*, 37.

23. Plato, *The Republic*, trans. Desmond Lee (London: Penguin, 1955), 14.

24. F. W. Sternfeld, *The Birth of Opera* (Oxford: Clarendon, 1993), 37.

25. Charles Altieri, "Pound's Vorticism as a Renewal of Humanism," *Boundary 2: An International Journal of Literature and Culture* 12, no. 3 (1984): 441.

26. Altieri, "Pound's Vorticism as a Renewal of Humanism," 441.

27. Altieri, "Pound's Vorticism as a Renewal of Humanism," 451.

28. Ezra Pound, *Antheil and the Treatise on Harmony* (New York: Da Capo, 1968), 24.

29. Pound, *Antheil*, 37.

30. Pound, *Antheil*, 38.

31. Pound, *Antheil*, 48.

32. Pound, *Antheil*, 49.

33. Pound, *Antheil*, 62.

34. Ezra Pound, *Literary Essays of Ezra Pound* (New York: New Directions, 1968), 74–75.

35. Fisher, *Pound's Radio Operas*, 38.

36. Fisher, *Pound's Radio Operas*, 15.

37. Fisher, *Pound's Radio Operas*, 144.

38. Pound, *ABC of Reading*, 37.

39. Pound, *ABC of Reading*, 61.

40. Pound, *Literary Essays*, 3.

41. Pound, *ABC of Reading*, 198.

42. Pound, *Literary Essays*, 91.

43. Ezra Pound, *Ezra Pound and Music*, ed. R. Murray Schafer (New York: New Directions, 1977), 473.

44. Pound, *Ezra Pound and Music*, 469.

45. Pound, *Literary Essays*, 9.

46. Pound, *Ezra Pound and Music*, 479.

47. Fisher, *Ezra Pound's Radio Operas*, 126.

48. Bucknell, *Literary Modernism and Musical Aesthetics*, 84.

49. Albright, *Untwisting the Serpent*, 547.

50. Pound, *Antheil and the Treatise on Harmony*, 44–45.

51. Pound, *Ezra Pound and Music*, 74.

52. Pound, *Literary Essays*, 44.

53. Pound, *Literary Essays*, 56.

54. Charles Bernstein, "Pound and the Poetry of Today," in *My Way: Speeches and Poems* (Chicago: University of Chicago Press, 1999), 161–62.

55. Bernstein, "Pound and the Poetry of Today," 160.

56. Bernstein, "Pound and the Poetry of Today," 161.

57. Altieri, "Pound's Vorticism as a Renewal of Humanism," 453.

58. Charles Bernstein, "Time Out of Motion: Looking Ahead to See Backward," in *A Poetics* (Cambridge, MA: Harvard University Press, 1992), 120.

59. For a detailed discussion of Bernstein's use of musical metaphors and their relation to his practice, see John Shoptaw, "The Music of Construction: Measure and Polyphony in Ashbery and Bernstein," in *The Tribe of John: Ashbery and Contemporary Poetry*, ed. Susan Shultz (Tuscaloosa: University of Alabama Press, 1995).

60. Charles Bernstein, ed., *Close Listening: Poetry and the Performed Word* (Oxford: Oxford University Press, 1998), 9.

61. Bernstein, *Close Listening*, 18.

62. *Shadowtime*, 8.

63. Albright, *Untwisting the Serpent*, 165.

64. Albright, *Untwisting the Serpent*, 165.

65. Synopsis for *Shadowtime*, 14.

66. Musical and Other Notes to *Shadowtime*: An Opera with Music by Brian Ferneyhough and Words by Charles Bernstein, 17.

67. Walter Benjamin and Knut Tarnowski, "Doctrine of the Similar (1933)," *New German Critique*, no. 17 (1979): 65.

68. Marjorie Perloff provides a quite different treatment of this and other sections of *Shadowtime* in her book, *Unoriginal Genius: Poetry by Other Means in the New Century* (Chicago: University of Chicago Press, 2010). Perloff aptly reads the proceduralism of the opera as a kind of quasi-Oulipian production in which "Bernstein is dramatizing the obsession with order in what is a curiously disordered life" (97).

69. See "amphibole" in the *Oxford English Dictionary*. https://www-oed-com.

70. Synopsis for *Shadowtime*, 14.

71. Benjamin and Tarnowski, "Doctrine of the Similar (1933)," 68.

72. Joel Bettridge, "Charles Bernstein's *Shadowtime* and Faithful Interpretation," *Textual Practice* 21 (2007): 750.

73. Charles Bernstein, *Shadowtime*, Compact Disc (NMC, 2006), 62.

74. Bernstein, *Shadowtime*, 68.

75. Bernstein, *Shadowtime*, 74.

76. Bernstein, *Shadowtime*, 20.

77. Brian Ferneyhough, "Words and Music," *Argotist Online*, April 15, 2007. https://argotistonline.co.uk.

78. Sternfeld, *Birth of Opera*, 8.

79. Sternfeld, *Birth of Opera*, 9.

80. Synopsis for *Shadowtime*, 15.

81. Carolyn Abbate, *In Search of Opera* (Princeton, NJ: Princeton University Press, 2001), 3.

82. Synopsis for *Shadowtime*, 13.

83. Abbate, *In Search of Opera*, 40.

84. Emmanuel Levinas, *The Humanism of the Other*, trans. Nidra Poller (Champaign: University of Illinois Press, 2006), 45.

85. Levinas, *Humanism of the Other*, 50.

86. Tony Davies, *Humanism* (Abingdon, UK: Routledge, 1997), 132.

87. Bernstein, "State of the Art," 8.

88. Ben Yarmolinsky, introduction to *Blind Witness: Three American Operas*, edited by Charles Bernstein (New York: Factory School, 2008).

Chapter 2

1. For a broad discussion of the role of improvisation and spontaneity in poetry, music, and other arts of the period, see Daniel Belgrad, *The Culture of Spontaneity: Improvisation and the Arts in Postwar America* (Chicago: University of Chicago Press, 1998).

2. For a discussion of the defining role of jazz in Baraka's practice, see William J. Harris, *The Poetry and Poetics of Amiri Baraka: The Jazz Aesthetic* (Columbia, MO: University of Missouri Press, 1985).

3. Allen Ginsberg, *Howl: 50th Anniversary Edition* (New York: Harper Perennial Modern Classics, 1986), 163.

4. Jack Kerouac, "Essentials of Spontaneous Prose," in *The Portable Beat Reader*, ed. Anne Charters (New York: Viking, 1992), 484–85.

5. Blanchot, *Space of Literature*, 99.

6. Gerald Bruns, *Material of Poetry* (Athens: University of Georgia Press, 2012), 70.

7. Blanchot, *Space of Literature*, 173.

8. Bruns, *Material of Poetry*, 70.

9. Bruns, *Material of Poetry*, 73.

10. Robert Creeley, *The Collected Essays of Robert Creeley* (Berkeley: University of California Press, 1989), 28.

11. Creeley, *Collected Essays*, 28.

12. Creeley, *Collected Essays*, 487.

13. Creeley, *Collected Essays*, 488.

14. Creeley, *Collected Essays*, 490.

15. Creeley, *Collected Essays*, 494–95.

16. Creeley, *Collected Essays*, 591.

17. Robert Creeley, "Appearing with John Ashbery in 'Attitudes Towards the Flame,'" PennSound, 1983, http://writing.upenn.edu.

18. For a discussion of the role of music in Creeley's serial poetry, see Joseph Conte's *Unending Design: The Forms of Postmodern Poetry* (Ithaca, NY: Cornell University Press, 1991).

19. Robert Creeley, *The Collected Poems of Robert Creeley: 1945–1975* (Berkeley: University of California Press, 1975), 41.

20. Creeley, *Collected Poems: 1945–1975*, 129.

21. Creeley, *Collected Poems: 1945–1975*, 129.

22. Creeley, *Collected Poems: 1945–1975*, 215.

23. In addition to "A Song," *For Love* (included in *Collected Poems: 1945–1975*) also includes four poems titled "Song" and numerous other poems whose titles directly imply the importance of music and song: "Chanson," "A Counterpoint," "Air: 'Cat Bird Singing,'" "A Folk Song," "Ballad of the Despairing Husband," "Sing Song," "The Song," "Jack's Blues," and "Air: 'The Love of a Woman.'"

24. Creeley, *Collected Poems: 1945–1975*, 112.

25. Creeley, *Collected Poems: 1945–1975*, 112.

26. Creeley, *Collected Poems: 1945–1975*, 112.

27. Creeley, *Collected Poems: 1945–1975*, 112.

28. Vladimir Jankélévitch, *Music and the Ineffable*, trans. Carolyn Abbate (Princeton, NJ: Princeton University Press, 2003), 79.

29. Jankélévitch, *Music and the Ineffable*, 83.

30. Creeley, *Collected Poems: 1945–1975*, 112.

31. Creeley, *Collected Poems: 1945–1975*, 165.

32. Creeley, *Collected Poems: 1945–1975*, 164.

33. Creeley, *Collected Poems: 1945–1975*, 164.

34. Creeley, *Collected Poems: 1945–1975*, 164.

35. Creeley, *Collected Poems: 1945–1975*, 164.

36. Robert Creeley, *Collected Poems: 1975–2005* (Berkeley: University of California Press, 2005), 633.

37. Creeley, *Collected Poems: 1945–1975*, 193.

38. Creeley, *Collected Poems: 1945–1975*, 245.

39. Creeley, *Collected Poems: 1945–1975*, 258.

40. Silverman, *Flesh of My Flesh*, 10.

41. Silverman, *Flesh of My Flesh*, 11.

42. Benjamin Friedlander, "'What Is Experience?,'" in *Form, Power, and Person in Robert Creeley's Life andWork*, ed. Stephen Fredman and Steve McCaffery (Iowa City: University of Iowa Press, 2010), 209.

43. Friedlander, "'What Is Experience?,'" 227.

44. Friedlander, "'What Is Experience?,'" 228.

45. Creeley, *Collected Poems: 1945–1975*, 272.

46. Creeley, *Collected Poems: 1945–1975*, 272.

47. Creeley, *Collected Poems: 1945–1975*, 272.

48. Creeley, *Collected Poems: 1945–1975*, 272.

49. Creeley, *Collected Poems: 1945–1975*, 272.

50. Creeley, *Collected Poems: 1945–1975*, 272.

51. Creeley, *Collected Poems: 1975–2005*, 394.

52. Creeley, *Collected Poems: 1945–1975*, 207.

53. Creeley, *Collected Poems: 1945–1975*, 207.

54. Rachel Blau Du Plessis, "The Hole: Death, Sexual Difference, and Gender Contradictions in Robert Creeley's Poetry," in *Form, Power, and Person in Robert Creeley's Life andWork*, ed. Stephen Fredman and Steve McCaffery (Iowa City: University of Iowa Press, 2010), 92.

55. Du Plessis, "The Hole," 92.

56. Silverman, *Flesh of My Flesh*, 4.

57. Robert Creeley, *Contexts of Poetry: Interviews, 1961–1971*, 1st ed. (Bolinas, CA: Four Seasons Foundation, 1973), 146.

58. Creeley, *Collected Poems: 1975–2005*, xi.

59. Creeley, *Collected Poems: 1975–2005*, 429.

60. Creeley, *Collected Essays*, 493–94.

61. Creeley, *Collected Poems: 1945–1975*, 409.

62. Creeley, *Collected Poems: 1945–1975*, 358.

63. Creeley, *Collected Poems: 1945–1975*, 358.

64. For a discussion of "My New Mexico," see Charles Altieri, "What Does *Echoes* Echo?," in *Form Power and Person in Robert Creeley's Life and Work*, ed. Fredman Stephen and McCaffrey Steve (Iowa City: University of Iowa Press, 2010).

65. Creeley, *Collected Poems: 1945–1975*, 389.

66. Creeley, *Collected Poems: 1945–1975*, 427.

67. Creeley, *Collected Poems: 1945–1975*, 427.

68. Creeley, *Collected Poems: 1945–1975*, 427.

69. Creeley, *Collected Poems: 1945–1975*, 402.

Chapter 3

1. Brad Haas, "John Taggart Flashpoint Interview," *Flashpoint Magazine*, February 2002, http://www.flashpointmag.com.

2. An important early consideration of this topic is Rochelle Ratner's essay, "The Poet as Composer: An Inquiry into the Work of John Taggart," which appeared in *Paper Air* 2, no. 1 (1974). Mark Scroggins also takes up the topic at the conclusion of his study, *Louis Zukofsky and the Poetry of Knowledge*, in which he notes that Taggart's penchant for Zukofsky-esque musical forms is balanced by an equal emphasis on voice. As he puts it, "Taggart's mature poetics, which have come to fruition in the years since 1979's Dodeka, are founded on both the Zukofskyan notion of the poem as melody, as musical composition, and Olson's Projectivist emphasis on the poet's voice as active performer of the poem"; see Scroggins, *Louis Zukofsky and the Poetry of Knowledge*, 303. More recently, Patrick Pritchett's "'Giant Steps,' John Taggart and Messianic Jazz" (https://jacket2.org) and Peter O'Leary's, "This Poem Is a Song an Act a Work of Love" (jacket2.Org/article/poem-song-act-work-love) both approach Taggart's relationship to music. Both of these essays are included in the *Jacket2* special issue from 2014, which is an indispensable resource for those interested in Taggart's work.

3. Gil Ott and Toby Olson, "Interview with John Taggart," *Paper Air* 2, no. 1 (1974): 49, eclipsearchive.org/projects/PAPER/PA2.1/contents.html.

4. As Mark Scroggins discusses in his treatment of Taggart in the conclusion of *Louis Zukofsky and the Poetry of Knowledge*, Taggart thus continues the Poundian tradition of invoking the fugue as a structural analogy to poetic composition.

5. Taggart, *Songs of Degrees*, 189.

6. Ott and Olson, "Interview with John Taggart," 50.

7. Taggart, *Songs of Degrees*, 126.

8. Taggart, *Songs of Degrees*, 197.

9. Taggart, *Songs of Degrees*, 112.

10. Zukofsky, *Prepositions*, 12.

11. Taggart, *Songs of Degrees*, 197.

12. Taggart, *Songs of Degrees*, 189.

13. John Taggart, *Is Music: Selected Poems* (Port Townsend, WA: Copper Canyon, 2010), 17.

14. Taggart, *Is Music*, 17.

15. Taggart, *Is Music*, 17.

16. Taggart, *Is Music*, 17.

17. Taggart, *Is Music*, 18.

18. For a close treatment of the relationship between Taggart's poem and Coltrane's song that inspired it, see Pritchett, "'Giant Steps.'"

19. Taggart, *Is Music*, 44.

20. Taggart, *Is Music*, 44.

21. Taggart, *Is Music*, 44.

22. Taggart, *Is Music*, 44.

23. Ott and Olson, "Interview with John Taggart," 50.

24. The importance of war as the crisis for which Taggart seeks peace in poetry is at the center of Robert Creeley's poem "John's Song," from *If I Were Writing This* (2003). Marrying his characteristic line and Taggart's repetition, Creeley writes, "If ever there is / if ever, if ever / there is, if ever there is / . . . No more war, dear brother, / no more, no more war / if ever there is" (*The Collected Poems of Robert Creeley: 1975–2005*, 598).

25. Toby Olson, "Spirit Image, Kerry Clouds, Peace on Earth: A Few Old Memories and New Thoughts About John Taggart," *Paper Air* 2, no. 1 (1979), 3. http://eclipsearchive.org.

26. Taggart, *Is Music*, 48.

27. Taggart, *Is Music*, 51.

28. Taggart, *Is Music*, 60.

29. Taggart's use of this image is a direct link to Robert Duncan's use of the same image in his "*Seventeenth Century Suite in Homage to the Metaphysical Genius in English Poetry (1590–1690)*," from *Groundwork*. Duncan quotes Robert Southwell's poem "The Burning Babe" and then mirrors Southwell's image of Christ as "a babe of fire" who purifies mankind's sins with the image of the napalm ravaged children of Vietnam, "I am looking upon burn faces / that have known catastrophe incommensurate / with meaning, beyond hate or loss or / Christian martyrdom, unredeemed. My heart / caves into a space it seems / to have long feard." See Robert Duncan, *Groundwork: Before the War, in the Dark* (New York: New Directions, 2006), 79.

30. Taggart, *Is Music*, 48.

31. Taggart, *Is Music*, 50.

32. Taggart, *Is Music*, 86.

33. Taggart, *Songs of Degrees*, 77.

34. Taggart, *Songs of Degrees*, 77.

35. As such, the project of "Slow Song" can be understood as in line with the painterly abstraction that New York School poets developed in response to their contemporaries in the visual arts. See Michael Davidson, "Ekphrasis and the Postmodern Painter Poem," *Journal of Aesthetics and Art Criticism* 42, no. 1 (1983): 69–79, https://doi.org/10.2307/429948.

36. Ott and Olson, "Interview with John Taggart," 48.

37. Ott and Olson, "Interview with John Taggart," 47–48.

38. Taggart, *Songs of Degrees*, 70.

39. Taggart, *Songs of Degrees*, 71.

40. Taggart, *Is Music*, 35.

41. Taggart, *Is Music*, 35.

42. Taggart, *Is Music*, 38.

43. Taggart, *Is Music*, 41.

44. Taggart, *Is Music*, 35.

45. Taggart, *Is Music*, 36.

46. Taggart, *Is Music*, 38.

47. Williams, *The Collected Poems of William Carlos Williams, Volume 2: 1939–1962* (New York: New Directions, 1991), 55.

48. Williams, *Collected Poems, Volume 2*, 55.

49. Taggart, *Is Music*, 39.

50. Taggart, *Is Music*, 41.

51. Taggart, *Is Music*, 43.

52. For a discussion of the technical relationship between the chapel and Feldman's piece, see Steven Johnson, "Rothko Chapel and Rothko's Chapel," *Perspectives of New Music* 32, no. 2 (Summer 1994): 6–53. As Johnson demonstrates, Feldman adopted formal procedures analogous to the structure of the chapel, in particular his use of discrete sections and of "vertical" and "linear time." These concepts come from the work of the musicologist Lawrence Kramer and designate two poles of time in the philosophy of music. In Kramer's framework, "vertical time," which he sites as the purview of Feldman, arrests the flow of chronological time and holds it in extended stasis, a process Johnson identifies with Feldman's use of extended single cords. By contrast, "linear time" is characterized by its directionality, as is found in melody.

53. Johnson, "Rothko Chapel and Rothko's Chapel."

54. Sheldon Nodelman, *The Rothko Chapel Paintings: Origins, Structure, Meaning* (Austin: University of Texas Press, 1997), 309.

55. Nodelman, *Rothko Chapel Paintings*, 330.

56. John Taggart, *Loop* (Los Angeles: Sun and Moon, 1991), 131.

57. Taggart, *Loop,* 132.

58. Taggart, *Loop,* 136.

59. For a discussion of the relationship between Kierkegaard's meaning of "repetition" and Taggart's practice, see Peter O'Leary, "This Poem Is a Song a Work of Love."

60. For a discussion of the role of Kierkegaard's "repetition" in the Rothko Chapel, see "Part III" of Nodelman, "The Meaning of the Chapel Installation," in *Rothko Chapel Paintings*, 333–38.

61. Soren Kierkegaard, *Fear and Trembling / Repetition*, trans. Edna Hong (Princeton, NJ: Princeton University Press, 1983), 131.

62. Kierkegaard, *Fear and Trembling / Repetition,* 294. Although Kierkegaard does not name Orpheus, he returns to the structure of the myth as he discusses the situation of a character at the heart of his tract on repetition, a young man who is melancholic over the change in his feelings about his lover. As Kierkegaard writes, "The young girl was not his beloved: she was the occasion that awakened the poetic in him and made him a poet. That was why he could love only her, never forget her, never want to love another, and yet continually only long for her. She was drawn into his whole being; the memory of her was forever alive. She had meant much to him; she had made him a poet—and precisely thereby had signed her own death sentence" (138). While Kierkegaard casts the poet as tragically

stuck in the mode of recollection, Taggart situates the task of the poet (and the musician) as that of repetition

63. Taggart, *Is Music*, 108.

64. Taggart, *Is Music*, 109.

65. During a class visit at DePaul University in 2005, Taggart told students, "If you read a poem silently, you have defeated the poem."

66. Taggart, *Loop*, 140.

67. Nodelman, *Rothko Chapel Paintings*, 313.

68. Taggart, *Loop*, 137.

69. Taggart, "Reading at the Rothko Chapel, Houston, TX, October 25, 2012."

70. Taggart, *Loop*, 137.

71. Taggart, *Loop*, 140.

72. Taggart, *Loop*, 140.

73. Taggart, *Loop*, 164.

74. Taggart, *Loop*, 142.

75. Taggart, *Loop*, 166.

76. Taggart, *Loop*, 170.

77. Taggart, *Loop*, 142.

78. Taggart, *Loop*, 143.

79. Nodelman, *Rothko Chapel Paintings*, 331.

80. Taggart, *Loop*, 153.

81. Taggart, *Loop*, 152.

82. Taggart, *Loop*, 153.

83. Taggart, *Loop*, 171.

84. Taggart, *Loop*, 171.

85. Olson, "Spirit Image, Kerry Clouds, Peace on Earth," 3.

86. John Taggart, *Pastorelles* (Chicago: Flood Editions, 2004), 3.

87. Taggart, *Pastorelles*, 2.

88. Taggart, *Pastorelles*, 2.

89. Taggart, *Is Music*, 98.

90. Taggart, *Pastorelles*, 104.

91. Taggart, *Pastorelles*, 93.

92. Taggart, *Pastorelles*, 93.

93. Taggart, *Pastorelles*, 93.

94. Taggart, *Pastorelles*, 95.

95. Taggart, *Pastorelles*, 95.

96. Taggart, *Pastorelles*, 97.

97. Taggart, *Pastorelles*, 97.

98. John Taggart, *There Are Birds* (Chicago: Flood Editions, 2008), 14.

99. Taggart, *There Are Birds*, 12.

100. Taggart, *There Are Birds*, 13.

101. Taggart, *There Are Birds*, 23.

102. Taggart, *There Are Birds*, 62.

103. Taggart, *There Are Birds*, 13.

104. Taggart, *There Are Birds*, 14.

105. Taggart, *There Are Birds*, 15.

106. Taggart, *There Are Birds*, 22.

107. Taggart, *There Are Birds*, 15.

108. Taggart, *There Are Birds*, 16.

109. Taggart, *There Are Birds*, 16.

110. Taggart, *There Are Birds*, 17.

111. Taggart, *There Are Birds*, 31.

112. Taggart, *There Are Birds*, 32.

113. Taggart, *There Are Birds*, 23.

114. Taggart, *There Are Birds*, 18.

115. Taggart, *There Are Birds*, 19.

116. Taggart, *There Are Birds*, 19.

117. Taggart, *There Are Birds*, 42.

118. Taggart, *There Are Birds*, 37.

119. Derrida, "A Silkworm of One's Own (Points of View Stitched on the Other Veil)," trans. Geoffrey Bennington, *Oxford Literary Review* 18, no. 1/2 (1996): 6.

120. Taggart, *There Are Birds*, 69–70.

121. Geoffrey Chaucer, John Strong Perry Tatlock, and Percy MacKaye, *The Complete Poetical Works of Geoffrey Chaucer* (New York: Macmillan, 1912), 443.

122. Taggart, *There Are Birds*, 73.

123. Taggart, *There Are Birds*, 73.

124. Taggart, *There Are Birds*, 87.

125. Taggart, *There Are Birds*, 88.

126. Taggart, *There Are Birds*, 89.

Chapter 4

1. Although Eurydice's role in the Orpheus myth is structurally in the service of his narrative, several later retellings address her role, beginning at least with the earliest surviving opera, Jacopo Peri's *Eurydice*, from 1600, and through Harryette Mullen's poem, "Eurydice," from *Sleeping with the Dictionary* (Berkeley: University of California Press, 2000). Mullen's poem casts Eurydice's plight as a tragedy in which she has a voice but is unheard; she is also identified with Blackness, as the poem reads, she "can't wait to be sprung from shadow, / to be known from a hole in the ground" (26). Mullen stops short of imagining Eurydice as claiming the poet's power of music, though, and instead concludes, "music sways her, she concedes, / as darker she goes deeper," both relinquishing the will Eurydice had expressed at the opening of the poem and returning her to the darkness with which she is identified.

2. For a discussion of Morris's shift from slam poetry to that of the sonically based avant-garde, see Christine Hume, "Improvisational Insurrection," in *American Poets in the 21st Century: The New Poetics*, ed. Claudia Rankine and Lisa Sewell (Middletown, CT: Wesleyan University Press, 2007), and Kathleen Crown, "Sonic Revolutionaries: Voice and Experiment in the Spoken-Word Poetry of Tracie Morris," in *We Who Love to Be Astonished*,

ed. Laura Hinton and Cynthia Hogue (Tuscaloosa: University of Alabama Press, 2002)

3. J. L. Austin, *How to Do Things with Words* (Cambridge, MA: Harvard University Press, 1962), 6–7.

4. The foundational step of Morris's reconfiguration of Austin is for her to claim the validity of poetry, including sound poetry. Austin explicitly excludes poetic and theatrical language on the grounds that such language is unserious. As he argues, "language in such circumstances is in special ways—intelligibly—used not seriously, but in ways *parasitic* upon its normal use—ways which fall under the doctrine of the *etiolations* of language" (22). The whole of Morris's career and, as she argues, that of many other Black artists, is grounded in the belief that precisely because of its visionary, creative potential, poetic language is, in fact, deeply serious and rejuvenative, not "parasitic."

5. Tracie Morris, *Who Do with Words: (A Blerd Love Tone Manifesto)* (Tucson, AZ: Chax, 2018), 49.

6. Austin, *How to Do Things with Words*, 160.

7. Morris, *Who Do with Words*, 67.

8. Morris, *Who Do with Words*, 96.

9. Morris, *Who Do with Words*, 67.

10. Morris, *Who Do with Words*, 78.

11. Morris, *Who Do with Words*, 67.

12. Morris, *Who Do with Words*, 15.

13. Morris, "Tracie Morris," PennSound, May 1, 2019, http://writing.upenn.edu.

14. The recording of Morris's performance is available at PennSound, the online audio poetry archive hosted by the University of Pennsylvania Center for Programs in Contemporary Writing. This archive is the most complete collection of recordings of Morris's live performances and is the source of all such performances discussed in this chapter, other than those published on Bandcamp.com in association with *Handholding: 5 Kinds: Sonic, Textual Engagements* (Tucson, AZ: Kore, 2018).

15. Austin, *How to Do Things with Words*, 6.

16. Hume, "Improvisational Insurrection," 417.

17. Fred Moten, *Black and Blur* (Durham, NC: Duke University Press, 2017), 82.

18. Walton Muyumba, *The Shadow and the Act: Black Intellectual Practice, Jazz Improvisation, and Philosophical Pragmatism* (Chicago: University of Chicago Press, 2009), 20.

19. Muyumba, *Shadow and the Act*, 129.

20. Fred Moten, *Stolen Life* (Durham, NC: Duke University Press, 2018), 49.

21. Morris, "Tracie Morris."

22. Moten, *Black and Blur*, ix.

23. Morris, "Tracie Morris."

24. Albert Glinsky, *Theremin: Ether Music and Espionage* (Champaign: University of Illinois Press, 2000).

25. Morris, *Who Do with Words*, 77.

26. For a close reading of this poem, see Hume, "Improvisational Insurrection."

27. Morris, "Tracie Morris."

28. This is a general rule. For instance, Morris describes her Akomfrah "handholding"

as "an erasure poem," and the Cage "handholding" is perhaps best understood as a conceptual poem, consisting as it does of several minutes of superimposed silence and near-silent ambient noise recorded at six separate locations.

29. Morris, *Handholding*, 118.

30. Morris, *Handholding*, 5.

31. Morris, *Who Do with Words*, 77.

32. Morris, *Handholding*, 57.

33. Morris, *Handholding*, 10.

34. Morris, *Handholding*, 58.

35. Morris, *Handholding*, 69.

36. Morris, *Handholding*, 69.

37. Morris, *Who Do with Words*, 22.

38. Morris, *Handholding*, 69.

39. Morris, *Handholding*, 69.

40. Morris, *Handholding*, 70.

41. Morris, *Handholding*, 70.

42. Morris, *Handholding*, 70.

43. Morris, *Handholding*, 71.

44. Gertrude Stein, *Selected Writings of Gertrude Stein*, ed. Carl van Vechten (New York: Vintage, 1990), 494.

45. Morris, *Handholding*, 71.

46. Morris, *Handholding*, 72.

47. Marjorie Perloff, *Poetics of Indeterminacy: Rimbaud to Cage* (Evanston, IL: Northwestern University Press, 1993), 108.

48. Juliana Spahr, *Everybody's Autonomy* (Tuscaloosa: University of Alabama Press, 2011), 44.

49. Elizabeth Frost, *The Feminist Avant-Garde in American Poetry* (Iowa City: University of Iowa Press, 2003), 18.

50. Priscilla Wald, *Constituting Americans: Cultural Anxiety and Narrative Form* (Durham, NC: Duke University Press, 1995), 271.

51. Wald, *Constituting Americans*, 273.

52. Mullen, *Sleeping with the Dictionary*, x.

53. Robin Tremblay-McGaw, "Enclosure and Run: The Fugitive Recyclopedia of Harryette Mullen's Writing," *MELUS* 35, no. 2 (Summer 2010): 72.

54. Deborah Mix, "Tender Revisions: Harryette Mullen's Trimmings and SPeRMKT," *American Literature: A Journal of Literary History, Criticism, and Bibliography* 77, no. 1 (March 2005): 86–87.

55. Morris, *Handholding*, 7.

56. Moten, *Stolen Life*, 243.

57. Morris's framing of her text in relation to Stein also recalls Mullen's discussion of literary call-and-response in the work of Frederick Douglass. In her landmark essay, "African Signs and Spirit Writing," Mullen draws attention to Frederick Douglass, "literally writing 'in the spaces' of his master's copybook," as he articulates a secular and political experience of language acquisition and identity formation (7). This interlineal identity is

both material and figurative, even allegorical in importance to Mullen's practice of writing in the context of a given literary tradition that is predominantly white. Morris's practice in *Handholding* should be understood as a continuation of this tradition. Douglass's work is performative in the way Morris recasts Austen's term: he performs an identity in and through his language use; similarly, first Mullen and later Morris continue to assert and recast claims to Black identity in the continuously evolving context of cultural, literary, political, and economic history.

58. Morris, *Handholding*, 73.

59. Morris, *Handholding*, 73.

60. Morris, *Handholding*, 73.

61. Morris, *Handholding*, 73.

62. There's no way to be sure, but "Sona" seems to be a reference to a character from the online multiplayer video game "League of Legends." As the "League of Legends Fandom" site describes, Sona's powers are, appropriately, acoustic, with her attacks including the "power chord," the "hymn of valor," the "aria of perseverance," the "song of celerity," and the "crescendo."

63. Morris, *Handholding*, 73.

64. To that incident, Morris responds, "what **she** said here is unfortunate. It isn't fortune and it isn't innate. I'll leave it there but it was a disappointment. I'll say that. (She won't). A 'a white old chat churner' after all" (102). Morris's voice in her performance of this passage registers her disappointment in Stein as she turns Stein's own words against her, Morris framing Stein's use of the epithet as evidence that Stein fell into the role of racist, gossipy white privilege.

65. Stein, *Selected Writings of Gertrude Stein*, 480.

66. Morris also seems to have this passage in mind in her preface to the piece. She notes that her "muse is off on her own, talking to other muses like . . . my ancestors' kitchen aesthetics. The way they manifested art in kitchens at home and homes away from home (two of my mother's aunts had their own restaurants). They had a whole other conversation about food that Stein could not enter. It was about the context in which they cooked, in which cooking was done, eating was done. It was a conversation about who cooked for whom" (*Handholding*, 71).

67. Morris, *Handholding*, 85.

68. Morris, *Handholding*, 86.

69. Moten, *Stolen Life*, 21–22.

70. Morris, *Handholding*, 105.

71. Morris, *Handholding*, 105.

72. Morris, *Handholding*, 105.

73. As Morris notes in the preface to "Resonatæ," "Ursonata" has been an important text for contemporary sound poets, with particularly well-known performances by Jaap Blonk and Christian Bök. The nationalities of these performers (Dutch and Canadian, respectively) is relevant, as it is for Morris, for how their relationships to both their own native languages and those they have acquired influence their performances.

74. Morris, *Handholding*, 118.

75. Morris, *Who Do with Words*, 61.

Chapter 5

1. See Caroline Abbate, "Music—Drastic or Gnostic?" *Critical Inquiry* 30, no. 3 (2004): 505–36. Accessed October 16, 2020. doi:10.1086/421160. For a treatment of Mackey's Gnosticism, see Peter O'Leary's *Gnostic Contagion: Robert Duncan and the Poetry of Illness* (Middletown, CT: Wesleyan University Press, 2002).

2. Mackey's writing resonates with Robert von Hallberg's analysis of the importance of music to lyric poetry, *Lyric Powers*. As von Hallberg writes, defending the sense of mystery that seems to inevitably imbue proposed definitions of the relationship between the arts: "That musicality is magical, unaccountably charming; that what musicians produce seems to correspond somehow to something heavenly or cosmic—these notions are needed still. One should remember, before dismissing Orpheus and the spheres as superstition, that modern secular musicology has no convincing account of the power of music. Music seems to correspond to some transcendent order, though one cannot define that order. Musicality is a sign of that order, but an indecipherable code. Paraphrase certainly won't do. Musicality corresponds *to* . . . It rather signifies the very idea of affective correspondence" (144, emphasis in the original).

3. Nathaniel Mackey series *From a Broken Bottle Traces of Perfume Still Emanate* (New York: New Directions, 2010) consists of the following volumes: *Bedouin Hornbook* (1986); *Djbot Baghostus's Run* (1993); *Atet A. D.* (2001); *Bass Cathedral* (2008); and *Late Arcade* (2017).

4. Mackey, *From a Broken Bottle*, 1–3:527.

5. Nathaniel Mackey, "Sound and Sentiment, Sound and Symbol," in *Discrepant Engagement*, 233–34.

6. For a discussion of his relation to Gnosticism, see Peter O'Leary, "Deep Trouble / Deep Treble: Nathaniel Mackey's Gnostic Rasp," in his book, *Gnostic Contagion*.

7. Norman Finkelstein, "Nathaniel Mackey and the Unity of All Rites," *Contemporary Literature* 49, no. 1 (2008): 52.

8. My analysis of musicality in Mackey's poetics is deeply indebted to those who have previously discussed his intense interest in music. In particular, Brent Hayes Edwards's analysis of Mackey's "poetics of reprise" (586), often lurks behind my argument, and I will return to his discussion in detail with respect to Mackey's use of under-the-line poems. See Brent Hayes Edwards, "Notes on Poetics Regarding Mackey's 'Song,'" *Callaloo* 23, no. 2 (2000): 572–91. Edwards's argument is exemplary both for its attention to the conceptual relationships between the poetry and the music and for its self-conscious reticence about being too focused on musicality. The relationship between Mackey's poetry and music is also demonstrated by his collaborations with musicians, as I discuss in the conclusion. The earliest recording of Mackey's collaborations was his 1994 album *Strick*, with musicians Royal Hartigan and Hafez Modirzadeh. Jeffrey Gray and Richard Quinn both discussed the album in their contributions to the 2000 special issue of *Callaloo* dedicated to Mackey. Gray and Quinn both argue that in Mackey's poetics, formal innovation is intimately tied to cultural critique. Arguing that Mackey's work is "identitarian" and "multicultural," respectively, Gray and Quinn both compellingly explore larger implications of the text-music interaction on *Strick*. Thus commenting that "Mackey's raspiness is in his prosody" (631), Gray argues that *Strick* operates as a site of contestation between the aural and the textual, "the heard and the written" (630). As such, it proposes "a musical rather than a chronological

way of cohering, dissolving the illusion of narrativity through which experience is usually forced to make sense" (624). Quinn similarly locates an "aural oscillation" in *Strick*, "a movement in sound which critiques word, thought, concept or category as rigid products" (609), and also concludes that Mackey's attack on categorization articulates a multicultural ethics.

9. Nathaniel Mackey, "Cante Moro," in *Sound States: Innovative Poetic and Acoustical Technologies*, ed. Adelaide Morris (Chapel Hill: University of North Carolina Press, 1997), 196.

10. Mackey, "Cante Moro," 196.

11. Mackey, "Limbo, Dislocation, Phantom Limb: Wilson Harris and the Caribbean Occasion," in *Discrepant Engagement*, 163.

12. Mackey, "Limbo, Dislocation," 195.

13. Mackey, "Limbo, Dislocation," 195.

14. Mackey, "Limbo, Dislocation," 199.

15. Mackey, "Limbo, Dislocation," 199.

16. Mackey, "Cante Moro," 198.

17. Bruce Fink, *The Lacanian Subject: Between Language and Jouissance* (Princeton, NJ: Princeton University Press, 1995), 90.

18. Fink, *Lacanian Subject*, 94.

19. Devin Johnston, "Nathaniel Mackey and Lost Time: 'The Phantom Light of All Our Day,'" *Callaloo* 23, no. 2 (2000): 563.

20. Paul Naylor, "An Interview with Nathaniel Mackey," *Callaloo* 23, no. 2 (2000): 647.

21. Naylor, "Interview with Nathaniel Mackey," 647.

22. Mackey, "Sound and Sentiment," 258.

23. Mackey, "Sound and Sentiment," 259.

24. Mackey, "Sound and Sentiment," 258.

25. Susan Stewart, "Letter on Sound," in *Close Listening: Poetry and the Performed Word*, ed. Charles Bernstein (Oxford: Oxford University Press, 1998), 33.

26. Stewart, "Letter on Sound," 34.

27. Nathaniel Mackey, "The Changing Same: Black Music in the Poetry of Amiri Baraka," in *Discrepant Engagement*, 46.

28. Mackey, "Changing Same," 40.

29. The first of the letters in this form was originally published as "Song of the Andoumboulou 6" in *Eroding Witness* (Champaign: University of Illinois Press, 1984), selected by Michael S. Harper for the National Poetry Series in 1985. The letter is not collected in the volumes of the fiction, and, unlike the letters in *From a Broken Bottle*, it is undated. The first letter collected in the fiction bears a compelling structural similarity to the story of Orpheus. As I discuss in the introduction, the oldest known reference we have to Orpheus, Ibycus's line "famous Orpheus," indicates that the renown of the archetypal poet extends well beyond our written records. Just so, Mackey's early letter from *Eroding Witness* begins with reference to a conversation that extends beyond our given pages; its first words are, "in one of your earlier letters" (50). Taken together, these early instances of the letters help to suggest the many ways in which they, like the poetry, engage with seriality as a way of questioning the boundaries of any individual work.

30. Mackey seems to play upon this insistent textuality of the epistolary form, as well as

the compulsion to configure aesthetic practice as premised upon loss, in the closing para-
graph of the first letter. N. writes in frustration to Angel of Dust—"This dialogue seems
hopelessly enmeshed in the very 'ontology of loss' of which you've insisted I disburden
myself"—and closes the letter with the admonishment, "please don't expect anything more
in the way of words" (4). Of course, tens of thousands of words follow.

31. Mackey, *From a Broken Bottle*, 1–3:43.

32. Mackey, *From a Broken Bottle*, 1–3:49.

33. Mackey, *From a Broken Bottle*, 1–3:43.

34. Mackey, *From a Broken Bottle*, 1–3:45–46.

35. Mackey, *From a Broken Bottle*, 1–3:46.

36. Mackey, *From a Broken Bottle*, 1–3:47.

37. Mackey, *From a Broken Bottle*, 1–3:47.

38. Mackey, *From a Broken Bottle*, 1–3:48.

39. Mackey, *From a Broken Bottle*, 1–3:475.

40. Mackey, *From a Broken Bottle*, 1–3:475.

41. Mackey, *From a Broken Bottle*, 1–3:481.

42. Mackey, *From a Broken Bottle*, 1–3:494.

43. The proximity of poetry and music in Mackey's work is a touchstone throughout
Fred Moten's *In the Break: The Aesthetics of the Black Radical Tradition* (Minneapolis: University
of Minnesota Press, 2003).

44. The title of this volume, *Atet A. D.*, relates to both a change in the name of N.'s
band and to the thematic concerns of this text. Having decided that their name, The Mystic
Horn Society, privileged woodwinds, and masculinity by extension, the band seeks a new
name. The renaming makes reference to Egyptian mythology, as "Aunt Nancy's idea was
that [they] call [themselves] the Maatet, or simply, Maatet, a name the Egyptians gave one
of the boats in which the sun sails across the sky, the one it boards at dawn, the morning
boat (the other being the one in which it completes its journey, Sektet, the evening boat).
Maatet joins Atet, a more common name for the morning boat, with Maat, the name of
the goddess of truth: Maat + Atet = Maatet" (43). The senses of heliocentric rebirth and
truth in this naming are then coupled with Lambert's suggestion for the band's new name,
The Molimo Sound Ensemble, which draws on "the molimo spirit" of the Mbuti, "a spirit of
mediation or reconciliation" (42). Through a series of substitutions, contractions, and apos-
traphizations, the band settles on the name "The Molimo m'Atet," a phrase that emphasizes
the gender uncertainty or androgyny of truthful rebirth.

The edenic drive behind this change in the band's name can also be heard in the rhyme
between the title of the book, *Atet A. D.*, and aetat AD. The prospect of performing a new
world also comes from N.'s mention of Julius Hemphill's piece "Dogon A. D." As N. writes
to Angel of Dust, Hemphill "says that 'A. D.' in the title of his piece . . . stands for Adaptive
Dance, that it came out of his reading an article about the Dogon deciding to reveal some
of their sacred dance rituals to attract the tourist trade. Before hearing this I took it to
mean Anno Domini, as most people probably do" (159–60).

45. Mackey, *From a Broken Bottle*, 1–3:404–5.

46. Mackey, *From a Broken Bottle*, 1–3:405.

47. Mackey, *From a Broken Bottle*, 1–3:405.

48. Mackey, *From a Broken Bottle*, 1–3:486.

49. Mackey, *From a Broken Bottle*, 1–3:487.

50. Mackey, *From a Broken Bottle*, 1–3:492.

51. Mackey, *From a Broken Bottle*, 1–3:493.

52. Conte, *Unending Design*, 53.

53. Ekkehard Jost, *Free Jazz* (Boston, MA: Da Capo Press, 1994), 153.

54. Jost, *Free Jazz*, 154.

55. Jost, *Free Jazz*, 162.

56. Mackey, *Eroding Witness*, 61.

57. Mackey, *Eroding Witness*, 60.

58. Mackey, *Eroding Witness*, 60–61.

59. Mackey, *Eroding Witness*, 60.

60. In classical prosody, amphimacers are also known as "cretics," associated with poetry characteristic of the island of Crete. The cretic is also discussed in book 3, part 3 of Plato's *Republic*, as a matter of concern for the role of music and poetry in education, as well as their relationship to one another. Socrates and Glaucon heartily agree that music should be subservient to poetry. Immediately after having banished the harp, zither, and flute from the republic because of their unnecessary and perhaps dangerous harmonic ranges, they agree that the lyre and the cithara should be retained for poetic accompaniment. After lauding the victory of Apollo's lyre over Marsyas's flute, Socrates and Glaucon go on to express their desire for regular rhythms, which "suit a life of courage and discipline" (101). Interestingly enough, while Socrates and Glaucon were able to locate preferable musical modes, rhythm is a mystery to them. Socrates says that the well-known musician Damon has vaguely described such a rhythmic pattern, and repeatedly states, "we'll consult Damon about it" (101). Thus, in Mackey's use of the cretic, we have a formal allusion to slippery, partially known musical terminology associated with an island.

61. It is not insignificant that the acoustic relationship between these words is reiterated in their semantic connection, with both "before" and "begins" serving as key terms establishing the poem's thematic concern with temporality.

62. Mackey, *Eroding Witness*, 60.

63. Mackey, *Eroding Witness*, 60.

64. Mackey, *Eroding Witness*, 60.

65. Mackey, *Eroding Witness*, 60.

66. Nathaniel Mackey, *School of Udhra* (San Francisco: City Lights, 1993), 44.

67. Mackey's use of this device clearly recalls that of Jack Spicer in *Heads of the Town up to the Aether*, included in his collected poems, *My Vocabulary Did This to Me*, as well as Ed Roberson in *Voices Cast Out to Talk Us In*.

68. Peter O'Leary, "An Interview with Nathaniel Mackey," *Chicago Review* 43 (1997): 42–43.

69. Edwards, "Notes on Poetics," 586.

70. Edwards, "Notes on Poetics," 585.

71. Edwards, "Notes on Poetics," 523.

72. Edwards, "Notes on Poetics," 585.

73. Jost, *Free Jazz*, 71.

74. Jost, *Free Jazz*, 83.

75. Jost, *Free Jazz*, 76–77.

76. Jost, *Free Jazz*, 77.

77. Jost, *Free Jazz*, 77.

78. Mackey, *School of Udhra*, 43.

79. Like "Alphabet of Ahtt," "Amma Seru's Hammer's Heated Fall" is unnumbered, though its place in the sequence indicates that it is effectively, "'mu' part nine."

80. Mackey, *School of Udhra*, 38.

81. Mackey, *School of Udhra*, 43.

82. Mackey, *School of Udhra*, 45. In an interview, Mackey comments that he was "also thinking of Olson's, 'That Island,'" when writing the "mu" series. Olson's poem reads: "That island / floating in the sea / just as the street-lights / come on," followed after several blank lines by the phrase, "*Moeurs de Societé*" (underlined in the original). As George Butterick tells us, this is most likely a reference to Ten Pound Island in Gloucester Harbor, which comes up elsewhere in *The Maximus Poems*. Perhaps the most compelling connection between this poem and Mackey's under-the-line poems is the interconnectedness of vision and invisibility. In Olson's piece, the island comes into being just as it falls from view—in the darkness of the night, beyond the fishbowl of the lighted streets.

The image of the "Floating Island" also resonates with Cecil Taylor's *Chinampa*, which is the subject of Fred Moten's exploration of "the beautiful distance between sound and the writing of sound" in his essay "Sound in Florescence: Cecil Taylor's *Floating Garden*," in *Sound States: Innovative Poetics and Acoustical Technologies*, ed. Adelaide Morris (Chapel Hill: University of North Carolina Press, 1997), 228.

After appearing at the end of "Poem for Don Cherry," the island becomes a recurring image throughout the "mu" series, particularly in the under-the-line (under-the-water?) poems. As the island imagery becomes more developed in the series, though such an analysis is beyond the bounds of the current discussion, the "mu" poems could certainly be very interestingly read as in conversation with the notion of *marronage*. See, for example, Aimé Césaire, "For Renée Depestre, Haitian Poet," as well as his *Discourse on Colonialism.*

Mackey's subsequent poetry collections, *Nod House* (New York: New Directions, 2011) and *Blue Fasa* (2015), continue the interweaving of "Song of the Andoumboulou" and "mu." Mackey's preface to *Nod House* discusses it as "a continuation of *Splay Anthem* and the work that came before it," xi. Noting the collection's "Eastern turn," he also describes its aspirations with respect to thematic resonances: "it wants to be a vibration society," xi.

83. Mackey, *School of Udhra*, 45.

84. Mackey, *School of Udhra*, 45.

85. Mackey, *School of Udhra*, 46.

86. Mackey, *School of Udhra*, 47.

87. Mackey, *Splay Anthem*, ix.

88. Mackey, *Splay Anthem*, xii–xiii.

89. Mackey, *Splay Anthem*, xiii.

90. Mackey, *Splay Anthem*, xv.

91. Mackey, *Splay Anthem*, 56.

92. Mackey, *Splay Anthem*, 87.

93. Mackey, *Splay Anthem*, 87.

94. Mackey, *Splay Anthem*, 116.

95. Mackey, *Splay Anthem*, 118.

96. Mackey, *Splay Anthem*, xiii.

97. Mackey, *Splay Anthem*, 30.

98. Mackey, *Splay Anthem*, 33.

99. Mackey, *Splay Anthem*, 3.

100. Mackey, *Splay Anthem*, 5.

101. Mackey, *Splay Anthem*, 7.

102. Mackey, *Splay Anthem*, 51.

103. Mackey, *Splay Anthem*, 57.

104. Mackey, *Splay Anthem*, 60.

105. Mackey, *Splay Anthem*, 72.

106. Mackey, *Splay Anthem*, 35.

107. Mackey, *Splay Anthem*, xvi.

Conclusion

1. Duncan, *Groundwork*, xiv.

2. O'Leary, *Gnostic Contagion*, 80.

3. O'Leary, *Gnostic Contagion*, 82.

4. For an important discussion of the role of the Vietnam War in Duncan's poetry and poetics, see Nathaniel Mackey's ranging, magisterial essay "Gassire's Lute: Robert Duncan's Vietnam War Poems," in *Paracritical Hinge*.

5. Robert Duncan, *Bending the Bow* (New York: New Directions, 1968).

6. For a discussion of the analogy between Duncan's poetics, Alexander Calder's mobiles, and Arnold Schoenberg's development of twelve-tone composition, see chapter 2, "Infinite Serial Form," in Conte, *Unending Design*.

7. Duncan, *Bending the Bow*, 7.

8. Duncan, *Bending the Bow*, 7.

9. Duncan, *Bending the Bow*, 8.

10. Duncan, *Opening of the Field*, 10.

11. Duncan, *Bending the Bow*, 16.

12. Duncan, *Bending the Bow*, 60.

13. Duncan, *Groundwork*, 16.

14. Duncan, *Groundwork*, 16.

15. Duncan, *Groundwork*, 17.

16. Spicer, *The House That Jack Built: The Collected Lectures of Jack Spicer*, ed. Peter Gizzi (Middletown, CT: Wesleyan University Press, 1998), 5.

17. As Gizzi notes in the introduction to *The House That Jack Built*, the film is "an underground camp classic" (188). For a discussion of the relationship between camp and the Orphic in Spicer's poetry, see Catherine Imbriglio, "'Impossible Audiences': Camp, the Orphic, and Art as Entertainment in Jack Spicer's Poetry," in *After Spicer: Critical Essays*, edited by John Vincent (Middletown, CT: Wesleyan University Press, 2011). Although Imbriglio does not elaborate in detail on Spicer's Orphic poetics and instead deploys the idea of the

Orphic as a foil for what she sees as Spicer's camp aesthetic, her discussion is useful for how she demonstrates Spicer deploying these contrary modes to destabilize one another and, thus, maintain an open and exploratory poetics.

18. Spicer, *House That Jack Built*, 7.

19. Gizzi, "Jack Spicer and the Practice of Reading," in *House That Jack Built*, 188.

20. Spicer, *My Vocabulary Did This to Me: The Collected Poetry of Jack Spicer,* edited by Peter Gizzi and Kevin Killian (Middletown, CT: Wesleyan University Press, 2008), xxii.

21. Spicer, *My Vocabulary Did This to Me*, 18.

22. Spicer, *My Vocabulary Did This to Me*, 18.

23. Maria Damon, *Dark End of the Street: Margins in American Vanguard Poetry* (Minneapolis: University of Minnesota Press, 1993), 200. As Damon demonstrates, "Spicer used the Orpheus myth in a specifically gay context, inextricably linking gayness with lyric poetry," 199.

24. Spicer, *My Vocabulary Did This to Me*, 20.

25. Spicer, *House That Jack Built*, 19.

26. Robin Blaser, "Practice of Outside," in *The Collected Books of Jack Spicer* (San Francisco: Black Sparrow, 1996), 321.

27. Blaser, "Practice of Outside," 323.

28. Lewis Ellingham and Kevin Killian, *Poet Be Like God: Jack Spicer and the San Francisco Renaissance* (Middletown, CT: Wesleyan University Press, 1998), 189.

29. Spicer, *My Vocabulary*, 254.

30. Spicer, *My Vocabulary*, 256.

31. Spicer, *My Vocabulary*, 259.

32. Spicer, *My Vocabulary*, 259.

33. In his poem "A Postscript to the Berkeley Renaissance," from the early 1950s, Spicer returns to the image of Orpheus after the loss of Eurydice, here lamenting his loss of the ability to sing: "I was a singer once. I sang that song. / I saw the thousands of bewildered birds / Breaking their cover into poetry / Up from the heart" (*My Vocabulary*, 45).

34. Spicer, *House That Jack Built*, 169.

35. Gizzi, "Jack Spicer and the Practice of Reading," in *The House That Jack Built*, 200.

36. Spicer, *My Vocabulary*, 69.

37. Spicer, *My Vocabulary*, 72.

38. Spicer, *My Vocabulary*, 72.

39. Spicer, *House That Jack Built*, 102.

40. Spicer, *My Vocabulary*, 421.

41. Spicer, *My Vocabulary*, 422.

42. Spicer, *My Vocabulary*, 422.

43. John Ashbery, *The Collected Poems: 1956–1987* (New York: Library of America, 2008), 185.

44. Ashbery, *Collected Poems: 1956–1987*, 536.

45. John Ashbery, *A Controversy of Poets*, ed. Paris Leary and Robert Kelly (New York: Anchor, 1965), 523.

46. Ashbery, *Collected Poems: 1956–1987*, 535.

47. Ashbery, *Collected Poems: 1956–1987*, 534.

48. Ashbery, *Collected Poems: 1956–1987*, 535.

49. Ashbery, *Collected Poems: 1956–1987*, 536.

50. As John Shoptaw has demonstrated in his study of Ashbery's poetry, *On the Outside Looking Out: John Ashbery's Poetry* (Cambridge, MA: Harvard University Press, 1994), while sexuality is as slippery a topic as any in Ashbery's oeuvre, the fact of his homosexuality frames what Shoptaw identifies as Ashbery's practice, "homotextuality." As Shoptaw argues, "although, or rather because, Ashbery leaves himself and his homosexuality out of his poetry, his poems misrepresent in a particular way which I will call 'homotextual.' Rather than simply hiding or revealing some homosexual content, these poems represent and 'behave' differently, no matter what their subject. With their distortions, evasions, omissions, obscurities, and discontinuities, Ashbery's poems always have a homotextual dimension" (4).

51. Duncan, "The Homosexual in Society," in *A Selected Prose* (New York: New Directions, 1995), 47.

52. Spicer, *My Vocabulary*, 74.

53. Spicer, *My Vocabulary*, 87.

54. Spicer, *My Vocabulary*, 94.

55. Pierre Joris, "Steve's Standards," 1985, http://pierrejoris.com.

56. Peter Kostakis, *"Son of Serious Fun."* Liner Notes for *Futurities II*, by Steve Lacy (Hat Hut Records, 1990).

57. Kostakis, *"Son of Serious Fun."*

58. Kostakis, *"Son of Serious Fun."*

59. Creeley, *The Collected Poems of Robert Creeley: 1975–2005*, 213.

60. Steve Swallow, *So There*, ECM, 2006.

61. Jeffrey Gray, "'Beyond the Letter': Identity, Song, and Strick," *Callaloo* 23, no. 2 (2000): 621.

62. Richard Quinn, "The Creak of Categories: Nathaniel Mackey's Strick: Song of the Andoumboulou 16–25," *Callaloo* 23, no. 2 (2000): 608.

63. Mackey, *Splay Anthem*, 56.

64. Mackey, *Eroding Witness*, 60.

65. Mackey, *Nod House*, 48.

Works Cited

Abbate, Carolyn. *In Search of Opera*. Princeton, NJ: Princeton University Press, 2001.
———. "Jankélévitch's Singularity." In *Music and the Ineffable*, by Vladimir Jankélévitch, translated by Carolyn Abbate. Princeton, NJ: Princeton University Press, 2003.
———. "Music—Drastic or Gnostic?" *Critical Inquiry* 30, no. 3 (2004): 505–36. Accessed October 16, 2020. doi:10.1086/421160.

Albright, Daniel. *Untwisting the Serpent: Modernism in Literature, Music, and Other Arts*. Chicago: University of Chicago Press, 2000.

Altieri, Charles. "Avant-Garde or Arriere-Garde in Recent American Poetry." *Poetics Today* 20, no. 4 (1999): 629–53.
———. "Pound's Vorticism as a Renewal of Humanism." *Boundary 2: An International Journal of Literature and Culture* 12, no. 3 (1984): 439–61.
———. *Self and Sensibility in Contemporary American Poetry*. Cambridge: Cambridge University Press, 1984.
———. "What Does Echoes Echo." In *Form Power and Person in Robert Creeley's Life and Work*, edited by Stephen Fredman and Steve McCaffrey. Iowa City: University of Iowa Press, 2010.

Ashbery, John. *A Controversy of Poets*. Edited by Paris Leary and Robert Kelly. New York: Anchor, 1965.
———. *The Collected Poems: 1956–1987*. New York: Library of America, 2008.

Austin, J. L. *How to Do Things with Words*. Cambridge, MA: Harvard University Press, 1962.

Baudelaire, Charles. "Richard Wagner and *Tannhäuser* in Paris." In *Selected Writings on Art and Literature*, translated by P. E. Charvet. London: Penguin Classics, 1995.

Belgrad, Daniel. *The Culture of Spontaneity: Improvisation and the Arts in Postwar America*. Chicago: University of Chicago Press, 1998.

Benjamin, Walter, and Knut Tarnowski. "Doctrine of the Similar (1933)." *New German Critique*, no. 17 (1979): 65–69. https://doi.org/10.2307/488010.

Bernstein, Charles, ed. *Blind Witness: Three American Operas*. New York: Factory School, 2008.

————. *Close Listening: Poetry and the Performed Word*. Oxford: Oxford University Press, 1998.

————. "PennSound: Charles Bernstein." PennSound. Accessed May 18, 2020. http://writing.upenn.edu.

————. "Pound and the Poetry of Today." In *My Way: Speeches and Poems*. Chicago: University of Chicago Press, 1999.

————. "Pounding Fascism." In *A Poetics*. Cambridge, MA: Harvard University Press, 1992.

————. *Recalculating*. Chicago: University of Chicago Press, 2013.

————. *Shadowtime*. Los Angeles: Green Integer, 2005.

————. "State of the Art." In *A Poetics*. Cambridge, MA: Harvard University Press, 1992.

————. "Synopsis" for *Shadowtime: An Opera with Music by Brian Ferneyhough and Words by Charles Bernstein*. NMC, 2006.

————. "Time Out of Motion: Looking Ahead to See Backward." In *A Poetics*. Cambridge, MA: Harvard University Press, 1992.

Bertoff, Robert. "On John Taggart's *There Are Birds*." Jacket2, 2014. jacket2.0rg/article/john-taggarts-there-are-birds.

Bettridge, Joel. "Charles Bernstein's *Shadowtime* and Faithful Interpretation." *Textual Practice* 21 (2007): 737–60.

————. *Reading as Belief: Language Writing, Poetics, Faith*. New York: Palgrave MacMillan, 2009.

Blanchot, Maurice. *The Space of Literature: A Translation of "L'Espace Littéraire."* Translated by Ann Smock. Lincoln: University of Nebraska Press, 1989.

Blaser, Robin. "Practice of Outside." In *The Collected Books of Jack Spicer*. San Francisco: Black Sparrow, 1996.

Bruns, Gerald. *The Material of Poetry*. Athens: University of Georgia Press, 2012.

Bucknell, Bradley. *Literary Modernism and Musical Aesthetics: Pater, Pound, Joyce, and Stein*. Cambridge: Cambridge University Press, 2002.

Butterick, George. *A Guide to the Maximus Poems of Charles Olson*. Berkeley: University of California Press, 1978.

Campion, Thomas. *Campion's Works*. Oxford: Clarendon, 1909.

Césaire, Aimé. *The Collected Poetry*. Translated by Clayton Eshelman and Annette Smith. Berkeley: University of California Press, 1983.

————. *Discourse on Colonialism*. Translated by Joan Pinkham. New York: Monthly Review Press, 2001.

Chaucer, Geoffrey, John Strong Perry Tatlock, and Percy MacKaye. *The Complete Poetical Works of Geoffrey Chaucer*. New York: Macmillan, 1912.

Conte, Joseph. *Unending Design: The Forms of Postmodern Poetry*. Ithaca, NY: Cornell University Press, 1991.

Cooperman, Matt. "'Reasons for Singing': On John Taggart." Jacket2, 2014. jacket2.org/feature/reasons-singing-john-taggart.

Couch, Randall. "A Eurydice Beyond My Maestro: Triangular Desire in Harryette Mullen's 'Dim Lady.'" *How2* 2, no. 4 (2006).

Creeley, Robert. "Appearing with John Ashbery in 'Attitudes Towards the Flame.'" PennSound, 1983. http://writing.upenn.edu.

————. *Contexts of Poetry: Interviews, 1961–1971*. 1st ed. Bolinas, CA: Four Seasons Foundation, 1973.

————. *Quick Graph*. Bolinas, CA: Four Seasons Foundation, 1970.

————. "Robert Creeley." PennSound. Accessed May 18, 2020. http://writing.upenn.edu.

————. *The Collected Essays of Robert Creeley*. Berkeley: University of California Press, 1989.

————. *The Collected Poems of Robert Creeley: 1945–1975*. Berkeley: University of California Press, 1975.

————. *The Collected Poems of Robert Creeley: 1975–2005*. Berkeley: University of California Press, 2005.

Crown, Kathleen. "Sonic Revolutionaries: Voice and Experiment in the Spoken-Word Poetry of Tracie Morris." In *We Who Love to Be Astonished*, edited by Laura Hinton and Cynthia Hogue. Tuscaloosa: University of Alabama Press, 2002.

Damon, Maria. *Dark End of the Street: Margins in American Vanguard Poetry*. Minneapolis: University of Minnesota Press, 1993.

Davidson, Arnold. "The Charme of Jankélévitch." In *Music and the Ineffable*, by Vladimir Jankélévitch, translated by Carolyn Abbate. Princeton, NJ: Princeton University Press, 2003.

Davidson, Michael. "Ekphrasis and the Postmodern Painter Poem." *Journal of Aesthetics and Art Criticism* 42, no. 1 (1983): 69–79. https://doi.org/10.2307/429948.

Davies, Tony. *Humanism*. Abingdon, UK: Routledge, 1997.

Derrida, Jacques. "A Silkworm of One's Own (Points of View Stitched on the Other Veil)." Translated by Geoffrey Bennington. *Oxford Literary Review* 18, no. 1/2 (1996): 3–65.

Donahue, Joseph. "Approaching Taggart Chapel: Ritual, Rothko, and Poetic Form." Jacket2, 2014. jacket2.org/article/approaching-taggart-chapel.

Du Plessis, Rachel Blau. "The Hole: Death, Sexual Difference, and Gender Contradictions in Robert Creeley's Poetry." In *Form, Power, and Person in Robert Creeley's Life and Work*, edited by Stephen Fredman and Steve McCaffery. Iowa City: University of Iowa Press, 2010.

Duncan, Robert. *Bending the Bow*. New York: New Directions, 1968.

————. *Groundwork: Before the War, in the Dark*. New York: New Directions, 2006.

————. "The Homosexual in Society." In *A Selected Prose*. New York: New Directions, 1995.

————. *The Opening of the Field*. New York: New Directions, 1960.

Edwards, Brent Hayes. "Notes on Poetics Regarding Mackey's 'Song.'" *Callaloo* 23, no. 2 (2000): 572–91.

Ellingham, Lewis, and Kevin Killian. *Poet Be Like God: Jack Spicer and the San Francisco Renaissance*. Middletown, CT: Wesleyan University Press, 1998.

Emerson, Ralph Waldo. *Emerson's Prose and Poetry*. Edited by Joel Porte and Saundra Morris. New York: W. W. Norton, 2001.

Ferneyhough, Brian. *Collected Writings*. Reading, UK: Harwood Academic, 1995.

————. "Words and Music." Argotist Online, April 15, 2007. https://www.argotistonline.co.uk.

————. "Musical and Other Notes to *Shadowtime*: An Opera with Music by Brian Ferney-hough and Words by Charles Bernstein." NMC, 2006.

Fink, Bruce. *The Lacanian Subject: Between Language and Jouissance*. Princeton, NJ: Princeton University Press, 1995.

Finkelstein, Norman. "Nathaniel Mackey and the Unity of All Rites." Contemporary Literature 49, no. 1 (Spring 2008): 24–55.

Fisher, Margaret. *Ezra Pound's Radio Operas: The BBC Experiments, 1931–1933*. Cambridge, MA: MIT Press, 2002.

Fitch, Fabrice. "Liner Notes to *Shadowtime*." Compact Disc. NMC, 2006.

Foster, Edward. "An Interview with Nathaniel Mackey." *Talisman* 9 (1992): 48–62.

Friedlander, Benjamin. "'What Is Experience?'" In *Form, Power, and Person in Robert Creeley's Life and Work*, edited by Stephen Fredman and Steve McCaffery. Iowa City: University of Iowa Press, 2010.

Frost, Elizabeth. *The Feminist Avant-Garde in American Poetry*. Iowa City: University of Iowa Press, 2003.

Ginsberg, Allen. *Howl: 50th Anniversary Edition*. New York: Harper Perennial Modern Classics, 1986.

Gizzi, Peter. "Jack Spicer and the Practice of Reading." In *The House That Jack Built: The Collected Lectures of Jack Spicer*. Middletown, CT: Wesleyan University Press, 1998.

Gizzi, Peter, and Kevin Killian. "Introduction." In *My Vocabulary Did This to Me: The Collected Poetry of Jack Spicer*. Middletown, CT: Wesleyan University Press, 2008.

Glinsky, Albert. *Theremin: Ether Music and Espionage*. Champaign: University of Illinois Press, 2000.

Gray, Jeffrey. "'Beyond the Letter': Identity, Song, and Strick." *Callaloo* 23, no. 2 (2000): 621–39.

Guthrie, WKC. *Orpheus and Greek Religion: A Study of the Orphic Movement*. Princeton, NJ: Princeton University Press, 1993.

Haas, Brad. "John Taggart Flashpoint Interview." *Flashpoint Magazine*, February 2002. http://www.flashpointmag.com.

Harris, William J. *The Poetry and Poetics of Amiri Baraka: The Jazz Aesthetic*. Columbia, MO: University of Missouri Press, 1985.

————. "'How You Sound?': Amiri Baraka Writes Free Jazz." In *Uptown Conversation: The New Jazz Studies*, edited by Robert G. O'Meally, Brent Hayes Edwards, and Farah Jasmine Griffin. New York: Columbia University Press, 2004.

Herrick, Robert. *The Complete Poetry of Robert Herrick*. Edited by J. Max Patrick. New York: Norton, 1968.

Hoppin, Richard. *Medieval Music*. New York: W. W. Norton, 1978.

Hume, Christine. "Improvisational Insurrection." In *American Poets in the 21st Century: The New Poetics*, edited by Claudia Rankine and Lisa Sewell. Middletown, CT: Wesleyan University Press, 2007.

Imbriglio, Catherine. "'Impossible Audiences': Camp, the Orphic, and Art as Entertainment in Jack Spicer's Poetry." In *After Spicer: Critical Essays*, edited by John Vincent. Middletown, CT: Wesleyan University Press, 2011.

Jankélévitch, Vladimir. *Music and the Ineffable*. Translated by Carolyn Abbate. Princeton, NJ: Princeton University Press, 2003.

Johnson, Steven. "Rothko Chapel and Rothko's Chapel." *Perspectives of New Music* 32, no. 2 (Summer 1994): 6–53.

Johnston, Devin. "Nathaniel Mackey and Lost Time: 'The Phantom Light of All Our Day.'" *Callaloo* 23, no. 2 (2000): 563–70.

Joris, Pierre. "Steve's Standards." Pierre Joris, 1985. http://pierrejoris.com.

Jost, Ekkehard. *Free Jazz*. Boston, MA: Da Capo Press, 1994.

Kerouac, Jack. "Essentials of Spontaneous Prose." In *The Portable Beat Reader*, edited by Anne Charters. New York: Viking, 1992.

Kierkegaard, Soren. *Fear and Trembling / Repetition*. Translated by Edna Hong. Princeton, NJ: Princeton University Press, 1983.

Kivy, Peter. *Osmin's Rage: Philosophical Reflections on Opera*. Princeton, NJ: Princeton University Press, 1988.

Kostakis, Peter. *"Son of Serious Fun." Liner Notes for Futurities II*, by Steve Lacy. Hat Hut Records, 1990.

Lacan, Jacques. *The Four Fundamental Concepts of Psycho-Analysis*. Edited by Jacques-Alain Miller. Translated by Alan Sheridan. New York: W. W. Norton, 1978.

League of Legends Wiki. "Sona." Accessed January 10, 2019. https://leagueoflegends.fandom.com.

Lee, M. Owen. *Virgil as Orpheus: A Study of the Georgics*. New York: State University of New York Press, 1996.

Levinas, Emmanuel. *The Humanism of the Other*. Translated by Nidra Poller. Champaign: University of Illinois Press, 2006.

Mackey, Nathaniel. "'A Reading by Nathaniel Mackey with Bassist Vattel Cherry,' Uploaded by Duke University." YouTube. April 15, 2015. www.youtube.com.

———. *Blue Fasa*. New York: New Directions, 2015.

———. "Cante Moro." In *Sound States: Innovative Poetic and Acoustical Technologies*, edited by Adelaide Morris. Chapel Hill: University of North Carolina Press, 1997.

———. *Discrepant Engagement: Dissonance, Cross-Culturality, and Experimental Writing*. Tuscaloosa: University of Alabama Press, 2000.

———. *Eroding Witness*. Champaign: University of Illinois Press, 1984.

———. *From a Broken Bottle Traces of Perfume Still Emanate*. Vols. 1–3. New York: New Directions, 2010.

———. *Nod House*. New York: New Directions, 2011.

———. *Paracritical Hinge*. Iowa City: University of Iowa Press, 2018.

———. *School of Udhra*. San Francisco: City Lights, 1993.

———. *Splay Anthem*. New York: New Directions, 2006.

Mix, Deborah. "Tender Revisions: Harryette Mullen's Trimmings and SPeRMKT." *American Literature: A Journal of Literary History, Criticism, and Bibliography* 77, no. 1 (March 2005): 65–92.

Moody, A. David. *Ezra Pound: Poet; A Portrait of the Man and His Work*. Oxford: Oxford University Press, 2007.

Mooney, Edward. "Repetition." In *Cambridge Companion to Kierkegaard*, edited by Alastair Hannay and Gordon Daniel Marino. Cambridge: Cambridge University Press, 1997.

Morris, Adelaide. *Sound Stats: Innovative Poetics and Acoustical Technologies*. Chapel Hill: University of North Carolina Press, 1997.

Morris, Tracie. *Handholding: 5 Kinds: Sonic, Textual Engagements*. Tucson, AZ: Kore, 2018.

———. "Tracie Morris." PennSound, May 1, 2019. http://writing.upenn.edu.

———. *Who Do with Words: (A Blerd Love Tone Manifesto)*. Tucson, AZ: Chax, 2018.

Moten, Fred. *Black and Blur*. Durham, NC: Duke University Press, 2017.

———. *In the Break: The Aesthetics of the Black Radical Tradition*. Minneapolis: University of Minnesota Press, 2003.

———. "Sound in Florescence: Cecil Taylor's Floating Garden." In *Sound States: Innovative Poetics and Acoustical Technologies*, edited by Adelaide Morris. Chapel Hill: University of North Carolina Press, 1997.

———. *Stolen Life*. Durham, NC: Duke University Press, 2018.

Mullen, Harryette. "African Signs and Spirit Writing." *Callaloo* 19, no. 3 (Summer 1996): 670–89.

———. *Sleeping with the Dictionary*. Berkeley: University of California Press, 2000.

Mullen, Harryette, and Arlene Keizer. "Incidents in the Life of Two Postmodern Black Feminists." *Postmodern Culture* 22, no. 1 (September 2011). https://muse.jhu.edu.

Muyumba, Walton. *The Shadow and the Act: Black Intellectual Practice, Jazz Improvisation, and Philosophical Pragmatism*. Chicago: University of Chicago Press, 2009.

Naylor, Paul. "An Interview with Nathaniel Mackey." *Callaloo* 23, no. 2 (2000): 645–63.

Nodelman, Sheldon. *The Rothko Chapel Paintings: Origins, Structure, Meaning*. Austin: University of Texas Press, 1997.

O'Leary, Peter. "An Interview with Nathaniel Mackey." *Chicago Review* 43 (1997): 30–58.

———. *Gnostic Contagion: Robert Duncan and the Poetry of Illness*. Middletown, CT: Wesleyan University Press, 2002.

———. "This Poem Is a Song an Act a Work of Love." Jacket2, 2014. jacket2.org/article/poem-song-act-work-love.

Olson, Charles. *The Maximus Poems*. Berkeley: University of California Press, 1983.

Olson, Toby. "Spirit Image, Kerry Clouds, Peace on Earth: A Few Old Memories and New Thoughts about John Taggart." *Paper Air* 2, no. 1 (1979). http://eclipsearchive.org.

Ott, Gil, and Toby Olson. "Interview with John Taggart." *Paper Air* 2, no. 1 (1979). eclipsearchive.org.

Ovid. *Metamorphoses*. Translated by Rolfe Humphries. Bloomington: Indiana University Press, 1968.

Oxford English Dictionary. 2nd ed. 20 vols. "Amphibole." Oxford: Oxford University Press, 1989. http://www.oed.com. Accessed June 5, 2020.

———. "Tath." http://www.oed.com. Accessed August 1, 2019.

Palmer, Michael. "Introduction." In *Ground Work: Before the War, in the Dark*. By Robert Duncan. New York: New Directions, 2006.

Perloff, Marjorie. "After Free Verse: The New Non-Linear Poetries." In *Close Listening: Poetry and the Performed World*, edited by Charles Bernstein. Oxford: Oxford University Press, 1998.

———. *Poetics of Indeterminacy: Rimbaud to Cage*. Evanston, IL: Northwestern University Press, 1993.

———. *Unoriginal Genius: Poetry by Other Means in the New Century*. Chicago: University of Chicago Press, 2010.

Perloff, Marjorie, and Craig Dworkin. *The Sound of Poetry / The Poetry of Sound*. Chicago: University of Chicago Press, 2009.

Plato. *The Republic*. Translated by Desmond Lee. London: Penguin, 1955.

Pound, Ezra. *ABC of Reading*. New York: New Directions, 1960.

————. *Antheil and the Treatise on Harmony*. New York: Da Capo, 1968.

————. *Ezra Pound and Music*. Edited by R. Murray Schafer. New York: New Directions, 1977.

————. *Literary Essays of Ezra Pound*. New York: New Directions, 1968.

————. *The Spirit of Romance*. New York: New Directions, 1968.

Prevallet, Kristin. "Jack Spicer's Hell in 'Homage to Creeley.'" Jacket2, 1999. jacketmagazine.com/07/spicer-prevallet.html.

Pritchett, Patrick. "'Giant Steps': John Taggart and Messianic Jazz." Jacket2, 2014. https://jacket2.org.

Quinn, Richard. "The Creak of Categories: Nathaniel Mackey's Strick: Song of the Andoumboulou 16–25." *Callaloo* 23, no. 2 (2000): 608–20.

Ratner, Rochelle. "The Poet as Composer: An Inquiry into the Work of John Taggart." *Paper Air* 2, no. 1 (1974). eclipsearchive.org/projects/PAPER/PA2.1/contents.html.

Reed, Anthony. *Freedom Time: The Poetics and Politics of Black Experimental Writing*. Baltimore, MD: John Hopkins University Press, 2014.

Rilke, Rainer Maria. *Sonnets to Orpheus*. Translated by Stephen Mitchell. New York: Simon & Schuster, 1986.

Roberson, Ed. *Voices Cast Out to Talk Us In*. Iowa City: University of Iowa Press, 1995.

Rothko, Mark. "The Romantics Were Prompted." In *Writings on Art*. New Haven, CT: Yale University Press, 2006.

Rothko Chapel, The. "The Rothko Chapel." Accessed August 1, 2018. www.rothkochapel.org.

Schopenhauer, Arthur. *The World as Will and Representation*. Translated by E. F. J. Payne. Mineola, NY: Dover, 1966.

Schwitters, Kurt. "Ursonata." PennSound. Accessed January 1, 2019. http://writing.upenn.edu.

Scroggins, Mark. *Louis Zukofsky and the Poetry of Knowledge*. Tuscaloosa: University of Alabama Press, 1998.

Sewell, Elizabeth. *The Orphic Voice: Poetry and Natural History*. New York: Harper & Row, 1971.

Shadowtime. Compact Disc. NMC, 2006.

Shepherd, Reginald, ed. *Lyric Postmodernisms: An Anthology of Contemporary Poetries*. Denver, CO: Counterpath, 2008.

Shoptaw, John. *On the Outside Looking Out: John Ashbery's Poetry*. Cambridge, MA: Harvard University Press, 1994.

————. "The Music of Construction: Measure and Polyphony in Ashbery and Bernstein." In *The Tribe of John: Ashbery and Contemporary Poetry*, edited by Susan Shultz. Tuscaloosa: University of Alabama Press, 1995.

Silverman, Kaja. *Flesh of My Flesh*. Palo Alto, CA: Stanford University Press, 2009.

Spahr, Juliana. *Everybody's Autonomy*. Tuscaloosa: University of Alabama Press, 2011.

Spanos, William. "The Fact of Firstness." *Boundary 2: An International Journal of Literature and Culture* 6, no. 7 (1978): 1–10.

Spicer, Jack. *My Vocabulary Did This to Me: The Collected Poetry of Jack Spicer*. Edited by Peter Gizzi and Kevin Killian. Middletown, CT: Wesleyan University Press, 2008.

———. *The House That Jack Built: The Collected Lectures of Jack Spicer*. Edited by Peter Gizzi. Middletown, CT: Wesleyan University Press, 1998.

St. John, David, and Cole Swensen, eds. *American Hybrid: A Norton Anthology of Poetry*. New York: W. W. Norton, 2009.

Stein, Gertrude. *Selected Writings of Gertrude Stein*. Edited by Carl van Vechten. New York: Vintage, 1990.

Sternfeld, F. W. *The Birth of Opera*. Oxford: Clarendon, 1993.

Stewart, Susan. "Letter on Sound." In *Close Listening: Poetry and the Performed Word*, edited by Charles Bernstein. Oxford: Oxford University Press, 1998.

Strauss, Walter. *Descent and Return: The Orphic Theme in Modern Literature*. Cambridge, MA: Harvard University Press, 1971.

Swallow, Steve. *So There*. ECM, 2006.

———. *Home*. ECM, 2019.

Taggart, John. *Is Music: Selected Poems*. Port Townsend, WA: Copper Canyon, 2010.

———. *Loop*. Los Angeles: Sun and Moon, 1991.

———. *Pastorelles*. Chicago: Flood Editions, 2004.

———. *Peace on Earth*. West Branch, IA: Toothpaste, 1981.

———. "Reading at the Rothko Chapel, Houston, TX, October 25, 2012." PennSound. Accessed November 1, 2018. writing.upenn.edu/pennsound/x/Taggart.php.

———. *Remaining in Light: Ant Meditations on a Painting by Edward Hopper*. Albany: SUNY Press, 1993.

———. *Songs of Degrees*. Tuscaloosa: University of Alabama Press, 1994.

———. *Standing Wave*. Providence, RI: Lost Roads, 1993.

———. *There Are Birds*. Chicago: Flood Editions, 2008.

Tremblay-McGaw, Robin. "Enclosure and Run: The Fugitive Recyclopedia of Harryette Mullen's Writing." *MELUS* 35, no. 2 (Summer 2010): 71–94.

Vacari, Patricia. "Sparagmos: Orpheus Among the Christians." In *Orpheus: The Metamorphosis of a Myth*. Toronto, CA: University of Toronto Press, 1985.

Virgil. *Virgil's Georgics*. Translated by Janet Lembke. New Haven, CT: Yale University Press, 2005.

Von Hallberg, Robert. *Lyric Powers*. Chicago: University of Chicago Press, 2008.

Wald, Priscilla. *Constituting Americans: Cultural Anxiety and Narrative Form*. Durham, NC: Duke University Press, 1995.

Warden, John, ed. *Orpheus: The Metamorphoses of a Myth*. Toronto, CA: University of Toronto Press, 1982.

Williams, William Carlos. *The Collected Poems of William Carlos Williams, Volume 2: 1939–1962*. New York: New Directions, 1991.

Willis, Elizabeth. "The Arena in the Garden: Some Thoughts on the Late Lyric." In *Telling It Slant: Avant-Garde Poetics of the 1990s*, edited by Mark Wallace and Steven Marks. Tuscaloosa: University of Alabama Press, 2002.

Žižek, Slavoj, and Mladen Dolar. *Opera's Second Death*. Abingdon, UK: Routledge, 2002.

Zuckerkandl, Victor. *Sound and Symbol*. Translated by Willard Trask. Princeton, NJ: Princeton University Press, 1969.

Zukofsky, Louis. *A*. New York: New Directions, 2011.

———. *Prepositions*. Berkeley: University of California Press, 1981.

Index